AMERICAN STILL LIFE

The Jim Beam Story and the Making of the World's #1 Bourbon

F. PAUL PACULT

FOREWORD BY FREDERICK BOOKER NOE III, KNOB CREEK BOURBON AMBASSADOR

WILEY

JOHN WILEY & SONS, INC.

Published by John Wiley & Sons, Inc., Hoboken, New Jersey.
Published simultaneously in Canada.

For general information on our other products and services, or technical support,
please contact our Customer Care Department within the United States at
800-762-2974, outside the United States at 317-572-3993 or fax 317-572-4002.

Wiley also publishes its books in a variety of electronic formats. Some content that
appears in print may not be available in electronic books. For more information about
Wiley products, visit our web site at www.wiley.com.

Library of Congress Cataloging-in-Publication Data:

Pacult, F. Paul, 1949–
   American still life: the Jim Beam story and the making of the world's
   #1 bourbon / by F. Paul Pacult.
      p.   cm.
   Published simultaneously in Canada.
   Includes bibliographical references.
   ISBN 0-471-44407-3 (cloth)
   1. James B. Beam Distilling Company.   2. Whiskey industry—United
States—Kentucky—History.   3. Liquor industry executives—United
States—Kentucky—Biography.   4. Liquor industry executives—United
States—Kentucky—Genealogy.   5. Beam family.   6. Kentucky—Genealogy.
   I. Title.
   HD9395.U47J367   2003
   338.7'66352—dc21

                                                        2003011340

Printed in the United States of America.

10 9 8 7 6 5 4 3 2 1

For Sue, forever gratefully connected to.

For Rick, forever gratefully guided by.

Contents

Foreword

While I thought I knew everything about my family, *American Still Life* taught me that you can always learn more about who you are and where you came from. I am proud to invite you into my world to learn about the first family of bourbon—our history and our rich heritage.

As the seventh generation Beam involved in producing award-winning bourbon, I have a keen understanding of the importance of tradition and heritage. It comes with being part of a family that can trace our bourbon-making roots back more than 200 years. The historical account describes my family's heritage—capturing our hopes, dreams, and ambitions in the process. *American Still Life* also offers an important history of bourbon, a history that at times reads like a novel.

Jim Beam is the No. 1 bourbon in the world, but as you'll see, it is also so much more. Jim Beam is pride, Jim Beam is determination, Jim Beam is quality. Jim Beam is America. And for generations of families working in our distilleries, Jim Beam is, has been, and always will be, a way of life. *American Still Life* captures this pride and the essence of who we are and what bourbon is all about.

When my great-great-great-great-grandfather, Jacob Beam, brought his first bourbon to market in 1795, he had no way of knowing what he was starting. He was a distiller, hoping to earn an honest living and provide for his family. In many ways, he was just like every other pioneer who had made his way westward in America. He wanted a better life and was willing to work hard to achieve it.

More than 200 years later, Jacob's bourbon has become an American Icon and the cornerstone to my family's time-honored bourbon-making tradition. Each generation has contributed to this legacy, adding unique skills and talents. Everyone has played an invaluable part, helping Jim Beam become a successful business focused on producing the world's finest bourbons.

When I finished this book, I had a terrific sense of pride in my family. I now have an even deeper respect for the challenges my family faced, the risks we took, and the long days we put in to make our whiskey just right.

I learned how to make bourbon from my father, Booker Noe, Jim Beam's grandson. Growing up, I joined my father at the distillery, watching the Beam craftsmen make the mash and barrel up the whiskey. When I was old enough, I joined in the family tradition working nights on the bottling line. My father taught me the business from the ground up. He also taught me the importance of keeping things honest and straight.

American Still Life is an honest and straight account of my family's history, our bourbon, and the Kentucky way of life. It celebrates a part of America that is gone and recognizes another part that is still going strong.

It was a pleasure for me to read and I hope you will enjoy it as well.

Fred Noe

Preface

Snapshots from the Album of an American Family

I DIDN'T COME TO appreciate and know whiskey well until 1989. Until that time, I had prided myself on being a wine journalist and instructor, surviving, even thriving in New York City. New York in the 1980s was a remarkable melting pot for the world's wines. As American consumer interest in fine wines exploded, wines poured in from everywhere: Australia, Chile, Hungary, Argentina, Greece, Washington State, Oregon, Israel. I wrote about wine for various publications, consulted for wine shops in the northeast about what they should buy and how they should sell it, and owned and operated a wine school, Wine Courses International, out of a loft in lower Manhattan. Life was good.

Whiskey, however, was foreign territory, a dark and, in my mind, inhospitable continent. Wine was white or red. Whiskey was, after all, brown.

Then, in the winter of 1989, a friend at the *New York Times,* Rich Colandrea, who had been attending my wine classes, hired me to create and write a special advertising section on Scotch whisky for the Sunday *Times Magazine.* To my astonishment, the 28-page section turned out to be an enormous hit with *Times* readers, advertisers, and the *Times* staff. The *Times* requested more special sections on Scotch and other distilled spirits in 1990 and 1991. I provided them. Within two years, I was writing as much about whiskey and distilled spirits in general as about wine. Cognac, Armagnac, Eau-de-vie, Vodka, Gin, Tequila, Rum, Liqueurs, Irish whiskey, Canadian whisky, Bourbon whiskey—all distilled spirits— suddenly fell within the scope of my view-finder. I was sampling and evaluating hundreds of distilled spirits a year on top of all the wines I was still analyzing.

In 1991, I kicked off publication of *F. Paul Pacult's Spirit Journal,* my subscription-only, advertising-free newsletter wherein I critiqued distilled spirits of all categories in as much detail as I had previously done with wine. That microscopic attention had evidently never before been afforded to spirits to any great extent. The *Spirit Journal*— liquor industry people and subscribers told me—finally gave an independent, unbiased voice to spirits, one that had been swamped during the "wine boom" decades of the 1970s and 1980s.

In 1992, I received a call from Jim Beam Brands, who were then, as they are now, headquartered in Deerfield, Illinois. I had come to know Jim Beam Bourbon as America's flagship bourbon, a hugely popular, iconic brand with a global presence. The previous year, I had reviewed in the *Spirit Journal* the company's four elite, super-premium "small batch" bourbon whiskeys, Booker's Bourbon, Basil Hayden's, Baker's, and Knob Creek. The Jim Beam management team asked me if I would consider touring the nation with Booker Noe, Jim Beam's grandson and the Master Distiller Emeritus of the James B. Beam Distilling Company, to introduce the company's small batch bourbons to audiences comprised of the public, trade, and press.

At the first opportunity, I hopped aboard the Booker Express. On and off for three years, as my schedule permitted, I toured the United States with this giant, affable man—Kansas City, San Diego, Boston, Miami, Dallas. You name the major city and, most likely, Booker and I were there at some point talking to jam-packed halls, ballrooms, and restaurants.

As I make clear in Chapter Six, the crowds we encountered were not present to see me. Maybe some were *Spirit Journal* subscribers, but the majority attended because they had heard of this unbelievable gentleman named Booker Noe.

What made Booker so appealing on our tours was his unbridled honesty, boundless enthusiasm for bourbon, and his good-humored, no-nonsense personality. Tall as he was wide of girth, Booker commanded the speaker's table merely by sitting there. While I would be discussing with each group the merits of Basil Hayden's, Baker's, and Knob Creek and describing to them what made the Jim Beam small batch bourbons different from mainstream bourbons, the audience would be itching to hear what Jim Beam's grandson had to say, what knowledge he could impart about the bourbons, especially his own, the fiery, four-alarm Booker's Bourbon.

Once Booker started talking in his rural Kentucky drawl about his whiskeys and how to make bourbon, or smoking hams, or fishing, or the spiritual importance of consuming lots of thick-sliced smoked ham on homemade biscuits, only an earthquake could stop him or, for that matter, compel the audience to vacate. The audiences were enthralled and amused by this massive, unassuming man who'd casually answer questions, saying things like, "Do I add water ta Booker's? At a hunnert twenty-six percent alcohol, you kiddin'? Don't an' it'll blow tha top o' your head right off. Hell, I pour some Booker's in a tall ol' glass 'bout one-third an' fill the rest with branch water and some ice. Call it Kentucky Tea. Clears the lungs, soothes the stomach . . . and lights a fire in your mind. All those things in jus' one glass. Yes sir, Kentucky Tea. Mighty good for what ails ya."

The public warmly responded to Booker because he came off as the real deal. He was authentic, unscripted. Booker Noe defined what people thought a Kentucky whiskeyman should be. Though Booker is now retired, receiving guests at his home in Bardstown, Kentucky (Jim Beam's old home) for lunch or dinner and a glass or two of Kentucky Tea and 10 to 12 smoked ham biscuits per person, he remains, along with his son Fred, the focal point of the Beam legacy.

But the unique story of Jim Beam Bourbon and how it became the best-selling bourbon whiskey in the world is about much more than Booker and Fred Noe and the company's small batch bourbons. The Jim Beam Bourbon saga, I came to realize over the years, is one part family history, one part riveting fireside tale about the opening of the western frontier, one part American memorabilia scrapbook, and one part international business opus. The Jim Beam Bourbon saga can only be told as a story that is inextricably interwoven into the tale of America becoming an independent nation and, in time, the world's foremost industrial and commercial power.

The tale begins with Johannes Jacob Beam (originally Boehm of German ancestry), who in the latter years of the eighteenth century left Maryland to homestead in the untamed frontier territory known as Kentucke. Beam's aim was to farm, distill whiskey, and raise a family. Not necessarily in that order. How a locally produced spirit made mostly of corn and sold by the individual barrel eventually became the world's number one bourbon whiskey over the course of seven generations and two centuries is a testament to the Beams' perseverance, ingenuity, and remarkable sense of family loyalty. Enduring frontier hardships, a fledgling country's growing pains, the Civil War, the temperance movement and Prohibition, financial difficulties, and World Wars, the Beam family story weaves together regional, national, and international commerce; rural American history and intimate family history. No other family in the international whiskey realm has had as deep an impact or has left as illustrious a legacy as the Beams.

A 1965 newspaper story that appeared in the *Austin Statesman* reported on the 170th anniversary of Jim Beam Bourbon described the adventure of the Beam family best when it said, "The story of the Beam family and its unique contribution to American industry can almost be linked to the progress of America itself. For the Beam family tradition of six generations in one business, in one industry—in a truly American industry—defies parallel."

An appropriate way to absorb and enjoy this account is to pour yourself a dram of Jim Beam Bourbon cut with mineral water, get comfortable in a big chair, and be time-warped back to when America was rambunctious, raw, adventurous, and the source of unlimited opportunities. The Beams are naturally skilled at keeping things simple, clear, and direct. I hope you find *American Still Life* as entertaining, genuine, and unaffected as the Beams are.

I recall well a late night dinner with Booker and his wife Annis somewhere in our travels a decade ago. We had just conducted another standing-room-only tasting, people shoehorned into an auditorium. Booker mused about the raucous, enthusiastic reception we had just experienced, saying as he looked at me, "Sometimes ah still don't see what all tha fuss's about. Hell, Paul, we've jus' been makin' whiskey outta corn for a little while. 'S all." I had come to know Booker well enough by that point to know that he wasn't being disingenuous. He's incapable of it.

Here's to the many future quaffs of Kentucky Tea yet to be shared with Booker Noe, grandson of Jim Beam, and Fred Noe, son of Booker.

F. PAUL PACULT

Wallkill, New York
June 2003

Acknowledgments

AMERICAN STILL LIFE WOULD never have happened without the help and support of the following people:

- Sue Woodley, my wife and partner, for proofreading, editing, rewriting, researching, and conceptualizing.
- Richard F. Pacult, for moral support on many fronts.
- Matt Holt, my editor at John Wiley & Sons, who first approached us with the business book idea, made it happen with our topic suggestions, then made many key editorial suggestions.
- Everyone else at John Wiley & Sons who is connected with the book.
- The amiable and able staffs at the Kentucky Historical Society, Special Collections in Frankfort; the Filson Historical Society in Louisville; the librarians at the Margaret I. King Library, University of Kentucky, Lexington; and the curators

of the Oscar Getz Museum of Whiskey History, and The Bardstown Historical Museum, Bardstown.

- Flaget Nally, Mary Hite, and Jo Ann Beam for a lovely stroll through a cemetery.
- Max Shapira, Harry Shapira, Jeff Homel, Larry Kass, Parker Beam, and Craig Beam of Heaven Hill Distillery, Bardstown.
- Frank Coleman and Patrick MacElroy of the Distilled Spirits Council of the United States (DISCUS), Washington, DC.

Though they had no stake in this book other than the basic storyline and no knowledge of the final content, the Jim Beam Brands Worldwide, Inc., group in Deerfield, Illinois, and Clermont, Kentucky, should be cited for their open and willing assistance with the research. Stephanie Moritz, our primary contact at JBBWorldwide, proved to be indispensable in helping to ferret out archival material, arrange for present and former staff member interviews, track down photos and related data, and assist with fact checking. Rich Reese, chief executive officer and president of JBBWorldwide, enthusiastically embraced the book concept from the very beginning. Other valuable assistance from JBBWorldwide came from Ron Kapolnek, Tom Maas, Tom Flocco, Kathleen DiBenedetto, Harry Groth, and Michael Donohoe of Future Brands, LLC. Linda Hayes, Jim Beam Noe, Jeff Conder, and Jerry Dalton at the Jim Beam Distillery in Clermont; Laura Dihel and Jim Kokoris at JSH&A should also be mentioned. Barry Berish, former chief executive officer of JBBWorldwide, and Norm Wesley, current chief executive officer, at Fortune Brands, Inc. were extremely supportive.

Of course, thanks to Booker and Fred Noe.

F.P.P.

PART ONE

The Foundations

Jacob Beam and Surviving in a Harsh Land

THE DISTILLED SPIRIT OF a nation epitomizes its people, its natural resources, and its commercial and political history. While Scotland has Scotch whisky, Ireland has Irish whiskey, France has cognac and armagnac, Russia has vodka, Italy has grappa, and Spain has brandy, the United States of America has bourbon whiskey. More than just a native beverage alcohol made from grain, yeast, and water, bourbon whiskey is presently an internationally recognized emblem of America. One bourbon, in particular, Jim Beam Bourbon, the world's leading brand, has more than any other come to symbolize the American culture. For over two centuries and seven generations, one family, the Beams, has more than any other whiskey-making clan guided not only the destiny of Jim Beam Bourbon but much of America's bourbon industry.

Launched in the 1780s by Jacob Beam, the Jim Beam Bourbon saga is based in the story of seventeenth- and eighteenth-century European immigrants leaving familiar surroundings, their trades, and families for the largely unexplored New World. From England, Scotland, and Ireland, from Germany, Switzerland, and France they came, escaping religious or class persecution, starvation or famine, poverty or plague, fleeing the filth, stench, and disease of over-crowded cities or the blight of over-farmed hinterlands. With them, the immigrants brought the inherent skills of making beer, wine, and spirits learned and perfected centuries earlier by their own grandfathers and great-grandfathers. The tale of Jim Beam Bourbon can be properly told only within the context of how the bourbon whiskey industry intertwined with the building of the United States.

A century and three-quarters before Jacob Beam sold his initial barrel of bourbon whiskey in Kentucky and three and a half centuries prior to bourbon being officially cited by Congress as the native distilled spirit of the United States of America, the first colonists were acknowledged to drink substantial amounts of alcoholic beverages routinely. They did so, in part, to fortify unbalanced diets; in part, to ward off the maladies brought on by impure drinking water and cold, drafty living conditions; in part, as an act of civic unity within the amiable confines of the town taverns. Records of the period, including store ledgers, wills, and shipping invoices, prove without a doubt that drinking alcoholic beverages was ingrained in the character of the American colonists. Drinking alcohol was habitual behavior related to European heritage as much as it was relevant to issues of sustenance, commerce, manners, and health.

Fortunately, possessing the skills necessary to produce beers, wines, and spirits was commonplace in the colonial period, an expertise that went hand-in-hand with the ability to cultivate fields and orchards. Many of the colonists, especially those from Ireland, Germany, England, France, and Scotland—nations with long-standing beer, wine, and distilled spirits traditions—were accomplished brewers, cider-makers, winemakers, and distillers.

Colonists wasted no time in tilling the soil and planting grains and fruit trees. Captain John Smith, leader of England's first permanent settlement in Jamestown, Virginia, wrote of the intense "toyle" involved with planting "corne" in 1607, the very year they landed in Virginia. The brave people of Jamestown needed fresh food and robust drink in the direst way. Only 32 of the original 105 members made it through the community's first winter of 1607–1608. Obviously, beverage alcohol would not have rescued all of the 73 fatalities, but it may have helped in saving a few.

Within the first two decades of New World colonization, orchards and cultivated fields matured and the colonists were successfully fermenting the juice of pears, peaches, cherries, quinces, and apples into ciders and brewing beer from the mashes made from rye and, to a lesser degree, corn. Indeed, bourbon whiskey's North American precursor was the beer made from Indian corn. Corn, the hallmark native grain of the Americas, was initially grown domestically in what is now Central and South America. Migrating Native Americans most likely brought corn with them as they moved into Mexico and the southern tier of what is now the United States probably between A.D. 800 and 1200, centuries before the first European explorers set foot on the continent. As we will see in the next chapter, without this tall-standing, vivid green plant, bourbon whiskey, as we know it, might never have been invented in the wilds of Kentucky.

As the ramshackle, mud, stone, and stick clusters of huts gradually evolved into thriving villages by the 1630s and 1640s complete with laws, dirt streets, wood buildings, merchants, and municipal governments, alehouses sprang up like mushrooms on a forest floor after three days of rain. These low-ceiling, candlelit taverns served food cooked over open fires in addition to libations that included "cyder," the sweet, thick fortified wines from the Portuguese-controlled island of Madeira, ale imported from England, "Caribee" rum, and even colonial concoctions such as "mobby punch." Mobby was a popular drink that blended, depending on who made it, local fruit brandies and perhaps even plantation rum imported from the English and French Caribbean colonies.

In Distill of the Night

The word *distill* comes from the Latin term, *distillare*, which means "to drip apart." This relates to the action of the vapors, or clouds of alcohol, that rise into the higher regions of the still and move through a cold copper coil, the so-called "worm," where the vapors condense back into high-alcohol liquid form. This raw, aromatic, colorless spirit is often distilled a second time to purify it further and to elevate the alcohol level. Spirits running off a second distillation normally range in alcohol content from 60 percent to 75 percent.

Another favorite alehouse wash-down was the "Yard of Flannel," a sturdy hot cocktail whose recipe called for rum, cider, spices, beaten eggs, and cream as ingredients. The Yard of Flannel was heated with the glowing bulb of a red-hot loggerhead, the metal bar with a ball at the end that was always kept burning in the fireplace. Interestingly, the phrase "at loggerheads," meaning two parties who have arrived at an impasse and are likely to quarrel, comes from this period, inspired by vigorous disagreements in which combatants would brandish loggerheads.

Alehouses became unofficial town halls, the community centers for the masses of seventeenth-century America. With suckling pigs or turkeys or legs of lamb roasting on spits in the huge flagstone fireplace and rounds of rum and ale being vigorously passed around, municipal issues were debated, business deals were transacted and closed, marriages were arranged or dissolved, local politics were shaped, and religious tenets argued. Lest we forget, by the last half of eighteenth century, the walls, corner tables, and hallways of alehouses across the American colonies echoed with the risky talk of revolution and independence from the English crown by men like Patrick Henry, Samuel Adams, Paul Revere, and others.

America's first commercial distillery was opened in the Dutch colony of New Netherland, or what is now Staten Island by Willem Kieft in 1640. Kieft was the Director General of the colony. It's likely that Kieft's fledgling distilling enterprise produced both fruit brandies and neutral grain spirits made from corn or rye. Applejack, a hearty type of apple brandy, was one of the day's most favored drinks on the northern reaches of the Atlantic seaboard. New Englanders often "frosted" their apple ciders, meaning that they would leave the cider outside unprotected on cold nights to create a frozen cap. Because the cap was mainly water from the cider, the alcohol would become very concentrated in the remaining liquid. They then drained the cider off from underneath the cap. The resulting applejack was particularly crisp, heady, and refreshing.

By 1645, the English colony of Virginia had become so active in ale and cider production that regulated price controls on the sale of beverage alcohol, termed "English strong waters," were introduced by the Virginia General Assembly. This event marked the first time that legislative action influenced the commercial side of beverage alcohol in the colonies.

New London, Connecticut, the active seaport village on the Long Island Sound, was by the 1660s a noted center of the New England rum distilling trade. Exporting their own goods in exchange for imported commodities, thirsty New Londoners imported molasses, a by-product of sugar production, from the Caribbean and distilled it into rum. In general, Caribbean rum was considered the better of the two and usually fetched a higher price. But, New England rum was certainly drinkable and every bit as ubiquitous. By the 1670s, New England boasted, with full justification, being the rum-producing capital of the New World, even though the base material of rum, sugar cane, was grown 1,500 miles to the south on the plantations that dominated the colonial islands of the West Indies.

Regrettably, the rum trade of the seventeenth century also gave rise to the slave trade—native Africans being kidnapped by ruthless European traders or captured by rival tribes then sold and shipped to the West Indies in brutal slave ships to work in the sugar cane fields, sugar refineries, and rum distilleries. While the colonists of New England were relishing their rum punches and toddies, the tribal chiefs of western Africa counted their gold fees, and the British, Spanish, and French plantation owners made fortunes selling sugar to Europe and rum to America. The transplanted native Africans, the defenseless prey of this unholy commercial trinity, were left to languish in horrific, dehumanizing, and frequently fatal conditions. Tens of thousands of slaves were stranded with no chance of returning home to Africa; left with no options but to toil in the tropical heat or be mercilessly lashed, maimed, or, worse, hanged. This repulsive blemish on the history of beverage alcohol in the New World is nothing to raise a glass to.

Stillhouses, Good Manners, and Houses of Worship

Although colonial villages had expanded into towns and modest cities by the eighteenth century, the majority of the populace continued to reside on farms. In the towns, stillhouses and alehouse breweries were as common as general merchandise shops, feed suppliers, blacksmiths, and cobblers. Rum continued to be the distilled spirit of choice, especially in New England. In 1750, 63 distilleries existed in the Massachusetts colony while 30 stills flourished just in the seaside town of Newport, Rhone Island.

With the inevitable population explosion and subsequent push into the western frontiers of Pennsylvania, western Virginia, and Maryland, the agrarian culture of the colonies took root in new territories whose landscape and inland climate were more suitable for the ambitious cultivation of grains, like corn, barley, and rye. As a matter of course, farmers distilled any grain production overrun into spirits. They sold their new spirits to alehouse proprietors or physicians who incorporated them into medicines rather than destroy the excess grain and realize no profit. Distilled spirits were likewise utilized as valid currency and as barter items. Horses were traded for barrels of whiskey; cloth, tobacco, and tools were exchanged for whiskey.

By the mid-1700s, the majority of farms of every size throughout the colonies, north to south, east to west, considered a pot still as standard equipment. The typical farm stillhouse was made of wood planks. It contained a copper kettle, probably with 25- to 50-gallon capacity, perched on a brick or stone kiln so that a wood fire could be kept lit beneath it. Copper tubing that curled like a corkscrew spiraled out of the pot still's swan-like neck. Referred to as the "worm," the water-cooled coil was used for the condensation of the alcohol vapors. No stillhouse was complete without a wood vat for the collection of the raw spirit. Stillhouses were as important to the welfare of the colonial farm as the barn, the wood shed, or the chicken coop. Distilling was more a matter of economic practicality and farm business efficiency than it was a luxury or a leisurely pursuit.

One Good Term Deserves Another

Is it *whiskey* or *whisky*? America's whiskey distillers have customarily employed the letter *e* when legally describing their whiskey. There are exceptions. The producers of Maker's Mark Kentucky Straight Bourbon and George Dickel Tennessee Sour Mash do not use an *e*. Likewise, the Irish have for centuries spelled the term, *whiskey*. In Canada and Scotland, the *e* is dropped. The term *whiskey* evolved from the ancient Gaelic word *uisge beatha*, which meant "water of life." *Uisge beatha* (pronounced, OOSH-key bay-hah) developed into *usquebaugh* (OOSH-kah baw), which became anglicized around the sixteenth century A.D. into *uiskie* (OOS-kee). By the early eighteenth century, uiskie became whiskie, which in short order was transformed into either whiskey or whisky.

The term *alcohol* is actually a derivative of the Arabic word *al-kuh'l*, which means "the antimony powder," or the brittle black powder used as a base in eye cosmetics of the Middle Ages by the Moors. The commonly used word in Europe for "still," *alembic*, comes from the Arabic *al-'anbik*, which translates to "the still," meaning, of course, the boiling kettle for distillation.

The enjoyment of spirits within the farming and village communities was not considered anything but ordinary. In fact, the mores of the era dictated that it was impolite *not* to offer houseguests a spirituous libation. In his book, *Kentucky Bourbon, The Early Years of Whiskeymaking*, author Henry G. Crowgey (1971, p. 12) recounts a report by an eighteenth-century gentleman by the name of Peter Cartwright who in his autobiography wrote, "From my earliest recollection drinking drams, in family and social circles, was considered harmless and allowable society . . . and if a man would not have it in his family, his harvest, his house-raisings, log-rollings, weddings, and so on, he was considered parsimonious and unsociable; and many, even professors of Christianity, would not help a man if he did not have spirits and treat the company."

Even the clergy of the period, those mortal conduits to the ear of the eternal spirit, freely partook of liquid spirits, the terrestrial essence of grain and fruit. Is it total folly, when you ponder it, to theorize that their Sunday morning homilies perhaps became more eloquent and animated following a brief trip to the cloakroom where a jug of perry, or pear cider, might be carefully stowed among liturgical vestments? Keeping a congregation rapt on the Sabbath in colonial times couldn't have been easy when the flock, seated on hard backless benches, was either shuddering in the cold of winter or sweltering from the summer heat and humidity. Some members of the clergy, however, had to be reined in when their zeal became misplaced and burned hotter for consumption than re-demption. In an effort to curb the worst cases of clerical inebria-tion, the Virginia General Assembly, for example, passed rules governing pastoral behavior in 1631 and again in 1676. Ministers found guilty of drunkenness were fined up to half a year's pay in the most grievous instances.

While open and free consumption by any adult of beverage alco-hol was viewed as acceptable behavior in the colonies, imbibing to excess in public was most assuredly not looked on favorably. Drunk-enness simply was not tolerated in these tight, small communities that regarded self-discipline, politeness, and restraint as high-level virtues. Inebriation was considered a display of bad manners, a prob-lem of the whole community, not just the offender and his or her family, and was usually dealt with harshly and swiftly by the commu-nity leaders. As communities grew, service regulations created for tavern owners as well as for drinkers were passed by local assemblies to punish repeat alcohol abuse offenders and their servers. Public house owners were urged to serve their patrons "by the smalls," indi-cating reasonable portions. Punishments for excessive drinking, in-cluding the lash, fines, and confinement in stocks in village squares, were often public and severe. Heavy-handed purveyors faced fines or, in the most serious breeches, temporary or permanent closures.

Drunk with Power

In 1772, Benjamin Franklin compiled a long list of words and phrases he heard in his local tavern that were synonymous with "drunkenness." Some of the best that Franklin came across were gassed, plowed, under the table, tanked, higher than a kite, blotto, smashed, soused, stewed, pissed, tipsy, sottish, skunked, pickled, canned, dipped, soaked, in one's cups, crapped, tight, half seas over, three sheets to the wind, pie-eyed, loaded, well-oiled, squiffy, plastered.

Eighteenth-Century Politics and the Coming of the Boehms

Social drinking was such a sanctioned and popular activity that by the eighteenth-century, politics and even the act of choosing candidates were directly affected by it. "Treating" was the custom of candidates supplying cider, ale, or brandy and other liquid treats like rum to voters on election day. Originally an English tradition, this dubious exercise became an acknowledged and widely practiced form of last-minute persuasion in the colonies. Politicians, or their representatives, in the 1740s, 1750s, and 1760s routinely sponsored "open houses" that were, not coincidentally, strategically located near polling stations. Some accounts report that barrels of beverage alcohol were seen *inside* some polling stations.

The purpose of this none-too-subtle concept was to "treat" the prospective voter to a wee nip of peery or brown ale or Caribbean rum before he voted (women weren't yet allowed to vote, of course) to help oil his decision-making machinery. While proponents of treating vociferously argued that the practice actually assisted in "getting out the vote" and should be viewed as a necessary indulgence, dissenters pointed to the fistfights, loitering, and predictable raucous behavior, sometimes including intimidation of voters by partisans, at the polling stations. They contended that treating disrupted the sanctity of the electoral process. Clashes born of retribution occasionally occurred when candidates discovered that voters who eagerly guzzled their cider and chowed down with gusto on their deer jerky had turned coat and voted for their opponent. Bare knuckles met jaws and ax handles said hello to skulls after many a colonial election when jilted candidates dispatched their thugs to gather information about who voted for whom.

Even George Washington's early political aspirations were reportedly affected, negatively at first, by treating, or more accurately, the absence of it. His initial two election bids to gain entry into Virginia's House of Burgesses in the early 1750s ended in defeat.

Some historians postulate that maybe it was Washington's refusal to prime the voters with libations that led to his surprising disappointments. After serving as an officer in the Virginia militia in the French and Indian War, Washington returned to Mount Vernon, his grand 100,000-plus acre family estate, and ran once again for the House of Burgesses in 1758.

Having learned a bitter lesson from his previous two failed office-seeking attempts, Washington, an avid distiller himself, made sure that his deputies provided ample cider, ale, rum, and brandy for the mouths of voters—169 gallons, to be precise, at a cost of over £34, which, in its day, was a princely sum. Washington won handily by the rather safe margin of 310 to 45. That 1758 election, anointed with beverage alcohol, launched a political and military career that contributed mightily to the transformation of a straggly bunch of colonies into an independent nation. Not without more than a little irony, Washington's career famously concluded with an eloquent speech to supporters and friends in a pub in lower Manhattan by the name of Fraunces Tavern.

In 1777, another giant of early American politics, James Madison, the fourth U.S. president, fumbled and lost an election because he would not lubricate with alcohol the throats and votes of constituents. Madison later observed, as told by Henry G. Crowgey in *Kentucky Bourbon: The Early Years of Whiskeymaking* (1971, p. 17), that "the people not only tolerated, but expected and even required to be courted and treated, no candidate, who neglected those attentions could be elected. . . ." Election reforms that dealt specifically with vote-influencing issues, in particular treating, were repeatedly put forth and passed in most major colonial houses of legislation throughout the decades immediately preceding the Revolutionary War. Most politicians, however, blatantly ignored the laws and provided alcohol, one way or another, on voting day.

Beverage alcohol likewise played a central role in the rations of the colonial militias. Troops that were dispatched to the Ohio frontier in 1754 and 1755 to fight on behalf of the British Crown in the

French and Indian War were supplied with rum. In fact, according to the book, *The Social History of Bourbon: An Unhurried Account of Our Star-Spangled American Drink* (1963, p. 9) author Gerald Carson claims that rum purveyors had the temerity to follow the troop encampments, surreptitiously supplying more rum when rations ran low or money was handy. This situation caused problems of intoxication in the ranks. Offenders were flogged with 20 lashes every day until they revealed the source of the secret and highly mobile rumrunners.

In the early decades of the 1700s, two emigrations that are considered crucial to American whiskey history commenced. Both groups brought with them strong agricultural and distilling backgrounds. The initial movement dawned in 1710 when thousands of German and Swiss families began landing on North American shores from northern Europe, fleeing religious persecution, horrid living conditions, or failing crops. These travelers gravitated to Pennsylvania, the Carolinas, Virginia, and Maryland. Those Germans and Swiss who made southeastern Pennsylvania their new home became known as the *Pennsylvania Dutch*. The immigrants from Germany included families named Boehm (sometimes Bohm, Bohmen), a clan who would in subsequent decades change the spelling of their surname to Beam, probably to make both the spelling and pronunciation simpler. One branch of the Beams, which would multiply prodigiously over the course of two centuries, would, in time, make an indelible impression on the world of whiskey and distilled spirits.

The second key migration occurred when a quarter-million Scots-Irish immigrants, commonly referred to as *Ulstermen*, escaped the paralyzing poverty of Northern Ireland and crossed the Atlantic between 1715 and 1775. The Ulstermen were born from a shotgun marriage arranged in 1611 by King James I of England, himself a Scot of the House of Stuart, when he by Royal decree forcibly transplanted hundreds of Scots and English subjects to County Ulster for the express purpose of making the Irish a bit tamer through the miracles of interbreeding and intermingling.

The British Crown's policy backfired, doing nothing to alleviate the crippling poverty, illiteracy, and famine that permeated the northern counties of Ireland. Unrest and turmoil, fueled by hopelessness, continued on decades after this ill-conceived relocation.

One century later, King George I of the House of Hanover presided on the British throne. Little had changed, however, in the Northern Ireland counties of Armagh, Down, Derry, and Antrim, and few alternatives seemed more attractive to the Scots-Irish than escape to the New World. In 1717, a disastrous harvest in the Northern counties made the decision to venture to North America all but certain for thousands of Scots-Irish. What the Ulstermen brought with them, along with a sound work ethic, a burning desire for better living conditions, a pugnacious nature, and raw ambition, was an inherent flair for distilling whiskey.

These ruddy-faced, fair-skinned immigrants, who by most reports appear to have been more Scottish than Irish, spread the gospel of grain-based spirits in a land where fruit-based ciders, wines, and brandies had dominated for a hundred years. Not to mention the fact that rum was the 800-pound gorilla of distilled spirits due, in large measure, to the endless supply of molasses from the Caribbean and the well-established rum-distilling industry in New England. During the period from 1760 to 1775, it is estimated that up to 12 million gallons of rum per year were pumped out of distilleries located in Massachusetts, Rhode Island, and Connecticut. Rum lust was so powerful, entrenched, and pervasive in the coastal colonies that no one really needed whiskey.

It is no mystery why prior to the Ulstermen's mass migration, whiskey was looked upon in the pre-Revolutionary War New World as, at best, a minor distilled spirit, a trifle, and a distraction that the few grain farmer-distillers on the eastern seaboard produced only in bumper crop years when extra grain was available. Saved for baking bread, farm stock feed, and brewing ale, not for distilling spirits, grain, whiskey's primary base material along with water and yeast, was difficult to grow along the North American coastline anyway. It wasn't until the expansion of the colonies into the western frontier where grains such as rye, wheat, barley, and, of course, corn, were easier to cultivate that whiskey gained its first firm footing in North America.

The German and Swiss immigrants, as well as their Scots-Irish counterparts, not only knew how but also where to grow grain. Consequently, the overwhelming majority eventually settled in the inland flatlands and arable river valleys of Pennsylvania, Delaware, Virginia, the Carolinas and, to a lesser degree, Maryland. Ultimately, it would be from these colonies that the exploration of Kentucky, the home of bourbon whiskey, and the dynasty of the Beams would be launched.

Magnificent, Savage Kentucke

Kentucke was Virginia's westernmost virgin territory for the majority of the eighteenth century. It was a place of mythical proportions in the minds of the colonists who were itching to venture into the western wilderness to establish new settlements. A few late-seventeenth century frontiersmen attempting to establish trade with the native tribes of the Ohio River Valley pushed into parts of Kentucke. Ultimately, however, it was the fabled Long Hunters of the 1750 to 1770 period, the intrepid trappers, explorers, and hunters like Thomas Walker, Christopher Gist, John Findley, James Knox, Benjamin Cutbird, Hancock Taylor, and, of course, Daniel Boone, who more thoroughly combed and charted this magnificent, savage frontier.

After returning home to the eastern seaboard colonies of Virginia, Maryland, and the Carolinas following their months-long hunting forays, the Long Hunters wove seductive fables that depicted Kentucke as an untouched land of dense, primeval forests teeming with elk, deer, and bear, of placid ponds and lakes with pristine water that rippled with trout and beaver, of navigable river highways and rushing streams, of rolling grasslands and pastures where gigantic bison grazed. Even if in their enthusiasm while peering into the rapt faces and wide eyes of their listeners the Long Hunters magnified and colored their stories more than a little bit, their descriptions weren't far from the reality. Kentucke *was* the heart of the relatively undisturbed continent.

It isn't reaching in the least then to conjecture that perhaps the newly wedded Jacob Beam caught wind of these amazing tales before emigrating to Kentucke himself from Maryland with his wife Mary Myers. The promise and mystique of Kentucke must have been tantalizing to a young, vigorous couple who were embarking on building a life for themselves in what had become just five years prior a new, robust nation. However, the Kentucky the Beams experienced upon moving there in 1787–1788 was a far cry from the Kentucke that the Long Hunters endured just 20 to 30 years before their arrival.

With the towns of the eastern colonies from Massachusetts to the Carolinas exploding in geographical size, population, and the necessary laws of governance and social conduct, colonists who yearned for bigger skies, larger tracts of land for farming, and less rules and civilization were doubtless intrigued by the vivid stories spun by the Long Hunters. But these rugged adventurers were careful to spice their fables with frank talk about the fierce warrior-hunters of the Shawnee, Wyandot, Delaware, and Cherokee nations. The Long Hunters had had frequent contact with all of these native tribes during their trips deep into Kentucke. Sometimes that contact was cautiously amiable. Other times it proved deadly.

Kentucke was considered by the native tribes as prime hunting ground, a sort of traditional wildlife preserve that had for centuries provided meat, furs, and skins to feed and clothe their families. Surprisingly, by the time the Long Hunters began arriving, Kentucke was not viewed as a location for year-round tribal residence.

Though tribal hunting camps would be active from several weeks to a few months at a time, by 1760, no native tribes permanently resided in Kentucke.

This hallowed place's name was, in fact, derived from the tribal term, *Kentucke,* which meant meadowlands to the Iroquois, the powerful confederacy of northeastern tribes whose influence flowed from the Hudson Valley into the Ohio River Valley, and it meant land of tomorrow to the Wyandot. Even before surveying parties plotted Kentucke's precise location in relation to the eastern colonies, it was known to be valuable, fortuitously situated real estate. The land of tomorrow was bordered on the north by the mighty southwest-flowing Ohio River, to the west by the even grander Mississippi River into which the Ohio deposited its milky brown torrent, and to the east by the craggy wall of the Appalachian Mountains. Kentucke was highly prized territory by both eighteenth-century Caucasian Americans and the region's native tribes because of the immensity and diversity of its natural bounty and resources and its excellent location. As the two disparate cultures collided and clashed over the domain of one coveted spot, blood from both was spilled.

A quarter-century before Jacob Beam started cultivating the corn, rye, and barley that would be fermented and distilled into his "Old Jake Beam Sour Mash" whiskey, the landmark progenitor of Jim Beam Bourbon, the Long Hunters had blazed a route, a hunter's highway called the Wilderness Road, into Kentucke through the Cumberland Gap (originally known as the Cave Gap). The Long Hunters came in groups of 20 to 30 men. After erecting a base camp inside Kentucke, which was maintained by older or infirm members of the group, the main hunting party split into smaller teams of three or four men who would then scatter to the four winds to trap raccoon and beaver and to track and slay herding animals with firearms that provided both meat and pelts. The principal targets of the Long Hunters were deer and elk, though the occasional buffalo was highly prized as well. The typical hunt took from two to four months.

The Long Hunters, who hailed mostly from Virginia and the Carolinas, had to regularly contend with the Shawnees and the Cherokees who bitterly resented them for invading what the tribal hunters perceived to be their hunting turf. In their eyes, the white-skinned Long Hunters were poaching their game. In reprisal, tribal hunting parties routinely stole pelts and packhorses from the Long Hunters and raided and destroyed base camps. By the 1760s, the white Long Hunters, who largely just desired to hunt and explore the territory without participating in skirmishes with the native tribes, presented the tribes with a steady stream of targets for mischief.

Daniel Boone (1734–1820) was the most illustrious and remembered of the Long Hunters. More than anything else, Boone relished being in the raw Kentucke wilderness by himself or accompanied by his brother, Squire. In 1773, Boone led a party of settlers into Kentucke for the express purpose of founding a settlement. Attacks by hostile Shawnees left the group terrorized, depleted, and defeated. Boone's son James was captured by the warriors and tortured to death. In 1774, Kentucke's initial pioneer settlement was established not by Daniel Boone, but by James Harrod who entered the territory from Pennsylvania via the Ohio River. That year was likewise noteworthy for the harvest of the first crop of corn by a settler named John Harman. That initial harvest marked the true beginning of distilling and whiskey-making history in Kentucke, even though it is almost certain that spirits were not produced from that inaugural yield. The earliest settlers were more occupied with retaining their scalps than with making corn spirits. The next year, 1775, Daniel Boone broke ground for Fort Boone, which was eventually renamed Boonesborough.

Problems with the native tribes reached their zenith in the 1770s as Shawnee warriors, especially, attacked white men, women, and children indiscriminately and pilfered or burned down settlements at will. They also set upon supply parties coming from the eastern colonies, killing and looting with abandon and scant chance of reprisal. With Revolutionary War preparation gearing up in the eastern colonies on the heels of Patrick Henry's "Give me liberty or give me death" speech to the Virginia Convention in March of 1775, the influx of able-bodied men slowed on the western frontier. This left the settlements insufficiently protected and, just as important, poorly fortified. The Caucasian population of Kentucke in 1775 was only about 150, mostly male. When the Declaration of Independence was signed on July 4, 1776, in a hot and humid Philadelphia, Kentucke's population had grown only to around 200. In 1778, it was 280.

The desperate war with Great Britain radically shifted the attention away from the expansion of the western frontier and back to the "mother ship" colonies and the fight for independent standing. The pioneers of Kentucke were left to fend for themselves against the increasingly perturbed and emboldened Shawnee as well as the lurking troops of the British, who were keen on establishing a military stronghold in the western territories to squeeze and distract the colonies. Dreams and ambitions of subduing the Kentucke wilderness were fading as the gun barrels of war grew hotter.

Treaties between native tribes and pioneers from earlier years had proven to be dismal failures. Regrettably, these fragile agreements were repeatedly broken either because the white settlers brazenly reneged or were ignorant of the details, which was the case more often than not, or because the tribal elders misunderstood the terms and fine print details of the treaties. Through no fault of their own, the tribes had trouble, in particular, grasping the concept of "land ownership." The culture and traditions of the native tribes of the eastern regions of North America dictated that using and taking care of the land wasn't the same as owning it. As more treaties were signed, more were broken. Bitterness on both sides led to mutual belligerence and eventual fierce fighting.

Fearing that the British, who were building troops north of the Ohio River, would team with the agitated tribes of the western frontier against the pioneers, the decision to take the offensive in Kentucke, Indiana, and Illinois was made in Virginia in 1778. The campaign to keep the British in check and to simultaneously quell the tribal uprisings in the west was led by George Rogers Clark, an adept negotiator and seasoned soldier.

Clark departed Virginia with a skimpy force of 150 enlistees and arrived on Corn Island near the Falls of the Ohio in June of 1778. Hoping to eventually reach and capture the British stronghold at Detroit, Clark confronted and defeated the British at Vincennes, Indiana, along the way, all the while trying to make constructive contact with native tribes whom he often dissuaded with siding with the British. During 1780 and 1781, Clark battled both the British and the native tribes in and around Kentucke. Though the tribes came to fear Clark and his troops, Shawnee hostility to the settlers, nonetheless, continued in the form of small surprise attacks rather than major confrontations. Homesteader supplies were looted, livestock was killed, crops were torched. The pioneers were hard-pressed to remain in the Kentucke wilderness. Dispirited, more than a few gave up and left, heading back across the perilous trails to the eastern colonies.

The pivotal American and French war victory at Yorktown where Washington decisively defeated General Charles Cornwallis heralded the winning of the Revolutionary War by the colonies and the dawning of a new geopolitical era. In Kentucke, a weary George Rogers Clark resigned his commission in 1783 and returned to Virginia. Disputes with the weakened but hardly disbanded Shawnee, however, continued well into the 1790s, the time when Jacob Beam was starting to sell his bourbon whiskey by the barrel.

The Start of the Beam Saga

In 1772, three years prior to the first hostilities between the colonies and Great Britain, the territory of Kentucke was made part of Fincastle County, Virginia. Then in 1776, Fincastle County was trisected into Kentucky (the *e* appears to have been replaced with the y in the spelling around this time), Montgomery and Washington Counties. In 1780, huge Kentucky County was itself divided into Jefferson, Fayette, and Lincoln Counties. Of course, after the signing of the Treaty of Paris in 1783, Kentucky was included as part of the new United States as a western portion of Virginia. The Commonwealth of Kentucky became the fifteenth state of the United States of America on June 1, 1792.

The rush to settle in Kentucky, which had all but ceased during the core Revolutionary War years of 1775–1781 when troop movements, both British and American, made long-range travel unappetizing and foolhardy, sprang to life again during the final months of 1784 and early 1785. Kentucky's population growth—though, *explosion* is a more appropriate word—from the conclusion of the Revolutionary War to 1800 was phenomenal. In 1778, Kentucky's population registered at 280. By 1790, astonishingly just a dozen years later, the official census recorded it as 73,077. The state census of 1800 officially logged 220,955 residents.

What makes these figures so mind-bending is the realization of how hard it was to travel long distances in the untamed, largely uncharted western wilderness. In the early Third Millennium when traveling hundreds of miles in a single day on land or through the air is commonplace, it is easy to overlook eighteenth-century difficulties. Five to eight miles a day with packhorses and wagons ferrying people, food, supplies, and household things was looked on as an outstanding day. Few trails, or *traces* as they were referred to in Kentucky, existed.

Transport by water was one way to enter Kentucky, which has more miles of navigable streams than any of the other 48 contiguous states. Lumbering flatboats and surface-knifing keelboats that originated in western Pennsylvania, Virginia, and Maryland made their deliberate way down the Ohio River, carrying families, their livestock, farming equipment, and other belongings to the frontier. Among those belongings and equipment often were copper pot stills, coiled copper worms, and wood collection vats, the fundamental distilling equipment that would forever alter the face of the American frontier. Fort Pitt, now Pittsburgh, was considered the optimum point of embarkation for river travel to Kentucky because of its well-fixed location at the confluence of the Ohio, Monongahela, and Allegheny rivers.

Flatboats, sometimes as lengthy as 40 feet and as wide as 20 feet, were awkward rectangular vessels with flat bottoms. They were constructed of lashed timbers. Flatboats, notorious for getting stuck on sandbars, almost always had a cabin for passengers and crew as well as pens for smaller livestock. Larger versions could transport up to 70 tons of cargo, including several score sheep, pigs, cows, or goats and even wagons. Because of their low, horizontal design, flatboats traveled only one way down the turbulent Ohio River, downstream. Keelboats, the design opposite of flatboats, were wooden hull, sail-less, river-going vessels that had a shallow draft and almost always boasted a long, central cabin for shelter. Propelled by teams of burly men who rowed, towed, or poled the boats through the current, keelboats were significantly more maneuverable on the Ohio than flatboats. They likewise had the advantage of being able to venture both up- and downstream. Still, other individualistic pilgrims gritted their teeth and paddled canoes and dugouts filled with their few possessions down the Ohio.

The more popular gateway from the 1750s through the early 1800s was the overland trail that naturally cut through the narrow confines of the Cumberland Gap. The Wilderness Road led to the Cumberland Gap. Though cramped and unpaved and, therefore, forbidding to wheeled vehicles especially when sodden or iced over, the Cumberland Gap offered Virginians, Pennsylvanians, Marylanders, and Carolinians the appealing chance to enter Kentucky without having to endure the white-knuckle ride provided courtesy of the Ohio River. Wagons required at least four horses or mules to complete the journey through this well-trampled notch in the Appalachians. Aside from bad weather conditions in the mountains, the two biggest problems for pioneers, similar to their river traveling peers, were attacks either from native war parties or from white high-waymen who could easily lie in waiting above the tight passageway.

Beams of Light

According to research done in 1919 by Jacob L. Beam (a different branch of the family from the Kentucky branch), then a Princeton professor, "The name Beam is the English spelling [according to the sound] of the German Boehm. *Boehm* is German for 'a or the Bohemian'." Professor Beam postulates that the name is ultimately derived from a fourth-century B.C. Celtic tribe, named Boii, who resided in the north of what is now Italy. Two hundred years before the appearance of Jesus, the Boii tribe relocated northeast. Then around A.D. 600 they moved south through Bavaria and on to what is today considered Bohemia, origination point for the Czechs. Beams, then, are fundamentally Slavic in nature, though for many centuries they did live in Germany and the German sector of Switzerland, which explains why they are frequently depicted as being of German or Swiss origin. Many of the Mennonite Beams who emigrated from Switzerland came to North America searching for religious freedom after being the butt of religious oppression. They remained in southeastern Pennsylvania in what is now Lancaster County.

The Cumberland Gap was the way by virtually all accounts that Johannes Jacob Boehm, the man who represents America's first generation of whiskey-making Beams, entered Kentucky with his copper pot still. Acknowledging that eighteenth-century American colonial record keeping was, in many instances, sketchy, at other times nonexistent or simply has in the meantime been lost, the available evidence is inconclusive as to whether Johannes Jacob Boehm was born in America or Germany or Switzerland. While several whiskey journalists and authors of the past have flatly claimed he was a German immigrant, no open-and-shut corroborated evidence exists for such an assertion.

Confusingly, an uncorroborated account called *Distilleries of Old Kentucky* from April 1935 written by Thomas E. Basham indicates that Maryland was Jacob's place of birth. Ship records discovered in a genealogical search sponsored by a Canadian branch of Beams who published their findings on the Internet show that droves of German and Swiss immigrants named Bohm, Beem, Bome, Behm, Bohme, and Bem arrived through the port of Philadelphia via England from 1710 to 1780, Some arrived at the request of William Penn, the founder of Pennsylvania, who was looking for workers with trade skills. Jacob, it turns out, was a common Christian first name of the era.

Data unearthed and pieced together for the writing of this book from county and church records, genealogical summaries, as well as from existing Beam family history and living members of the Kentucky branch points more in the direction that Johannes Jacob Boehm's birthplace was likely to have been in Pennsylvania circa 1755 to 1760 and that he was, in actuality, a first- or even second-generation American of German descent. Indeed, another separate body of genealogical research done in 1997 stipulates through records of The Lutheran Church of New Hanover of Montgomery County, Pennsylvania that Jacob and his brother Conrad P., whose pension records show fought in the Revolutionary War for the Continental Army for three years, hailed from Berks County, Pennsylvania.

At the Jim Beam American Outpost, the official visitor's center at the distillery complex in Clermont, Kentucky, the family tree depicts Jacob as being born on February 9, 1760 in Bucks County, Pennsylvania, to Nicolaus Boehm and his wife, Margaretha. Lutheran Church baptismal records state that Nicolaus and Margaretha had five children, with Johannes Jacob listed as the fourth child. This record contains no mention of Johannes Jacob's brother, Conrad P., though it is altogether possible that Nicolaus and Margaretha relocated either before or after the birth of the five

children listed in the baptismal record. Another tidbit is that
Conrad P. in his military records lists Bucks County, Pennsylvania,
as his birthplace. Conrad P., likely Johannes Jacob's elder brother,
might well have been born in a different location earlier than
Johannes Jacob. One record states that a Nicolaus Bohm landed
in Philadelphia on October 23, 1752. Could this be Johannes
Jacob's father?

Issues and questions, whose numbers seemed to multiply as
each new shred of data was collected, arose from these strands of
information that now resemble a platter of cooked spaghetti. Had
Nicolaus and Margaretha Boehm themselves emigrated from Germany by way of England during the massive immigrations of the
middle decades of the eighteenth century, or had *their* parents accomplished that feat one or two decades earlier? If, in fact, Johannes
Jacob Boehm was born in Pennsylvania, was his place of birth Berks
or Bucks or Montgomery County? With so many hundreds of German and Swiss immigrants flooding North America during the
1700s, it is now beyond question that there were multiple sets of
Boehm/Boem/Beam clans. Therefore, some of this unearthed data
doubtless crosses over from family branch to family branch. DNA
sampling is likely the only method remaining to make final deter-
minations as to Johannes Jacob Beam's precise ancestry.

It's probable that we will never know for certain the details of
Johannes Jacob Boehm's beginnings. In light of all this sometimes
contradictory, almost always confounding information, one last
salient question surfaces: Does the exact birthplace of Johannes
Jacob Boehm, who evidently preferred to be known as Jacob Beam,
or his pre-Kentucky years critically impact the grand scheme of the
story of how a single family influenced the whiskey-distilling industry in America more than any other? No, absolutely not.

Three undeniable facts that *are* vitally important are:

1. Jacob Beam had been well-schooled in the arts and sciences
   of farming, milling, and distillation;

2. Beam married Mary Myers (1765–1830), daughter of Jost Myers, in Frederick County, Maryland, on September 20, 1786; and

3. Jacob and Mary moved from Maryland to Lincoln County, Kentucky, in either 1787 or 1788, having advanced overland through the Cumberland Gap and over the next two decades had 12 children, nine boys and three girls.

Another ironclad historical fact is that Jacob and Mary Beam are listed in the 1790 *First Census of Kentucky* as residents initially of Lincoln County. To further substantiate their presence in Lincoln County in 1790, Jacob is cited as a witness to a bill of sale that exists. Sometime after 1790, however, Jacob and Mary Beam moved to Washington County to live on Hardin Creek. Deed records from the period of 1792 to 1803 reveal a rather cockeyed inheritance of 100 acres of land by Mary Myers Beam in the late 1790s. Mary's windfall came, according to county records, courtesy of her brother Jacob Myers. The land was a parcel from a 1500-acre tract originally owned by Mary's father Jost Myers, who disbursed 800 acres of the land among his children in a will dated March 18, 1797. The official county tabulation records an indenture, or written agreement, between Jacob Myers of Lincoln County and Jacob Beam of Washington County, dated August 5, 1799, "conveying 100 acres on Pottinger Creek for 40 pounds. . . ."

This county record implies that Jacob Beam either bought the parcel for Mary from his brother-in-law for £40, or that there existed some costs involved with the transfer of ownership that Jacob Beam was willing to pick up. This odd transaction leaves one wondering, though, if in that period sons preceded daughters in the inheritance pecking order or if Mary had somehow been left out of her father's will.

Whatever the case, it is now indisputable that Jacob and Mary Beam were living in Washington County by the time that Jacob got to liking his corn whiskey enough to begin selling it by the barrel in 1795. While no recording of this genuinely momentous event in American whiskey and business history has ever surfaced, virtually every source of information mentions that particular year as the commercial launch of the Beam family whiskey dynasty. The ripple effect of that initial business transaction, the innocent selling of a barrel of whiskey made from corn, would reverberate through seven generations of Beams over two centuries . . . and, eventually, the global marketplace.

Kentucky's First Bourbon Whiskeys and a Rebellion

Claims as to who produced Kentucky's first bourbon whiskey fly as high as NOAA weather balloons. The issue of whether or not Jacob Beam distilled the first Kentucky bourbon whiskey can be put to bed at the outset. He positively, unequivocally *did not*. No members of the Beam family have ever said otherwise and nothing in all the archival material of bourbon history even hints that he did. All indications are that stills were up and percolating well before the Beams ever set foot in Kentucky in 1787–1788. With the cultivation of corn beginning in 1774, it is likely that distillation preceded 1785; maybe even 1780, when the first mentions of whiskey begin appearing in county and court records with some regularity in Kentucky County.

Some elementary deductions and assumptions regarding Jacob Beam can be put on the table without breaking much of a sweat or the elasticity of truth. With his German ancestry, it makes complete sense that he would possess the skills of a farmer-miller-distiller by the time he and Mary arrived in Kentucky. Several stories claim that the Beams brought a pot still and a worm with them from Maryland. Following that line of thought, it likewise seems correct and fitting that they established a farm with a gristmill in Lincoln County almost immediately upon their arrival. In the decades that sandwiched the Revolutionary War years, farming, milling, and distilling were interdependent farm activities that extracted the greatest benefit from the grain crop. Farmers typically utilized excess grain in the making of spirits to use for barter or trade. Whiskey was a form of rural currency.

But whiskey made from Kentucky corn wasn't the New World's first native whiskey. Whiskey made from rye, the small grain that imparts a spicy taste to whiskey, was prevalent in the colonies that surrounded the Kentucky territory, including Virginia, the Carolinas, Maryland, and, most prominently, Pennsylvania. Distilling whiskey from rye gained momentum in the 1750s and continued well into the 1800s. Rye whiskey was America's true breakthrough whiskey and, though, it would be eclipsed in popularity by corn-based bourbon whiskey later on in the nineteenth century, it has remained a favorite selection of spirits connoisseurs.

Rye whiskey, as it turns out, was also a focal point of a post-Revolutionary War crisis that was centered mostly in western Pennsylvania. The Whiskey Rebellion, a tense and potentially disastrous situation that tested the presidency of George Washington in its first term, grew out of public disgust and disdain, especially in the grain farming communities of Pennsylvania, Virginia, and Maryland, of a national tax on distilled spirits that was passed into law on March 3, 1791, and enforced starting July 1, 1791. The problem stemmed from national debt incurred mainly through the funding of the American Revolution, not by any moral decree relating to alcohol issues.

George Washington's Secretary of the Treasury Alexander Hamilton estimated the national debt of the new United States in 1790 to be $50 million to $54 million, a staggering total for the era. Hamilton was rightfully anxious to rid the fledgling nation of such a massive, crippling debt as quickly as possible. But why he chose to tax only distilled spirits rather than all alcoholic beverages is open for serious discussion, even skepticism. Cynics claimed that due to subtle pressure on Hamilton from the old eastern seaboard state power brokers, who produced much of the nation's fermented but not distilled beers, ciders, and fruit wines, distilled spirits came into his sights as a plausible alternative revenue generator. Other observers cite as a possible source of Hamilton's inspiration the excessive taxation of whisky and stills in the Scottish Highlands and Lowlands by the British Parliament throughout the 1770s and 1780s when legislation was amended or introduced five times.

Kentucky wasn't nearly as populated as Pennsylvania, hence the immediate effect of the Excise Act was minimal to most Kentuckians. Jacob Beam and his peers were probably more concerned and occupied with establishing their farms and crops and fending off the remnants of the Shawnee rather than distilling grain. Distilling hadn't yet become a major factor in Kentucky in the first half of the 1790s. That is not to say, however, that federal excise agents were not on the prowl, collecting duties or hunting down scofflaws, in and around the young settlements that perched on the banks of the Ohio and Kentucky rivers. Some agents were attacked. Kentucky's chief excise collector, Thomas Marshall, had his effigy dragged and hanged in Lexington.

Other western states and territories, however, such as Pennsylvania (which attained statehood in 1787) and Maryland (declared a state in 1788) were prime grain-growing paradises and were burgeoning. Rye was the most plentiful commodity both in solid and liquid form west of the Allegheny Mountains. A packhorse could transport only four bushels of unadulterated, unprocessed rye. When rye was transformed into whiskey, that same packhorse could carry the equivalent of 24 bushels. The farmer-distiller could, in turn, realize a handsome profit. Turning rye grain into Monongahela Rye whiskey was simply good business done on the western frontier.

In Alexander Hamilton's eyes, criticism generated from the western frontier states was easier to deal with and deflect because of the sheer distances involved. The basic idea was to levy a tax on the farmer-distillers in the hinterlands on the capacity of their stills at from 54¢ to 60¢ per gallon and any spirits made in cities, towns, and villages at from 7¢ to 25¢ per gallon depending on the proof.

The farmers were to willingly pay up their tax to excise agents because they were true, uncomplaining patriots and citizens. Federal
agents were to carry the funds back to the treasury. The concept
when diluted and dressed-for-market probably looked feasible to all
in the highest echelons of government.

Hamilton and Washington, however, grossly underestimated
how loudly the western territories would bark in protest. Compared
to the eastern states, these areas were still primitive territories
largely settled in the mid-1770s by the mess-with-me-and-you're-
dead Ulstermen. The Ulstermen lived by the words of Scotland's
beloved poet, Robert Burns, who wrote "Whiskey and freedom gang
thegither" (*Oxford Concise Dictionary of Quotations*, 3rd ed., p. 81).

By the summer of 1792, antigovernment meetings were being
attended by increasing numbers of disgruntled farmer-distillers
who felt betrayed by the federal government. The discussions soon
turned more radical in tone. People were publicly warned by the
protesters not to take up employment as excise agents. To appease
the protesters, the Excise Act was altered with an amendment that
slightly lowered the distilling tax. No matter. The damage had been
done. Citizens who paid the tax lived under the threat of having
their stillhouses destroyed by antitax dissenters. Federal U.S.
marshalls were deployed from Philadelphia in July of 1794 by the
highly annoyed Hamilton to serve protesters with writs demanding
that they appear in court in the City of Brotherly Love to explain
why they weren't fulfilling their lawful obligations. This action further inflamed western Pennsylvania farmer-distillers who could not
easily leave their farms for weeks at a time to appear in federal court
hundreds of miles away.

Another amendment to the Act in 1794 adjusted the tax
downward with little or no positive response from the inflamed
farmer-distillers. The talk of insurrection accelerated to the point
at which some of the more strident and persuasive rebels wanted
western Pennsylvania to secede from the union. Hamilton finally
lost all patience. He suggested to Washington that an army of

militia be sent to the frontier. Washington and the other members of his cabinet agreed. In haste, Washington had his military staff gather 13,000 men from four states—New Jersey, Maryland, Virginia, and Pennsylvania—in the late summer of 1794.

By October, the force, led by Hamilton himself, arrived in western Pennsylvania where they were greeted by unexpected quiet and calm. One hundred seventeen of the most vehement protesters were rounded up and arrested. Only one-quarter of those taken into custody ever had their cases reach federal court. All others were quickly released with full amnesty after being detained. In the end, only two of the men whose cases advanced to trial were convicted. They were both sentenced to death, but were pardoned by President Washington himself.

Through his patient but stern dealing with the Whiskey Rebellion uprising, George Washington assured that his presidential power would never be threatened again. In 1797, Washington completed, with customary grace, his second term in office and returned home to Mount Vernon, where he once again took up being a gentleman farmer . . . and a country distiller. In 1802, the Excise Act was repealed. Distilling and distilled spirits would remain tax-free in the United States from 1802 until 1862.

The 1790s in Kentucky and Matters of Integrity

A positive repercussion of the Whiskey Rebellion for the state of Kentucky was the scores of disgruntled and disenfranchised Pennsylvanian, Marylander, and Virginian farmer-distillers who packed up and relocated to Kentucky. Also, Revolutionary War veterans, many of whom had been paid with land grants in the western frontier, were gravitating to Kentucky to claim their compensation. Consequently, Kentucky's population tripled from 1790 to 1800.

The steady stream of Scots-Irish and Germans coupled with the establishment of towns and villages plus the dedication to the cultivation of corn all came together during the pivotal decade of 1791 to 1800. Top these salient factors off with Kentucky's pristine ground water that's filtered for decades through the natural limestone substrata that supports the northern stretches of the state and you have a winning formula for grain distilling. These fundamental building blocks served as the cornerstones for the founding of the whiskey industry in Kentucky.

Why Kentucky Whiskey Is Called Bourbon

Present-day Bourbon County, Kentucky is minute compared to when it was instituted as part of Virginia in 1785. Many of Kentucky's earliest corn-based whiskeys were produced in Bourbon County and, consequently, were first described as "Bourbon County whiskey" to set it apart from the other types of so-called "western whiskeys" of the late eighteenth century and early nineteenth century, like the popular rye whiskeys of Maryland, Virginia, and Pennsylvania. That moniker was shortened to "bourbon whiskey."

Jacob Beam, meanwhile, was busy working his land and raising his family on Hardin Creek. Family lore relates how he set up a water-powered millstone to grind his corn and other grains like rye and barley. The milled grains when added to water made the mashes that were fermented and distilled. Nearby forests of chestnut, pine, hickory, maple, poplar, hemlock, ash, and beech doubtless provided the logs, bark, and planks needed to erect sturdy outbuildings, fences, barns, pens, and stillhouses. Beam, most probably, constructed a wooden collection vat for his spirits dripping fresh and perfumed off his copper pot still. The wood was likewise used to make barrels for storage of salted meats, rainwater, and whiskey.

Good water from reliable sources, like Hardin Creek, is central to founding long-lasting communities and, certainly, to producing good whiskey. Few places in North America are as blessed with pure water as Kentucky. The state, bordered by the Ohio River to the north and the Mississippi River to the west, is a web-like network of clear-running streams, creeks, and branches. Natural springs, whose aquifers are embedded deep in the limestone shelf, supply much of the state's fresh water, now as then. Limestone water, whose taste is frequently described as being sweet or smooth, is especially good for whiskey-making because it is rich in calcium carbonate. The calcium component works particularly well with yeast cells during the fermenting stage when the farmer-distiller is making his distiller's beer.

It can be deduced from available information that Beam was proactive in making a name in the distilling business by the late 1790s and early 1800s. His pride and joy was known as "Old Jake Beam Sour Mash" and was viewed by local imbibers as a fine dram. All reliable indications are that he sold his first barrel of bourbon whiskey in 1795. The modern convenience of glass bottles hadn't yet taken hold in Kentucky. As a result, the earliest bourbon whiskeys were sold directly from the barrel. Barrels would be stored in a barn or storehouse by the purchaser who, when the hankering for bourbon became too great, would simply station his pewter mug beneath the spigot and marvel at the clear to pale amber liquid as it cascaded from the barrel.

Late eighteenth-century bourbon whiskey was a raw and fiery distillate on the tongue. To the sense of smell, bourbon whiskey was flowery, prickly in the nostrils, and grain-scented. Bourbon whiskey warmed the breast in the cold months and soothed the aches and pains incurred being a farmer at any time of year. The longer it remained trapped inside the barrel, the better bourbon whiskey became as it mingled with the wood. Extended periods in wood barrels likewise encouraged the color to deepen from limpid clarity to pale amber because of oxidation and the interaction of the spirit with the natural chemicals, like tannin and lignin, in wood.

Boil and Bubble

It is widely accepted that ancient alchemists and scientists in the pre-Christ civilizations of China, India, Tibet, Greece and Egypt dabbled with the distillation of fermented mashes of rice, millet, herbs, or flowers. The advanced and inventive dynastic Egyptian culture perhaps even passed along its secrets of crude distillation to the Hebrews, Assyrians, and Babylonians. Most distilled spirits authorities agree that it was the Moors of the Middle Ages who perfected the art of distillation to the contemporary standard. These technologically and culturally sophisticated North African nomads of Berber and Arabic ancestry introduced distillation to Europe when they occupied much of the Iberian Peninsula following Tarik's invasion of Spain in A.D. 711.

Distilled spirits, such as bourbon whiskey, are the outcome of fermentation followed by distillation, or intense heating, in pot stills. Alcohol boils at a lower temperature than water, 173.1 degrees Fahrenheit versus 212 degrees Fahrenheit. Boiling generates vapors, or ethyl alcohol in gaseous form. The hot vapors condense when cooled through cold metal coils. The resultant liquid, the distilled essence of the fermented base material, is high alcohol "spirits."

Though scant profit was to be made from selling whiskey in the waning years of the eighteenth century, Beam seems to have been active and successful enough to become renowned and respected as a whiskeyman. Perhaps early on he realized that Kentucky bourbon whiskey was a harsh spirit when immature and that maybe it improved and smoothed out with some added time in the barrel. Other distillers of the 1790s were coming to the same conclusion.

Or, maybe Beam's reason for early acceptance of his bourbon whiskey was his particular choice of grains and yeast culture. Perhaps it was his recipe—the ratios of corn, rye, and barley—for Old Jake Beam Sour Mash that set it apart. Corn, a large, sweet grain, was simple to grow and was, therefore, the most widely planted grain in Kentucky. Rye, wheat, and barley, all small grains, were cultivated to lesser degrees and, as a result, have customarily been responsible for smaller percentages in bourbon whiskeys.

In terms of social conduct, Jacob Beam set the tone for the succeeding generations of Beams. The Beam family traits of being straightforward, self-effacing, industrious, and honest took seed with Jacob. *The Nelson County Record of 1896*, published about 60 years after his death, describes Jacob Beam as a "man of sterling worth and integrity . . ." Jacob and Mary had a dozen children. In order of age from oldest to youngest, they were George, Henry, Isaac, Jacob Jr., John, Margaret, Matilda, Sarah, Thomas, David, James, and Lewis, their last child, born in 1810.

From the time of the first offspring of Jacob and Mary Beam to the last, Kentucky was well on its way to becoming a whiskey culture. By 1810, tables, incomplete in nature, compiled by the U.S. marshalls of the Kentucky Federal District stated that at the minimum seven thousand pot stills were known to be operating in the Commonwealth of Kentucky. If this official accounting was acknowledged as being unfinished, just how many stills were simmering in the hollows, glens, and forests of the Bluegrass State in the first decade of the nineteenth century?

Double, double toil and trouble; Fire burn and cauldron bubble . . . like crazy.

David Beam and
Pre-Civil War Kentucky

DAVID BEAM WAS THE tenth child of Jacob and Mary Beam. Born in 1802 in Washington County, Kentucky, David was described, in the vernacular of the day, as a "chip off the old block." David is remembered within the Beam family circle as an intelligent, quick-witted person and a true reflection of Jacob Beam in his willingness to work hard and to skillfully carry on the family businesses of farming, milling, and distilling. Family history for this period, passed on largely by word of mouth, maintains that Jacob handed the reins of the family business to David in 1820 when David was only 18 years of age. While 18 might to us seem to be a tender age to assume command of a small but flourishing family business, circumstances in nineteenth-century America frequently afforded such opportunities to capable and enterprising young men.

In 1820, the Beam household celebrated Jacob's sixtieth year. It is reasonable to surmise that after running the family farm, grist mill, and distillery, providing for 13 dependents for 35 years, and being a participant in Washington County affairs, it was time for Jacob to step away and allow younger, stronger backs and more agile minds to cope with the fast-changing social and economic landscape of Kentucky and the nation. Four years after assuming command of the Beam farm and the descriptively named Old Tub Distillery, David Beam married Elizabeth Settle on July 19, 1824, in nearby Nelson County. David and Elizabeth Beam eventually had 11 children: Joseph B., Martha, David M., Sarah M., Isaac, John H., Nancy E., George W., William P., Jacob L., and Emily. One offspring of special note, with regard to the nascent Beam bourbon whiskey legacy, was David M., born in 1833. His generation's pivotal part of the Beam story forms the core of the next chapter.

In 1829, Jacob and Mary Beam bestowed the Pottinger Creek tract of 100-acres to George Beam, their oldest son. Either a provision in the conveyance or a verbal agreement between the parties stipulated that George was to ensure the welfare of Jacob, Mary, and their daughter and sixth child, Margaret. Frail Margaret passed away that same year. It is speculated that Mary Myers Beam, authentic pioneer woman and matriarch of the Jacob Beam clan, died soon after her daughter in 1830. The Washington County Census of 1830 listed Jacob Beam at the age of at least 70 as residing with his son George. Mary Beam was not mentioned. After Jacob took up residence with his oldest son, another son, John, the fifth child of Jacob and Mary, died in 1834.

Not surprisingly, in view of the paucity of reliable early nineteenth-century records, the exact date of Jacob Beam's demise is not clear and, as a result, is up for debate in some quarters. One unsubstantiated source lists his death as occurring in 1834. We could find no corroborating data for that year. Other sources claim he passed away as late as 1839. Visits to cemeteries in Nelson and Washington counties shed no useful light on the fate or final resting place of the Jacob Beam, though other men of the same name who passed away much later in the mid-1800s were located. At this juncture, we can only safely assume that the man whose name occupies the top box of the flow chart that illustrates the Beam family bourbon whiskey dynasty died after his wife, sometime between 1830 and 1839.

Precious little documented material exists about David Beam, Jacob's anointed successor, or, for that matter, the Beam family as a whole from 1800 to the time of David's death in February of 1852. An accurate composite can, however, with a little effort be drawn of the typical farmer-distiller's life in pre-Civil War north-central Kentucky and then applied to the Beams, who had before David was born, become well-established and even prominent citizens in Washington County.

Large families, such as Jacob and Mary Beam's brood of 14 and David and Elizabeth Beam's clan of 13, were considered normal, even compulsory in the 1700s and 1800s. Practical, everyday matters like working the family property, protecting kin and property in a still hostile environment, and, perhaps most important of all, ensuring succession in the family trade and inheritance of the amassed assets outweighed family planning considerations. Mortality rates among newborns and young children were predictably high on the frontier and, therefore, it was vital for young married couples to generate as many offspring as soon as possible after their marriage. Kentucky's population in the early 1800s was overwhelmingly rural. Qualified physicians were few in number in the countryside and were frequently located days away by horse-drawn carriage in Kentucky's larger towns like Louisville, Lexington, and Frankfort. Families dealt with births mainly on their own; grandmothers, aunts, and daughters helping mothers, neighbors assisting neighbors. Midwives played a central role in birthing.

In addition, the physical demands of agrarian life made it imperative that women bear children while they were still robust and able-bodied. Bright, strong children were viewed as a sign of a family's prosperity on the burgeoning frontier. Weak or infirm tots were looked upon, sometimes with unthinkable cruelty, as unfortunate liabilities, children to be ignored and passed over in favor of those who were hearty and able to wield a scythe, work a pot still, or milk a cow.

The perspective of early Kentuckians and all frontier Americans re-garding the various roles of family members would today probably be viewed as callous. In fairness, the demands that were inescapably im-posed by the severity of life on the frontier left little time or room for sentiment or special attention for feeble offspring. Though Charles Darwin (1809–1882) didn't publish *On the Origin of Species by Means of Natural Selection* until 1859, his survival of the fittest the-ory accurately depicted life on the Kentucky frontier in the first half of the nineteenth century. If the new United States was going to prosper, the culture in pre-Civil War states like Kentucky dictated that labor pains should bring capital gains.

Duties between the sexes were clearly defined and adhered to. Field work, metal and blacksmith works, logging, erecting and re-pairing buildings, carpentry, and livestock tending and butchering were tasks that were almost always the exclusive domain of men and boys. The male members of the family were also responsible for fer-menting and distilling whiskeys and brandies. Whiskey accounted for the lion's share of farm distilling, with fruit brandy playing a minor role.

Boys were expected to remain at home to help their fathers until they were in their late teens and early twenties. Then the boys were encouraged to get married—routinely through marriages arranged by family elders—as soon as possible to a strapping young woman and start having healthy babies. David Beam, a pertinent example, was 22 when he married and became a father.

Kentucky women, like Mary Myers Beam and her daughter-in-law Elizabeth Settle Beam, generally did not participate in the exterior chores of the farm in the early 1800s. Women and girls made, mended, and washed clothes; prepared and cooked meals; cured meats; and reared and gave rudimentary educations to the family's children. Women frequently were married by their mid-teens for childbearing considerations. Life for Kentucky females was fundamentally an indoor existence that was otherwise highly localized to the family property, which often totaled in the hundreds of acres. Travel outside the immediate environs was arduous and, therefore, prohibitive. Journeys to the nearest villages were infrequent, at best.

Kentucky's Green Goddess

Kentucky's mushrooming communities, in what is now referred to as the Bluegrass Region, revolved around the cultivation, the near worshipping of the plentiful, willowy green plant, Indian corn. An easily cultivated crop, corn was usually seen growing tall in long, dense rows that extended to the horizon. The indigenous coarse grain that was so prized initially by the native tribes of the Americas, corn was the quintessential crop for a remarkably fertile area that boasted well-drained soils rich in calcium and phosphorus, a climate with ample rainfall, balmy temperatures, much sunshine throughout the growing season, and plenty of pure, iron-free ground and creek water. Kentucky's remarkably pristine water, a highly beneficial component of whiskey distilling, was naturally supplied courtesy of the subterranean limestone shelf atop which rested the Bluegrass Region. As opposed to other grains like the small grains of wheat, rye, and barley, good-natured corn could be planted on unplowed, rocky soil and newly cleared land.

In stunning abundance, corn supplied solid and liquid food for humans and superior sustenance for livestock. In properly tilled fields, corn allowed other crops to co-exist and flourish. It was not uncommon in the nineteenth century to walk into a cornfield in Kentucky or anywhere in America's great heartland and stumble across thriving rows of string beans or melons or berries or peas running parallel to the erect, green marching bands of corn. Corn was doubtless the high-grade oil in the engine of nineteenth-century agriculture in America's developing central states.

In the late summer of every year, cornhusking festivals abounded throughout the farming communities of Kentucky. The yearly jubilees celebrated the passing of another growing season. Farming communities would gather en masse over the span of several days to strip the downy husks from thousands upon thousands of yellow, gold, and white corncobs. Steaming, hot cornbread baked fresh in big country brick ovens and boiled corn-on-the-cob slathered in freshly churned butter were devoured with gusto alongside roast suckling pig, turkeys, and chickens and washed down with tonsil-tingling corn-based spirit. The raw grain spirit, bourbon whiskey's immediate predecessor known as "white lightening" or "white dog," was as crystal clear as rainwater, stinging in the nose, and had the bite of an ornery plow horse on a sweltering midsummer day.

Farmers and their wives, brothers and sisters, cousins, uncles and aunts, neighbors and friends, deacons and preachers square-danced and jigged around tented corn stalks that were set alight at sundown. Those who couldn't or wouldn't wiggle a leg sang the well-known farming songs of England, Germany, Scotland, or Ireland. Infectious music, what we now call bluegrass, was provided by farmer-musicians playing fiddles, jugs, concertinas, harps, banjos, and drums. The corn harvest revelry became an annual milestone, a signpost marking the conclusion of Kentucky's summer season and the beginning of the long, cold, dark months.

Corn harvests were incredibly voluminous. Something had to be done with all of it. Large allotments of the annual corn harvest were stored whole and husked in barns, storage sheds, and silos and used as feed for livestock throughout the winter. Another significant portion was delivered to millers, like David Beam, who for trade or cash money converted the grain into grist that was then turned into flour for baking bread, piecrusts, biscuits, and cakes. The percentage of the grist that was not sold off for feed or the making of flour was used by distillers to create a mash that would be fermented into a low alcohol liquid for the making of whiskey. Purely as a result of timing, whiskey distilling in Kentucky as well as other states was considered a wintertime activity on the farm. With fieldwork being put off until the spring thaw, the time was available to make repairs on farm equipment and to distill whiskey in the stillhouse often on a daily basis. Grain and water were plentiful and the weather was cool. A seasonal project then, most modern distilling is now a year-round activity.

To produce a mash, the grains were mixed with fresh spring or branch (stream or creek) water plus a small portion of spent beer from the previous batch in a covered vat, most typically made of wood, to create a soupy, fragrant liquid, the color of turbid, muddy water. The addition of yeast, known for two centuries as "jug yeast," initiated the fermentation that would last from three to three and a half days. In less typical cases, fermentation would take four days. Rarely more. The resultant, relatively clear liquid, the fermented mash, was, by definition, beer. While Scotland and Ireland's distillers referred to the low alcohol liquid as "wash," their counterparts in Kentucky called it "distiller's beer." Aromatic and perfumed to the point of being flowery, distiller's beer ranged in alcohol content from 4 percent to no higher than 8 percent by volume prior to being distilled in copper pot stills. Seven to 8 percent was normal.

Fermentation, as these experienced brewers and distillers intimately knew, is a violent process of biochemical transformation where a copious amount of bubbling and burbling, popping and frothing occurs inside the covered vat, or fermenter, as sugar converts to alcohol. During the fermentation period, the unleashing of carbon dioxide overtakes the available oxygen. Kentucky's small, crude backwoods stillhouses where space was often extremely limited were places where eyes welled up with tears and noses ran uncontrollably on fermentation days.

Because of the profusion of corn in the region, the primitive whiskeys of early Kentucky were composed chiefly of corn. Some accounts do report, however, on the wide presence of Kentucky rye whiskey in the late 1700s and early 1800s. This occurrence was likely a holdover since more than a few of the farmer-distillers had relocated to Kentucky following the Whiskey Rebellion and Revolutionary War from places such as Pennsylvania, Maryland, and Virginia. Rye had been the dominant grain in those states but in Kentucky corn was simpler to grow and, as a result, became the preferred grain. The early mashes were, in all probability, comprised of a mixture of corn and lesser amounts of milled rye and malted barley.

Over the five decades before the Civil War, farmer-distillers such as the Beams learned through trial and error that the blending of corn with rye and barley malt at the mashing stage produced a more palatable, less aggressive and hence more commercially appealing whiskey. As the whiskeymen spent more time experimenting in their nineteenth-century stillhouses, they began to develop individual and unique mash recipes that suited their own tastes. The majority of the closely guarded formulas included corn, rye, and barley. Wheat was available but was included less than and rarely, if ever, with rye. Rye and wheat are compatible for neutral grain spirits, such as vodka, that are not matured. They are not, however, considered complementary grains by distillers for the creation of whiskey.

Some of the mash recipes from the early 1800s still exist and continue to form the core of certain bourbon whiskey brands. The Beam family claims that Jacob Beam's original mash recipe is still employed by the distillers at the Jim Beam Distillery 208 years later. From Jacob Beam's Old Jake Beam Sour Mash of two centuries ago to present-day Jim Beam Kentucky Straight Bourbon, Beam family bourbons have featured the corn-rye-barley trinity of grains.

As Kentucky's population grew, so did the number of stillhouses. One estimate claims that in 1810, a full decade before David Beam turned 18, 2,200 distilleries were in operation in Kentucky, cranking out over two million gallons of grain whiskey a year. When David Beam did take the helm of the family business, farm distilleries were rudimentary operations that were, for safety reasons, erected far from the property's residences, barns, sheds, livestock pens, corrals, and other valuable structures. Because of the inherent volatility and gaseous nature of fermenting and distilling and the use of intense heat, stillhouses were acknowledged to be potentially dangerous, sometimes deadly places. Most stillhouses had one or more sides open to the elements to reduce the risk of gas build-up. Explosions and fires, though, were common even when distillation was being conducted under the eye of the most conscientious distiller. Death and maiming from severe burns occurred with regularity in distilling communities. Ethyl alcohol, the goal of any distillery, is one of the most flammable, manmade compounds known. A tiny spark anywhere within the stillhouse could ignite the alcohol, creating a destructive fireball.

Kentucky's early whiskeys were distilled a single time in metal, copper-lined kettles that were topped by pewter coils that cooled and condensed the alcohol vapors. As the push for better whiskey swept the middle decades of the 1800s, a second distillation was added to further purify the spirit by eliminating congeners and fusel oils as well as to elevate the alcohol level. Nowadays, virtually all bourbon whiskeys in Kentucky undergo a two-stage distillation process, using continuous stills called *singlers* for the initial round of boiling and then copper tank pot stills known as *doublers* or *thumpers* for the second boil.

Abraham Lincoln: Native Kentuckian, Illinois Tavern Owner, 16th President

Thomas Lincoln, Abraham Lincoln's father, was illiterate but he was as handy with wood as he was with a plow. A Hardin County, Kentucky, farmer and a carpenter, Thomas tended his farm, made barrels for his farmer-distiller neighbors, crafted furniture and, on occasion, helped out at Wattie Boone's Nelson County distillery. On February 12, 1809, his wife Nancy Hanks Lincoln bore him a son, Abraham, in their log home.

Seven years later in 1816, Thomas Lincoln exchanged his Hardin County farm for $20.00 and 10 barrels of whiskey and set out with his family for Spencer County, Indiana, where they settled. In 1830, when young Abe was 21, the Lincolns relocated to Macon County, Illinois. In 1832, Abe ran for the Illinois State Legislature and was defeated. About a year later, he opened, with two partners, William Berry and John Bowling Green, a tavern and mercantile store in New Salem, Illinois. The name of the tavern/store was Berry & Lincoln.

According to the memory of a hired clerk who worked in the store for several months (as recounted in *Whiskey: An American Pictorial History* by Oscar Getz, 1978, pp. 91–92), the stock of Berry & Lincoln leaned heavily to spirited liquids, especially whiskey. Lincoln sold his whiskey for 6¢ a glass. The clerk contended that Berry & Lincoln had stocked foodstuffs before his arrival but offered only beverage alcohol during his brief tenure.

In 1834, Abe ran again for the State Legislature and won, serving four consecutive terms before leaving to practice law in 1842. In 1861, he became the nation's 16th president.

Up until the 1810s to 1820s, the most common heat source for farm pot stills was a wood fire. The fires were located within a brick and mortar oven beneath the copper pot still that rested on the oven. Wood fires, which were notorious for generating uneven heat, were labor-intensive and because of wayward sparks and embers, they were sometimes hazardous. Whiskey production in such primitive conditions was limited to making minute amounts of fresh spirit. Farmer-distillers in the nineteenth century typically measured their production by how many "wine gallons," or 3.785 liters, of spirit were produced per bushel of grain. A relatively efficient distilling operation in the 1820s, like the Beam family's Old Tub Distillery, would average from two and a half to three wine gallons of pure grain spirit per bushel of grain. By the end of an average day of distilling in the 1820s and 1830s, David Beam would have 30 to 40 wine gallons of fresh spirit resting quietly in a wood storage barrel. A very good, if infrequent, day at Old Tub would produce 50 to 60 wine gallons off the still.

While whiskey and other distilled spirits had been, by custom, stored, transported, and sold in wood barrels well before Kentucky was settled and admitted to the Union as a state, it wasn't until the last years of the eighteenth century that American distillers began to notice that wood barrels did more than just store the whiskey. Like most of the lore concerning the evolution of bourbon whiskey, determining which distiller first deduced that the character of bourbon dramatically improves when it is stored in oak barrels for extended periods will forever be mired in uncertainty. Between 1780 and 1800, Kentucky farmer-distillers started maturing their whiskeys in charred oak barrels for longer terms than what would be considered normal storage. The reason was that aged-in-oak whiskey was significantly mellower and less fiery on the palate. It was likewise slightly tinted in color, displaying a straw yellow, slightly reddish amber hue. The tawny hint of red inspired Kentuckians to nickname bourbon whiskey "red likker," "red eyeball likker," and "red-faced liquor." These monikers may have been influenced, as some historians think, by the physical reaction to them by the heavy-drinking sector of the population.

The beneficial effect of the wood barrels had everything to do with the fact that coopers, the skilled men who made barrels out of wood, torched the inside of the half-made barrels to make the staves more pliant and workable. Heat makes hardwoods like oak, the favored wood used for barrels, more malleable. In order to be made water tight, half-constructed barrels were maneuvered over pits of open flames and seared on the inside before metal hoops were fitted over them. Coopers also liked to char the insides of the barrel to singe off splinters, ridding the staves of parasites and smoothing rough edges and grains.

In American barrel-making circles, there were four levels of charring, level four being the most deeply charred. The deeper the char, the greater the flavor impact on the new spirit. Whiskeys matured in barrels that were charred to levels three or four, where the toasting invaded the wood layer from one-sixteenth up to one-eighth of an inch, sometimes took on a sweet, vanilla-like or even sap-like taste. That's because the innate sugars in the wood caramelized under intense, prolonged toasting, creating what coopers and distillers called the "red layer." The red layer is the thin membrane of caramelized sugar that lay just beneath the surface of the stave. As the whiskey was absorbed into the barrel, especially during the heat and humidity of summer when barrels and whiskey expand, the spirit took on some of the sweet, toasty characteristics of the red layer.

The recognition by Kentucky's pre-Civil War distillers, among them Jacob and David Beam, of the effect of long-term maturation in charred oak barrels was a key turning point in the history of bourbon whiskey, one that would, in time, become part of the legal definition of bourbon whiskey.

Cue the Industrial Revolution

As modernization on many fronts erupted in the 1820s and 1830s across the United States and Europe as the Industrial Revolution approached full-speed, numerous distilling advancements became available to David Beam and his peers. Better grades of copper, shipped in large sheets from England and Holland, were appearing on the docks of Boston, Philadelphia, and Baltimore. Coppersmiths were moving into the hinterlands from the eastern seaboard. Consequently, pot stills were increasingly available for sale in the general merchandise stores of Louisville and Lexington as well as on the dry goods-laden flatboats of the roving peddlers who journeyed up and down the Ohio and Kentucky Rivers hawking their wares. Farmer-distillers, many of whom before the 1820s, operated patched-up, dilapidated, and dangerous pot stills with capacities of only 30 to 40 gallons or less were able to purchase new, shiny copper pot stills whose inner chambers had double, even triple the capacity of the old-fashioned, out-dated kettles.

Notable progress in the distilling arena, however, didn't stop with improved and more capacious equipment. The age-old method of heating pot stills with wood fires was being gradually replaced by the use of steam heat, a more efficient and constant heating process. Steam-generated heat was also a much safer option for distillers than open wood fires from which flying embers could easily start a fire, any distiller's worst nightmare. As a reliable source both for power and heat, steam was a scientific revelation, an authentic technological breakthrough in the opening decades of the nineteenth century.

Not only did steam power improve the farmer-distillers' lot for the production of bourbon whiskey, it also made a benchmark commercial impact through the invention of river-going, paddle-driven steamboats. With the Louisiana Purchase in 1803 by Thomas Jefferson, the nation's third president, the hold of the United States on the vast area west of the Mississippi River up to approximately the Continental Divide in the Rocky Mountains was secured. Up until Jefferson wrangled the huge tract of land away from France's Napoleon for the reasonable sum of roughly $15 million, the Mississippi and Missouri River basins were unprotected and dangerous places, dominated alternately by the French, British, and Spanish. Much of the territory was unexplored at the time of the exchange.

In one deft, visionary motion, Thomas Jefferson doubled the size of the United States. After Lewis and Clark on their renowned 1804 expedition leading the intrepid Corps of Discovery charted the northern reaches of the region along the Missouri River, settlers began moving west. One of the biggest gains of the Louisiana Purchase was without question the opening of the Mississippi River from St. Louis to New Orleans to greater commercial traffic that no longer was hounded by French or Spanish troop patrols. By the steam-powered paddlers ability to transport, both up- and down-river, large volumes of cargo from river port to river port, steamboats helped revolutionize the distribution and sales of Kentucky bourbon whiskey.

As terrestrial modes of transportation increased, Kentucky's bourbon whiskeys grew rapidly in commercial importance to Kentuckians. While the inventions of the steam locomotive and steam-powered paddleboat would eventually be crucial to the distribution of bourbon whiskey, pragmatic farmer-distillers like David Beam who dealt with life in the here and now initially relied on roads to get their whiskeys to market. Originally, Kentucky was a place sparingly crisscrossed by *traces*, or trails, worn into the ground over centuries by buffalo, deer, or native tribal hunting parties. It was clear, however, when mass immigration started after the Revolutionary War that more roads would have to be built to connect the villages and communities of Kentucky. Better roads meant increased civilian travel and movement of marketable goods, like bourbon whiskey.

In 1797, two years after David Beam's father sold his first barrel of Old Jake Beam, the Kentucky General Assembly approved meager funds for existing road maintenance as well as for new road construction. That same year, Kentucky's first tollgate went up at Cumberland Ford. But funds collected from a few tollgates would never be enough to launch the kind of energetic road-building campaign that Kentucky's citizens demanded and the territory's future required. Land was cleared and roads were built, according to historians Lowell H. Harrison and James C. Klotter, co-authors of A New History of Kentucky (1997, p. 125), largely by unpaid labor through the system known as *corvée*. The corvée system dictated that each year all Kentucky men aged 16 and older worked free of charge on the road system for a designated number of days to repair existing roads and establish new ones.

The system worked in an extraordinarily successful fashion. By 1837, Kentucky had invested $4.5 million and had 343 miles of surfaced roads to show for it. By 1849, the state boasted 962 miles of paved roads, an admirable achievement considering the lack of mechanization. The stone-surfaced roads allowed Concord stagecoaches (the customary coach frequently seen in western films) to travel back and forth from Louisville to Nashville in two days, ferrying up to six passengers, a cache of mail, and modest amounts of freight. The one-way cost was $12.00 per head, which included an overnight stay with a meal at Bell's Tavern midway in the 180-mile journey. With the opening of the road network, bourbon whiskey, the most cherished cottage industry in Kentucky, began to take on the trappings of a bona fide industry.

David Beam and his fellow farmer-distillers could for the first time do more than just imagine selling their bourbon whiskeys beyond the immediate confines of the counties where it was being produced. By the mid-1830s, barrels of Old Jake Beam Sour Mash and other whiskeys started showing up in taverns in nearby Kentucky towns that perched on the Ohio River such as Louisville, Owensboro, and Paducah, not to mention Evansville, Indiana. How long might it be before the citizens of major cosmopolitan river towns like Memphis, Vicksburg, Natchez, Baton Rouge, and, the south's premier city, New Orleans, or towns like Nashville connected to Louisville by paved roads would be relishing the breast-warming delights of bourbon whiskeys such as Old Jake Beam Sour Mash, Old Crow or Old Pepper?

Distilleries and bourbons were becoming more plentiful as north-central Kentucky was transformed from a remote and treacherous eighteenth-century wilderness into an advanced agricultural region in the nineteenth century. Kentucky's prime heartland location made it a vibrant and unavoidable crossroads between the established eastern states and the ever-expanding push to the west as well as between Ohio, Illinois, Indiana, Michigan, and Pennsylvania to the north and Tennessee, Mississippi, Arkansas, and Louisiana to the south. Kentucky was primed and able, due to its fortunate situation and the inherent creativity of its diverse population, to absorb the free-flowing bombardment of newfangled concepts and inventions that heralded the inevitable coming of modernization in the commercial, social, financial, and educational sectors.

Jacob Beam's Deep (But Light and Savory) Secret

The Beam family through seven generations has kept the recipe for Jim Beam Bourbon a closely guarded secret. Jacob Beam, the first Beam to distill whiskey in Kentucky, was said to have loved one beverage more than his own Old Jake Beam whiskey, the predecessor of Jim Beam Bourbon that was popular for a century. The secret? Jacob, being of German descent, enthusiastically relished beer. It's said within the family circle that Jacob thought whiskey was too harsh. In fact, some family members claim that Jacob actually set out first to make a light, palatable beer and then ended up distilling it to make Old Jake Beam Sour Mash. His friends were so impressed with Old Jake Beam Sour Mash that Jacob felt compelled to continue making whiskey.

David Beam's foremost strength, and maybe the most compelling reason that Jacob Beam selected him over his brothers to run the family business, was his openness to and fascination with contemporary ideas. David Beam wasn't afraid to break with tradition as long as it meant furthering the fortunes of the family business. The extraordinary four-decade period of 1810–1850 that preceded the Civil War demanded that a vigorous and forward-thinking David Beam lead the "Old Tub Distillery," adapting and tinkering as new technologies emerged and as business opportunities presented themselves. Around 1830–1832, he enlarged the Old Tub Distillery on Hardin Creek to meet the demand. By all accounts, David Beam listened and reacted very well indeed since the family's distilling business substantially grew in volume sales and reputation under his guidance.

. . . And the Word Was "Bourbon"

With Kentucky's communities growing rapidly during David Beam's tenure, businessmen, including distillers, began advertising their goods and services in regional newspapers and other periodicals. According to Henry G. Crowgey's book *Kentucky Bourbon: The Early Years of Whiskeymaking* (1971, p. 60), newspaper ads touting bourbon whiskey began appearing in Kentucky in the early 1820s. Public notices would sometimes advertise enormous lots of whiskey for sale. One such advertisement by a distiller named General Green Clay offered 3,000 gallons of whiskey and four casks of peach brandy. Crowgey cites another print advertisement (p. 120) dated June 26, 1821, and appearing in the *Western Citizen*, a periodical from Bourbon County. The copy enticed readers to purchase a barrel or keg of BOURBON WHISKEY. The advertisement was placed and sponsored by the company of Stout and Adams of Maysville, Kentucky. While this lone event may not seem significant, the use of the words "bourbon whiskey" is, in fact, very important because of the public identification of the singular whiskey produced in north-central Kentucky specifically known as bourbon whiskey.

By the late 1830s and early 1840s, it wasn't just the locals calling their whiskey bourbon, it was much of the population in the Ohio and Mississippi river basins. By the time the first shots of the Civil War rang out in April of 1861, bourbon whiskey was widely recognized throughout the eastern half of the nation as the hallmark whiskey from Kentucky.

But, why was this corn-based spirit referred to as bourbon whiskey in the first place? Why not just as plain old Kentucky whiskey or even more elaborately as Kentucky sour mash corn whiskey? Bourbon whiskey is so named because originally Bourbon County, Kentucky, was an immense area that encompassed many of the subsequent counties in which whiskey was distilled 20 years hence. The Virginia Assembly created vast Bourbon County in

1786 out of Fayette County, in part, to flatter France, its monarch, Louis XVI, and the country's aristocracy. Louisville, the city, was named after Louis XVI. During the Revolutionary War, France had doled out financial, military, and arms assistance to the colonies. The French helped the American cause for independence not so much because they felt compassion for the seemingly overmatched colonists, but because they vigorously detested the British, their traditional archenemy. They also wanted to expand and prop up their own sagging influence in North America. The support of the French, though largely self-serving, was nonetheless critical.

We can, without great exertion, conclude that Kentuckians opted to call their native spirit *bourbon whiskey* merely to differentiate it from the era's other major style of whiskey, Old Monongahela rye. Pennsylvania's famous rye-based spirit predated Kentucky's bourbon whiskey by a minimum of a half-century, so the onus of drawing distinctions between the two competing whiskeys rested squarely on the shoulders of the Kentuckians. More an issue of convenience than of chauvinism, the people of Kentucky were astute merchants and were quick to realize that commercial success with their whiskey could be theirs if they made it stand alone.

What Is the Sour Mash Process?

Kentucky's bourbon whiskey distillers have for over a century and a half held back as much as a quarter of the mash from one fermentation and, then, added it to the next mash slated for fermentation. The distillers' reason was that the sour mash, or "backset" as it is also referred to, helps to maintain a consistency in quality from batch to batch. They likewise asserted that the backset combats wild yeast cells floating in the air and provides a measure of the yeast required for the subsequent fermentation. Most American whiskey experts agree that a celebrated and innovative Scotsman by the name of Dr. James Crow started the sour mash process in the 1830s. All Kentucky distilleries currently employ this method in the making of straight bourbon whiskey. The Old Crow Kentucky Straight Bourbon Whiskey brand is incidentally owned by Jim Beam Brands, who makes the whiskey according to Dr. Crow's recipe.

By the end of the 1820s, some of Kentucky's more elite bourbon whiskeys began to be described by actual brand names in newspaper ads and on the chalkboards that stood outside the doors of general merchandisers. For the first time in American whiskey history, the identities of whiskey distillers were becoming calculated selling points: Jacob Speare's Old Whiskey, Old Jake Beam Sour Mash, Solomon Kellar's, John Bedford's Whiskey. The distillers' names were beginning to be linked to their distillates. This direct connection, probably unintentional at first, gave the impression of better quality. The reasoning was textbook Marketing 101: If the distiller's name was seen on the barrel or the ceramic jug, the message was clear: *This person has enough confidence in his whiskey to put his name on it. It must be good.*

Industrialization and modernization also meant that farmer-distillers were about to receive a startling, if harsh dose of reality dispensed by businessmen who, after seeing how warmly Kentucky bourbon whiskey was being received by the drinking public, envisioned creating an entire trade out of commercial distilling. The first commercial whiskey distillery to be built in Kentucky was the Hope Distillery, supported by the bulk and influence of a reported $100,000 bankroll by a company headquartered in New England but incorporated in Kentucky. The imposing Hope Distillery opened in Louisville at Main Street and Portland Avenue in the summer of 1817 to much local fanfare and, we can imagine, some measure of trepidation by small-output local farmer-distillers like the Beams.

Sam K. Cecil reports in his book, *The Evolution of the Bourbon Whiskey Industry in Kentucky* (1999, p. 83), that the humongous plant boasted the latest in steam technology for its power in the form of a 45-horsepower engine. Its mechanized grain-processing station automatically did the work of tens of laborers. Hope Distillery's enormous trio of copper pot stills were imported from England and, together, tipped the scales at over 20,000 pounds. The pot stills' unheard of capacities were 1,500 and 750 gallons. Hope Distillery's mammoth pot stills were said to produce from 1,200 to 1,500 gallons of raw spirit per day. This was a prodigious, unprecedented amount when compared to the "well, no fire in the hole so it's a good day" average of 20 to 30 gallons a day tallied by most farmer-distillers. And, that was on the days when their farm pot stills were even operating. "Is Hope Distillery a signal of the beginning of the end for farmer-distillers?" some small distillers must have wondered as they stood looking in awe at the huge plant.

With so much funding underwriting the ambitious endeavor and so many innovative ideas in place, things started out promisingly for Hope Distillery. The Louisville business community was abuzz about its immediate impact as a budding landmark. Hope Distillery chugged briskly along for about three years. Then it suddenly began stumbling along for another 12 to 18 months before finally closing down for good. To the horror of the Louisville community and the gleeful delight of the small-fry farmer-distillers of north-central Kentucky, the New Englanders expressed their regrets, packed up, and high-tailed it back to the Northeast. All the latest technology and state-of-the-art equipment couldn't save Hope.

Some observers have claimed that in the end Hope Distillery was, in reality, undercapitalized and that the owners hadn't properly anticipated the high costs involved with such an ambitious start-up. Other people have reasoned that the age of big business distilleries simply hadn't yet come around to agrarian America. Still other authorities have postulated that whiskey drinkers flat-out rejected the "factory" whiskey in favor of the handcrafted, more intense whiskeys from the farmer-distillers to which they had become accustomed. From the various accounts and reports, it's fair to conclude that Hope Distillery failed due to a full menu of reasons, including the aforementioned three. Louisville lost Hope

Distillery in the early 1820s but Louisville's best whiskey days were still ahead of it.

Viewing this episode from another vantage point, Hope Distillery's very presence and the fact that it rose from nothing and operated for over four years did in its own way herald the future of bourbon whisky distilling in Kentucky and distilling, in general, for the United States. Even though the Hope Distillery venture collapsed, bourbon whiskey manufacturing itself was beginning by the mid-1820s to incrementally shift from being a seasonal sideline undertaking of small farmer-distillers to being a focused industry led by full-time, profit-driven businessmen-distillers.

The nation was in the midst of the greatest upheaval in terms of new, daring ideas, use of natural resources, and technological innovations that it had ever experienced. The four decades of the 1810s, 1820s, 1830s, and 1840s were remarkable for the amount and sheer variety of scientific, medical, commercial, technological, and industrial advancements. Samuel Morse invented the telegraph in 1834. Over the span of the next two decades, 23,000 miles of telegraph lines connected the major metropolitan centers of America by wire. Cement was created in 1824. Hydraulic turbines were invented in 1849, as were safety pins. Other inventions and critical events of the period, to cite just a handful include: vulcanized rubber was developed in 1839; the first Colt revolver appeared in 1836; the sewing machine debuted in 1846; the reaper changed farming forever beginning in 1834; the first steam locomotive was rolled out in 1825; the Baltimore & Ohio railroad line opened in 1828; the Erie Canal opened in 1825; California and New Mexico were obtained in 1848; gold was discovered in the Sierra Nevada foothills in California in 1848; the first postage stamps were used in 1847; the first anesthetic was applied in 1842; aspirin was invented in 1849; and Robert Fulton's first steamboat appeared in 1807.

North-central Kentucky, America, and the world were about to change in ways never before dreamed of because of the dual impact of the Industrial Revolution and America's unwavering dedication to the principles of democracy and free enterprise. David Beam's 30-year reign at Old Tub Distillery drew to a close in 1850 when in failing health he passed the baton to his third child, David M. Beam, Jacob Beam's grandson. David Beam died in 1852 at the age of 50.

But the demise of his father wouldn't affect David M. Beam nearly as much as the nascent clouds of dissent and anger which were forming in the southern skies as the nation began to grapple with the intense issues of slavery and states' rights.

David M. Beam and the
Debris of War

SPRING-BOARDING FROM THE preceding 40 years of development
and expansion, the 1850s were an especially vibrant period of social, economic, cultural, and commercial advancement in Kentucky
and all the central states of the Union. Unfortunately, the decade
was also remembered as a period of keen anxiety and grave concern
due to the trouble brewing 600 miles to the west in the Nebraska-
Kansas territory as the scalding hot and inextricably intertwined
topics of slavery and states' rights spurred talk on the streets, in taverns, and around dinner tables.

Within the Bluegrass State itself, however, life was improving at
a hell-bent pace, both for established citizens and newly arrived Kentuckians. Previously obscure hamlets such as Bardstown in Nelson
County were evolving into busy and renowned, if still countrified,
whiskey centers. Formerly sleepy villages like Bowling Green, Owensboro, Covington, Frankfort, and Lexington were developing into
strategically important towns for railroads and steamboat lines. These

five communities, in particular, were labeled as Kentucky's "depot" and, perhaps more poetically, "whistle stop" towns. Louisville was the state's showcase community, though. A lively, cosmopolitan, and bustling commercial, mercantile, and transportation hub, Louisville's steady growth had been helped substantially by both its vigorous steamboat traffic and its own flourishing steamboat construction industry. *A New History of Kentucky* by Lowell H. Harrison and James C. Klotter (1997, p. 130) reports that by the time calendars had turned from 1849 to 1850 "boats totaling 14,820 tons were registered at the Falls City." Louisville, with its commanding location at the Falls on the Ohio, lorded over the course of private and commercial traffic to the west from the Falls to the Mississippi River and to the east through to Cincinnati and Pittsburgh.

Louisville's prominence and urbanity immeasurably enriched and contributed to the opening up of north-central Kentucky's regional treasures to the rest of the nation. Fine bourbon whiskey, beautiful, well-read women, courtly, sophisticated gentlemen, and the nation's finest country for breeding thoroughbred horses were ballyhooed and touted in books and periodicals as the north-central Kentucky's most illustrious natural resources. By the last quarter of the nineteenth century, these attributes would become icons, nationally acknowledged emblems of the Bluegrass Region. Irvin Cobb, the Paducah, Kentucky-born humorist, circuit judge, and prolific author of more than 50 books, described the bourbon whiskies of the nineteenth century as being "properly qualified to caress a gentleman's palate as only a gentleman's palate should be caressed" and as "mellow as the moonlight."

Quicker communication between communities became a reality with the spread of Morse's telegraph, the growth of newspapers and magazines and the gradual augmentation of postal service even into the state's more rural corners. The ability of Kentuckians to journey to neighboring towns and even bordering states was made significantly simpler by the network of newly paved toll roads, regular steamboat service schedules, and the expanding Louisville &

Nashville (L&N) Railroad. Whiskey distillers in the "limestone water zone" counties of Nelson, Washington (including the Beams' well thought of Old Tub Distillery), Spencer, Bullitt, and Anderson counties took full advantage of this unprecedented era of modernization by enlarging their existing distilleries, by upgrading their pot stills to state-of-the-art status, or by erecting new facilities and warehouses to meet the expanding regional and national demand.

Bourbon whiskey was now being regularly transported back east across the Appalachians, where the hankering for rum and Madeira had finally run its course and been supplanted by the itch for the new-fangled, American-made grain whiskey made in Kentucky. Bourbon whiskey was the beneficiary of surging mid-nineteenth century buzz circulating around the period's taverns, general merchandise stores, and pubs. Kentucky bourbon dominated Pennsylvania's Monongahela rye in production volume by a healthy margin of over three-to-one. Bourbon whiskey shipments were likewise climbing in the northern tier states of Indiana, Illinois, Ohio, and Michigan as well as further west into Missouri and the still relatively untamed Nebraska-Kansas territory. The city of St. Louis, in particular, developed into a bourbon whiskey center, with virtually every public house and tavern offering multiple choices of Kentucky whiskey.

The states of the Deep South, most notably, Louisiana, Georgia, the Carolinas, Virginia, Mississippi, Alabama, and Arkansas were, however, the decade's most fertile and vibrant consumer market for Kentucky bourbon whiskey. Shipments of bourbon whiskey by steamboat from Louisville to New Orleans and later by 1860 by rail from Louisville to Nashville and points beyond were large, regular, and profitable.

By the 1850s, whiskey making in Kentucky was no longer perceived as being an adjunct farming activity leftover from the late eighteenth century, or as a part-time method of disposing of excess grain during the slow, chilly winter months. The production of bourbon whiskey was now turning into a modern, self-sustaining industry in north-central Kentucky. Brands of bourbon whiskey were taking shape and taking hold. In addition to David and David M. Beam, both highly acclaimed distillers of their day, some of the other benchmark whiskey distillers in bourbon history—Oscar Pepper and Dr. James Crow (James E. Pepper and Old Crow bourbon whiskeys), J. W. Dant (J.W. Dant and Yellowstone bourbon whiskeys), Taylor William Samuels (Maker's Mark bourbon whiskey), George T. Stagg (Ancient Age Distillery), Henry McKenna (Henry McKenna bourbon whiskey), W. L. Weller (W.L. Weller bourbon whiskey) as well as David's other son and David M.'s sibling, John H. Beam (Early Times)—were becoming keenly active in distilling during the years leading up to the Civil War.

The public profile of Kentucky bourbon whiskey as a distilled spirit of quality was dramatically improving in large measure because of these dedicated, steady, and innovative distillers who each strove to refine their product. *The Nelson County Record of 1896* reports that "David Beam . . . from 1820 to 1850 made excellent whisky. About this time the Beams were known all over Nelson and adjoining counties as among the best producers of whisky in this territory." The account goes on to describe David M. Beam, the third generation, as "one of Nelson's most honored citizens (who) succeeded his father (in 1853), and made a great success by his knowledge of how to make a good whisky."

In the pre-Civil War decades, whiskey was transported and sold for the most part directly out of the barrel in which it was aged and stored, though bulky ceramic jugs, glass decanters, and crude handblown glass bottles were slowly making their way into the marketplace. Not all the merchants, tavern owners, and innkeepers who sold bourbon to their patrons were paragons of integrity, according to Gary and Mardee Haidin Regan, authors of *The Book of Bourbon and Other Fine American Whiskeys* (1995, p. 40). Write the Regans, "The distillers supplied bars and saloons with decanters and bottles that bore the distillers' names and could be used to pour their product, but it wasn't at all uncommon for cheap whiskey to be poured from its cask into decanters that advertised a more expensive product." As bourbon whiskey grew in popularity during this era, cheating even bled over into the distilling ranks. Rogue distillers, who were out to reap a fast and easy profit at the expense of the ill-educated and unsuspecting masses, made bogus bourbon by surreptitiously blending minute amounts of real bourbon whiskey with greater portions of characterless, totally raw neutral grain spirits. The concept of whiskey brands and the sense of reliability that brands instilled in the eyes of the consuming public became all the more important at this stage in bourbon history as *rotgut,* the so-called "shadow whiskeys," proliferated in some markets.

The Second Most Important Revolution in Distilling History

When Aeneas Coffey patented his refinement of Robert Stein's still design in 1830, it heralded the dawn of a new era in distillation. Only the creation of the first primitive pot still, circa A.D. 800 to 1000, can be considered a more monumental event in the history of spirits. For approximately a millennium, spirits were distilled in one solitary way, in the bellies of metal pot stills. Pot still distilling is a touch romantic, in that, each distillation is its own entity, its own individual batch, and, therefore, can be said to exhibit a unique character. Continuous distillation in column stills, on the other hand, can be described as producing more faceless, more uniform spirits that don't normally display the same types of idiosyncratic characters of pot stilled spirits.

The primary attraction of column stills is their inherent ease of operation compared to fiddly pot stills. Column stills in Kentucky, where they are referred to as "singlers" for their single distillation process, are typically made of copper, stainless steel or, less prevalently, iron. They may stand as tall as 40 feet high and frequently consist of two columns. The first column, which separates the spirit from the fermented beer, is known as the analyzer. Its companion column, the rectifier, serves as a purifying vessel, removing fusel oils from the spirit.

Virtually all Kentucky bourbon distillers today employ column stills for their first distillation and a pot still, or "doubler," for their second distillation.

Distilling on the whole, however, was being transformed into a respectable trade, one in which a distinct regional thumbprint could be placed and recognized with pride by skillful distillers who dedicated the majority of their working lives to creating a high-grade product. Suddenly, the image of a state industry that would assist in the welfare of the north-central quadrant of the state, in particular, seemed to be getting easier and clearer to those who had the power or the insight to envision it. The natural and plentiful ingredients were corn, rye, barley, wheat, pure limestone water, and yeast; the wood for barrels was white oak; the distillate was bourbon whiskey; the place of origin was north-central Kentucky; and the potential marketplace was the whole of North America.

It appears by many of the accounts that chronicled whiskey production in Kentucky during the middle decades of the 1800s that the established whiskeymen were amiable with one another and, at times, very cooperative as their industry took root deep in Kentucky soil. That is not to imply, however, that they were not competitive because that would be misleading. In an article written by Colonel Thomas E. Basham, titled "Kentucky Marches On," from the 1935 periodical called *Distilleries of Old Kentucky*, the observation is made that ". . . the old-time Kentucky distiller never recognized competition in his line, save as from his neighbor distiller. His greatest ambition was to see how much better whiskey he could turn out—but not how much more whiskey he could make than his Kentucky competitor. There was probably no other group of manufacturers in the world who so vied with each other in their efforts to produce a better article than was the old-time, and the present day Kentucky, distiller."

Though Colonel Basham's language might admittedly suffer from a bit of period puffery and a dash of prideful exaggeration, the underlying message is fundamentally accurate. The north-central Kentucky distilling community was close-knit, communicative, sometimes collaborative, and apparently well aware of its place in local commerce, politics, and society. Their intramural rivalry, in some instances like the one between siblings David M. Beam at Old Tub and his brother John H. Beam at Early Times, in all likelihood advanced the cause of bourbon whiskey every bit as much as all the technological, communication, and scientific developments.

From a cottage industry, bourbon whiskey blossomed into a major industry from 1820 to 1860.

The Third Generation Comes On-Watch

Approximately a year after his father's death in February of 1852, David M. Beam, the third child of David and Elizabeth Settle Beam and the grandson of Jacob Beam, assumed full and legal control at the age of twenty of Old Tub Distillery on Hardin Creek in Washington County, Kentucky. David M., born in Washington County in 1833, was tall for the period, regal in his bearing as was the manner of many prominent Kentucky gentlemen, his lean face bearded. As an adult, he was reportedly fastidious about his appearance and always presented himself well in both private and public settings. His parents had made sure he was educated close to home in Washington and Nelson County public schools.

Alongside his father, whose reputation as an adept distiller had spread throughout the Bluegrass Region by the time he was born, David M. honed his own distilling skills working at Old Tub beginning in his early teen years. With acknowledged facility and flair, he comprehended well the crucial importance of maintaining the integrity of the family grain mash and jug yeast recipes that had been created by his grandfather in the late 1780s. From the start of his apprenticeship, David M. was taught that repeat patronage depended solely on consistent quality and the strict adherence to the secret and trusted Beam family formulas. By the time that David Beam was grooming his successor in the 1840s, the Beam's bourbon whiskey had become more widely known throughout Kentucky as "Old Tub" rather than "Old Jake Beam" as it was originally referred to in the earliest years of the nineteenth century.

While his two generational predecessors had taken enormous care to first establish a family trade in the wilderness and then to develop an individual bourbon whiskey style, David M.'s responsibilities and challenges, with accompanying headaches, achievements, and fears, to continue and increase the family business took far different twists and turns as everyday life in Kentucky and the United States markedly changed. Contemporary accounts depict David M. Beam as a thoughtful man who embraced the present and looked forward to the future. He was undaunted by radical change, either in its implementation or consequence. In virtually all aspects—personality, skill, demeanor, and intelligence—David M. was the ideal choice to lead Old Tub Distillery.

Upon taking the helm—and the spigot—at Old Tub in 1853, David M. realized almost immediately that the modern advancements in bulk cargo transport, specifically through steam-powered boats and railroads, were going to greatly impact, if not revolutionize, Kentucky's growing bourbon whiskey industry. If bourbon whiskey was indeed destined to expand far beyond the limestone water zone counties, it would be have to be carted on the rails and stowed in the storage holds of steamboats. A New History of Kentucky by Lowell H. Harrison and James C. Klotter (1997, p. 132) unequivocally states "Kentucky's most successful railroad of the era was the Louisville and Nashville . . ." The L&N was formed as an entity in 1850 and was funded with nearly $4 million worth of capital raised by the very communities that would be affected by its presence. During its construction all through the 1850s the talk of being able to travel the 185-mile distance from Louisville to Nashville in a third of the time that it took by Concord stagecoach propelled the massive project forward. Spending 10 hours on a nicely appointed, smooth-running train was an attractive prospect when compared to enduring 30 bumpy hours on a stagecoach, choking most of the journey on clouds of dust being kicked up by the team of horses. Little wonder then why public support for the L&N was so strong and across-the-board.

Rumors about the L&N and potential stations circulated throughout north-central Kentucky. In 1854, news reached David M. that the railroad was considering opening a branch line to Springfield, Kentucky, in roughly five years time, one that would run near or through the whiskey town of Bardstown in neighboring Nelson County. The lack of association, even in the talking stages, between the L&N and Washington County caused him concern about his distillery's future. David M. wanted the north-to-south running steel tracks of the L&N as a potential freight carrier for barrels of Old Tub. If the L&N Springfield extension line was going to be a day's ride or more by wagon from Old Tub Distillery, his Bardstown competitors would have a leg up on him. Once the plan for the Springfield/Bardstown line was confirmed by L&N officials, David M. made his most important decision as the head of Old Tub. In 1856–1857, the Old Tub Distillery, the whiskey house founded by his grandfather and fostered by his father, and the David M. Beam family relocated to Nelson County from its original and only location of Washington County.

Period Time Line: Taking It Literally

The literary output of America's finest authors, writers, and thinkers in the mid-nineteenth century was astounding. Here in chronological order is a smattering of the most enduring—not bad for an eight-year span:

1847: Ralph Waldo Emerson, first book of poems; Henry Wadsworth Longfellow, *Evangeline*.

1849: Nathaniel Hawthorne, *The Scarlet Letter*.

1851: Herman Melville, *Moby-Dick*.

1852: Harriet Beecher Stowe, *Uncle Tom's Cabin*.

1854: Henry David Thoreau, *Walden*.

1855: Walt Whitman, *Leaves of Grass*.

By the time that the Springfield/Bardstown extension of the L&N opened on March 19, 1860, the Beam family distillery was ready to ship its first freight. Additionally, the business was no longer named Old Tub. It had been renamed D.M. Beam & Company. The new distillery, up and running for at least two years, was situated a mere two miles north of Bardstown, next to Nazareth College and Convent. Owing more to innate shrewdness than to luck, David M. Beam's brand new, larger distillery was likewise situated only yards away from the L&N extension tracks. Though David M. changed the name of the company, the brand name of the bourbon whiskey remained Old Tub. Shipping barrels of Old Tub south to Nashville and north to Louisville began almost immediately, courtesy of the L&N Railroad. Along with Jacob Beam's selling of his initial barrel of whiskey in 1795 and James Beauregard (Jim) Beam's participation starting in the 1880s, the astute relocation of the distillery proved without a doubt to be the third most important business decision in the first century of the Beam family saga. The L&N carried Old Tub to newer and wider audiences. Business was booming. David M.'s wealth was growing.

David M. wasn't the only son of David Beam, however, to be making a name for himself as a respected young whiskey distiller in Bardstown around 1860. John Henry Beam, known to all as "Jack," was David M.'s younger brother. Jack worked within the familiar confines of Old Tub Distillery with his brother until the late 1850s. Realizing that his older brother was firmly in control of the family business, Jack decided to strike out on his own. He founded the Early Times Distillery in Bardstown that same year. Jack's distillery, which had a 50-bushel per day capacity, proved to be a success. Conveniently located on the L&N line at Early Times Station, just 43 miles south of Louisville, the distillery thrived for 60 years, producing classic brands of early Kentucky straight bourbon, like Early Times, Jack Beam, and A.G. Nall. The Beam family whiskey tree was growing branches.

Unfortunately, in 1880, Jack lost control of the Early Times Distillery when his distributor bought him out and took command. The new owners wisely kept him on as vice president and master distiller. Jack's unrivalled skill at distilling bourbon whiskey forced the owners first to double, then to quadruple the capacity of the distillery to keep up with the rousing demand. Some of Jack's distilling secrets were revealed in the *Nelson County Register of 1896.* "He is a great believer in the early time methods of making whisky, which includes mashing the grain in small tubs, and boiling the beer and whisky in copper stills over open fires," wrote the *Register.* Then they added, "What he doesn't know about distilling isn't worth knowing."

The brand of Early Times, which is no longer considered a straight bourbon whiskey by law because of its use of used barrels in maturation, is part of the whiskey portfolio of Brown-Forman Beverages Worldwide of Louisville, the venerable whiskey company founded by George Garvin Brown, a near-contemporary competitor of Jim Beam.

In 1861, on the threshold of the opening hostilities of the Civil War, David M. married Margaret Ellen Phillips of Washington County. David M. and Margaret had eight children, neatly divided between four girls and four boys. Their third and fourth sons were, respectively, James Beauregard (Jim), born in 1864, and William Parker (Park), born in 1868. Though two other brothers, George and Tom, preceded them, Jim and Park were, as we shall discover shortly, the inheritors of the Beam bourbon whiskey tradition and secrets.

One of David M. and Margaret's daughters, Nannie, would also play an interesting and pivotal role in the Beam story, but not before Kentucky would become an unwilling pawn between the forces of the Union and the Confederacy.

A Nervous State on the Brink

1856. While David M. Beam dismantled his old Washington County distillery, Old Tub, in order to re-establish it as well as the family headquarters in nearby Nelson County to be closer to the Louisville & Nashville Railroad, John Brown, the unstable zealot and radical abolitionist who was determined to abolish slavery by sword rather than by word in the territories of Nebraska and Kansas and eventually the country as a whole, murdered unarmed pro-slavery homesteaders camped near the Pottawatomie River in eastern Kansas. In one stroke, Brown sensationalized the swelling discord between the states and territories that championed slavery and those that had already condemned and outlawed it.

In the eyes of the pro-slavery states and territories, what was at stake every bit as much as the right to own slaves was the right of self-determination. The southern tier of states and the western territories, who argued that slavery was a necessary element of their agrarian culture and, therefore, economic stability, was firmly against interference from the federal government on virtually any matter. The hot-button issue of "Free State or Slave State" confronted every territory that applied for statehood from 1820 to 1850. The thorny, blood-stirring debate reached an apex at midcentury with The Compromise of 1850. The Act's authors, Senators Henry Clay of Kentucky and Daniel Webster of Massachusetts, worked out under the terms of The Compromise that California would enter the Union without having to serve an interim period as a territory, but would enter only as a free state. Any of the other far western territories, like Utah and New Mexico, that were scooped up as the booty of the Mexican War would have the option to decide individually via voter referendum whether or not they preferred to be a free or slave state. The clause in The Compromise that really stuck in the craw of the pro-slave lobby, however, was the formal ending of slavery in the District of Columbia, which the South considered one of its own.

But, more was to be heard from the notorious John Brown. A masterful and clever instigator, Brown believed, or so he claimed, that the Almighty Being had personally selected him to flush the nation of slavery at any cost utilizing any method. Deluded, yet like many zealots, Brown was oddly compelling. Brown planned his most infamous episode as he quietly moved east across the nation in 1857 and 1858, raising cash and arms, and converting a few new followers.

In the autumn of 1859, D.M. Beam & Company employees were preparing a loading dock for the transfer of whiskey barrels to L&N boxcars directly from the distillery plant in Bardstown. David M. Beam's vision was close to turning into reality. Meanwhile, John Brown, with a group of 21 male followers, 16 of them white and 5 of them African American, captured an armory and a rifle factory in Harper's Ferry, Virginia (now West Virginia), on October 16. The siege collapsed on October 18 as U.S. Marines, led ironically by Lieutenant Colonel Robert E. Lee of the U.S. Army, recaptured the compound in less than four minutes. Brown was injured by a Marine's sword in the assault and was taken into custody. John Brown was charged with treason by the State of Virginia. The following December 2, he was hanged. But the nation would not soon recover from the shock of Brown's rampage. Though John Brown's fundamental intent was correct, that slavery in any form for any reason at any time is wrong and immoral, his ruthless, deranged methods served more to galvanize the anti-Union feeling in the South than they discredited the concept of slavery. The worthwhile message was lost in the murk of Brown's repugnant and counter-productive actions.

By the time that the L&N Springfield extension line was up and running in the early spring of 1860, David M. Beam came to accept the chilling fact that conflict between the states appeared all but inevitable. The cultural rift was growing between North and South; the vitriolic rhetoric was flying in state houses, the Congress, and newspapers; and, most frightening of all, patience was shortening. Kentucky though technically a slave state was viewed by both sides as a "border" state, one whose intentions—and men—could go either way when the blood started soaking the earth and lives and fortunes were put in jeopardy. The edginess between the industrial, wealthier North and the agrarian, poorer South careened toward disaster.

The stark reality was that Kentuckians were sharply divided on the matters of slavery and self-determination. Between December 20, 1860, and February 1, 1861, seven southern states seceded from the Union. In order, they were South Carolina, Mississippi, Florida, Alabama, Georgia, Louisiana, and Texas. Because of Kentucky's tenuous position as a prime crossroads to both North and South and, as a result, a cultural blend of both regions, the majority of Kentuckians wanted the state to declare itself neutral and to abide by that decree no matter how long a war lasted. Then on April 12, 1861, Confederate forces fired on Fort Sumter, a South Carolina garrison of the U.S. Army. The American Civil War hostilities were afoot.

The wrenching decision whether to as a state remain neutral or to choose a side tore apart many Kentucky communities and families as well as representatives in the state legislature. Finally, after weeks of heated discussion, the Kentucky House voted on September 11, 1861, to support the Union and to expel Confederate loyalists despite the fact that most Kentuckians desired continued neutrality. Throughout the remainder of 1861 and the first seven months of 1862, Kentucky was fortunate enough to stay away from most of the early skirmishes. That blissful status came crashing down when in mid-August 1862, Confederate Major General Edmund Kirby Smith and 12,000 troops brought the war to north-central Kentucky by capturing first Lexington, then on the following day Frankfort.

Kentucky's bourbon whiskey distillers, including newly married David M. Beam, were naturally concerned about the effects an extended conflict would have on their budding industry. As the war progressed, the L&N Railroad was employed for commercial purposes only when it wasn't being used for troop or military supply movements. With steamboat traffic significantly curtailed on the Mississippi River by orders of the Union Army, the importance of the railroads as a transportation lifeline dramatically rose.

Direct impact generated by the war on the Kentucky bourbon whiskey industry took several telltale forms. Since right before the conflict had ignited, the South had evolved into the preeminent market for the bourbon whiskey distillers and many of the whiskeymen had come to rely heavily on that fertile commercial turf. Some Kentucky distillers, loyal to the culture of the South and to the friendships they had established through commercial channels, even went to fight for the Confederate cause. Though enlistment records sometimes contradict, some estimates claim that 25,000 to 40,000 young Kentuckians volunteered and fought in the Confederate Army while 90,000 to 100,000 teenage boys and young men were drafted or volunteered for service in the Union Army. The sudden disappearance of so many young males from the farms was the primary reason for much lower grain harvests in terms of volume throughout the state from the autumn of 1861 to the autumn of 1865. Less grain and manpower meant much less scrupulously produced bourbon whiskey, as well.

Early in the war, the Confederate States took the posture of imposing an outright ban on the sale of all distilled spirits on a state-by-state basis. The official wartime prohibition in the South was instituted, in large measure, to keep enough whiskey and spirits inventories at hand for the purposes of treating, cleansing, and anesthetizing the wounded through crude battlefield triage. As historical accounts have so vividly depicted, Civil War battlefields were little more than slaughterhouses as the tide of the conflict ebbed and flowed. Another reason for the restrictions was to stock enough whiskey for daily rations to the battered troops. Aside from being utilized to assist in the treatment of the wounded and as a soothing ration, whiskey was also viewed as a valuable medicine to help deal with other mounting ailments among the troops, including measles, fever, neuralgia, gonorrhea, syphilis, and rheumatism.

Much of the southern tier marketplace had shriveled up for the Kentucky distillers by late 1862 and early 1863. To add insult to injury, President Lincoln, the former Illinois tavern owner, decided in 1862 to impose an excise tax on spirits and whiskey to aid in offsetting the mounting expenses the Union was incurring by conducting a major war. Short of manpower, grain, and a regular stream of business, some north-central Kentucky distillers decided to board up their plants and ride out the war while others like D.M. Beam & Company continued to distill whiskey as best they could. With production down and scarcity a harsh reality, bourbon whiskey prices had skyrocketed by the summer of 1863. Whiskey of any sort was an especially coveted commodity on the black market where a gallon of top-grade bourbon whiskey like Old Tub could fetch an astonishing $35 for a gallon. That identical gallon cost a mere 25¢ in prewar 1860.

The Union had not forbidden the sale of whiskey or other spirits during the war years throughout the North. Indeed, well-heeled Union officers became some of the best customers for the bourbon whiskey distillers. The huge Union Army consumed vast quantities of whiskey, flour, and tobacco on a daily basis. The average Union soldier was also considerably more flush with cash than his Confederate counterpart and so was more liable to purchase a jug of bourbon whiskey to supplement his own daily ration and that of his friends. Though in 1830 the United States Army had abolished the daily ration tradition, this war was so horrific in its barbarism that commanding officers were left to decide for themselves whether or not to maintain that order. In light of the extreme circumstances, most Union officers simply looked away when they spotted one of their fatigued soldiers downing a tot of whiskey.

After a shaky start due to inept planning and unsteady military leadership, the Union Army by the final months of 1864 was, at last, turning the fickle tides of war in their favor. It was becoming painfully evident that the Confederate South, depleted of money, men, and supplies, was no match for the mighty Union North juggernaut over a protracted period. On March 9, 1864, President Lincoln turned over the running of the war effort to Lieutenant General Ulysses S. Grant, who was both a ruthless win-at-all-cost warrior and a serious admirer of Kentucky bourbon whiskey. Grant's fearlessness, strategic capabilities, and grim determination in the face of heavy casualties changed the tone of the war. When concerned advisors close to Lincoln bitterly complained about Grant's habitual imbibing even though he changed the direction of the war, Lincoln reportedly uttered something like, "Find out what brand of whiskey Grant drinks and have a case of it delivered to all my other generals." General Grant was, incidentally, an enthusiastic fan of Old Crow Bourbon.

The year 1864 was notable as well, one to be earmarked by all lovers of whiskey, for the David M. Beam household since their third of four sons, James Beauregard Beam, was born in Bardstown. The birth of Jim Beam would ultimately enhance not only the Beam family legacy but the distilling industry in America as a whole from the early 1880s to the present day. His father, David M., while doubtless thrilled with his new son born among the ruins of war, had other things to deal with as the war was furiously being fought to a desperate conclusion. North-central Kentucky, indeed the entire state, was a shambles. Supplies were nonexistent. Young men aged from eighteen to twenty-five all seemed to fall into one of three ghastly categories: dead, missing, or maimed. The L&N was limping along with irregular service. Steamboats moved troops and the sick and dying. Farms all around the Beam home in Nelson

County and numerous counties beyond lay fallow. Both Union and Confederate soldiers had sacked homes, barns, and businesses on much-dreaded overnight stays, leaving little in terms of grain stores, whiskey inventories, clothing, and livestock. The civilian population in Kentucky was defenseless.

As fewer and fewer able-bodied troops were seen marching through the Bluegrass Region, a new scourge was emerging with bloodcurdling regularity: lawlessness. In the vacuum left behind by departing Union and Confederate troops, bands of renegades, frequently deserters from both sides, were plundering farms and stores, taking everything that could be stowed on a horse or a wagon. With so much devastation and economic ruin, the black market for all types of goods was flourishing in the towns along the Ohio River. Those Kentuckians left behind needed to continue their lives and were willing to pay dearly for staples such as grains, livestock, guns and ammunition, horses, and mules. The outlaws like the infamous raiders of William Clarke Quantrill sowed terror in an already brutalized land. How many late nights in 1864 and 1865 did Margaret Beam find her husband David M. sitting alert in his chair facing the door, a shotgun resting in the crook of his arm?

On April 9, 1865, the illustrious and soft-spoken Confederate supreme commander General Robert E. Lee formally surrendered his 27,800 troops to General Ulysses S. Grant at Appomattox Court House, Virginia. Five days later, Abraham Lincoln was shot in the head by Confederate sympathizer John Wilkes Booth in Washington, DC. The last of the Confederate troops gave up their arms on May 26. On December 6, Congress ratified the Thirteenth Amendment that once and for all abolished slavery. The worst manmade destruction and premeditated strife ever known on the North American continent was over. But the effects, still rippling out from that April night in 1861 at Fort Sumter, were not.

The four hideous years of Civil War in which over 600,000 Americans had died had ripped apart families and whole communities in both North and South. The conflict had laid waste to businesses and the networks of commerce and trade, had put an abrupt, if temporary, halt to private and commercial transportation, and had, for all intents and purposes, set a match to much of the remarkable progress made in Kentucky during the five-decade period just prior to the war. Almost 20 percent of the young Kentuckians, the pride of the state, that went off to war did not return. Others returned home without limbs, with deep psychological disorders or were otherwise terribly incapacitated. Questions understandably arose in Kentucky in the summer of 1865. Could the unbridled rancor that divided brother from brother, father from son be overcome? Could Kentucky's Bluegrass Region and its farming, distilling, educational, and business sectors recover?

Moonshine, Sunshine, Rebuilding

By the summer of 1870, the Bluegrass Region was thought to be gradually bouncing back from the physical, economic, and emotional trauma wrought by the Civil War. The state's population stood at slightly more than 1.3 million people. Roads were being repaired. Newer paved roads were being constructed. Steamboat and railroad transportation was largely reintroduced to both private and commercial traffic. Damage to farms, shops, and villages was still evident but as a whole Kentucky was on the mend.

In Kentucky bourbon whiskey circles, some distilleries never reopened because restarting a distillery plant was costly and money for loans was scarce. Undercapitalization was rampant in all business sectors throughout the Bluegrass Region from 1865 to 1870. In 1860, one published estimate unearthed at the Kentucky Historical Society archives in Frankfort states that prewar Kentucky boasted 207 whiskey distilleries. By 1880, that total had dropped off to 153. Another contributing factor to the loss in distilling output was the excise tax first imposed in July of 1862 by President Lincoln. During the subsequent postwar decades, this tax was tweaked and poked and prodded by Congress and the Treasury Department as much or more than any other piece of federal legislation in the late 1800s. Typically, to help pay off the national debt, the duty's direction had to go higher.

"Got debt? Tax whiskey" had grown to be the habitual solution of the American and British governments mired in financial straits during the eighteenth and nineteenth centuries. The excise duty in the United States reached the $2 per gallon mark on January 1, 1865. A ludicrous amount for the era when one considers how economically crippled the country was. Not only were the costs of restarting distilleries high but now duty had to be paid in cash to federal agents on all fresh production—a classic double whammy courtesy of inept governing.

Running for the Roses

Seven years before the young Jim Beam began working for his father at the D.M. Beam & Company, the first Kentucky Derby was held on May 17, 1875, at Churchill Downs. Jockey O. Lewis rode the sleek Aristides across the finish line.

Consequently, the surviving whiskey distillers were generally either the well-established firms like D.M. Beam & Company, H. Wathen, Early Times, and J.W. Dant or the newer mavericks with deep pockets. Some entrepreneurs who had done well in other industries such as finance and banking, industry or law began entering the distilling trade during the postwar period because they could see the enormous potential as the nation was righting itself. The other effect the escalating excise tax had on the whiskey trade was the significant rise in illegal distillers, or moonshiners, who wanted to make money from their illicit whiskey but didn't want to pay the government-imposed duty to the excisemen. The Kentucky backwoods were dotted with illegal still operations, mostly small, easily concealed, crude copper kettles, beginning in 1865. One postwar Bluegrass wisecrack went, "Wherever there's smoke, there's bound to be a kettle."

Moonshine whiskey, aka "skull-pop," "baldface," "field whiskey," "soda pop moon," "white lightening," "brain-scorch," "white dog," "red eye likker," "bug-eye," and "squirrel liquor," was the illicit high-alcohol, high-octane, harsh, and raw corn spirits born in unlicensed stills hidden beneath trees and bushes in the hollows and forests of rural Kentucky. Moonshiners would color white lightening with pigments in an attempt to make it roughly resemble genuine bourbon whiskey to the untrained eye. Appearances can be remarkably deceiving, as we all acknowledge. Ersatz coloring aside, the dead giveaways, though, were the pungent odor and the fire-breathing taste, neither of which echoed real bourbon whiskey's sophisticated and smooth qualities. For better or for worse, skull-pop was a reality with which the legitimate, tax-paying bourbon whiskeymen had to co-exist.

The 1880s were a particularly pivotal decade in the chronicle of American whiskey. As fresh capital started to become available again from banks, the larger distillers began modernizing their facilities with a new type of distilling method, column distillation. Column stills were originally invented and patented in the 1820s (1827) by Irishman Robert Stein but were perfected by Aeneas Coffey, another Irishman, who patented his version in the early 1830s. Coffey's ingenious design dictated that a fermented grain mash, or beer as Kentucky's distillers know it, be distilled in a continuously flowing metal still shaped into tall, interconnected columns. The efficient method heated the beer, causing alcohol vapors to rise into the columns, condense, fall into the next column, and repeat the process until the new spirit reached the final column where it was drained off. This fresh spirit was called "low wines." The distiller could either leave the low wines as is or distill it again in a traditional pot still to raise the alcohol level further as well as to additionally purify the spirit. This result of this second distillation, or doubling as the bourbon distillers termed it, was high wines, or very pure grain spirit.

This five-decade-old technology was transforming the whisky industry in Scotland in the latter half of the nineteenth century as blended Scotch whiskies, or whiskies comprised of column still whisky and pot still whisky, were taking England by storm. Spirit volumes were greater with column stills than pot stills since they ran without stopping. The distilling operation itself was less labor-intensive and, therefore, more efficient. The major bourbon whiskey players had come to the collective conclusion that the United States was about to enter a period of unprecedented prosperity and expansion. If they were going to claim their part of the pie, they had to modernize. Many of the best Kentucky whiskymen began betting heavily that column stills would revolutionize their industry as well. With the opening of the western states and territories, Kentucky distillers realized that increased output was absolutely necessary and, therefore, so was expansion.

Other industrial advancements of note in the 1880s that were applied to mainstream Kentucky whiskey distilling included more efficient methods of grist-milling, like roll mills, fermentation tanks that had copper lining for most consistent fermentations and better hygiene through easier cleaning, and condensation coils that were either made entirely from copper or, at the minimum, were copper-lined. By contrast, Kentucky's moonshiners, the bandit white-doggers, were still ducking and praying every time they lighted the wood fire beneath their old, primitive copper kettle, hoping that it wouldn't blow them in chunks and pieces to neighboring counties and states.

With the nation poised to leap into an exciting, promising new epoch of growth, back in Bardstown David M. Beam was starting to ponder taking life a mite easier. D.M. Beam & Company was booming in the last quarter of the nineteenth century. Old Tub, its now-famous bourbon whiskey brand, was one of the nation's most popular libations and could be purchased in markets such as Boston, New Orleans, Philadelphia, and Chicago. Under David M.'s watchful eye, Old Tub with the help of the L&N Railroad had evolved since the Civil War into an authentic national bourbon whiskey brand. David M.'s reputation as a master distiller was golden and widespread both within and outside of the distilling community. With business humming along so well, David M. doubtless thought that it was time to begin the process of gradual transition from within the ranks.

Overlooking his two oldest sons, George and Tom, David M. began grooming his quick-witted and personable third son James Beauregard in the early 1880s to possibly take over the family distillery at some time in the future. Little by little, James Beauregard learned the family distilling secrets and recipes from his father. James Beauregard was said to wince any time someone called him "James" or "JB" or worst of all, "Jim Beau." He liked to keep things simple and straightforward. He made it known that he liked to be called "Jim." Just Jim Beam. Two syllables. Direct. Nothing fancy or elaborate. Jim Beam. Little did he know how far that name would carry him and his family's whiskey enterprise.

PART TWO

The Dynasty

Jim Beam and the Making of a Bourbon Whiskey Brand

DAVID M. BEAM DID not have to compel, bribe, threaten, or cajole his third and fourth sons Jim and Park to work with him at what was then still known in the 1880s as D.M. Beam & Company in Nelson County. The boys naturally and willingly participated in the workings of the distillery. Jim, born in 1864 in Bardstown, came on as an Old Tub Distillery regular in 1880 at the age of sixteen after attending Nelson County schools. William Parker, four years younger than Jim, entered the family business a few years later. Both were bright, self-confident, curious yet unassuming young men who exuded charm, in particular, the more gregarious and outgoing Jim. Bardstown was home. Family and friends were manifold and close by in this tightly knit community. D.M. Beam & Company and the Beams were acknowledged cornerstones of Bardstown. David M.'s savvy business sense, his optimistic vision of the future, and inherent distilling expertise had made bourbon whiskey the backbone of the family enterprise. Old Tub Bourbon Whiskey was one of the few nationally distributed distilled spirits brands by 1880, no small feat.

The rejuvenation, restoration, and healing of Kentucky after the devastation of the Civil War on so many social and economic fronts was still underway in the 1880s. Though the mood of the state's populace was growing more hopeful and forward-looking with each passing year, fundamental problems such as widespread poverty, a lack of elementary educational facilities, little steady employment, poor transportation, and the absence of basic hygiene in many communities plagued most of Kentucky's rural hamlets. The exception was Louisville, which had weathered the Civil War well and in the South's period of reconstruction had actually flourished as a pivotal crossroads and transportation center. The major bourbon whiskey families, the Beams, Dants, Browns, Bernheims, Peppers, and Moores, experienced, in general, a far better standard of living than many citizens in north-central Kentucky because of their expanding and maturing industry.

Yet, compared to the late 1860s and early 1870s, America, in 1880, was poised as a whole to boom. Even small pockets of the reconstructed South were beginning to flourish, though the majority was still in severe recovery. The year that Jim Beam joined his father at Old Tub, the population of the United States passed the 50 million mark. The Commonwealth of Kentucky alone counted more than 1.6 million citizens in the census of 1880. While millions more immigrants were pouring into the states of the east and the north, especially from Ireland and continental Europe, Kentucky's immigration rate remained comparatively stable through the 1880s and 1890s. In a sense, this was a blessing because it allowed Kentucky time to recuperate without the added burden of more mouths to feed, more jobs to fight for, and more housing and schools to erect. The infrastructure of the state was incrementally rebounding, allowing for natural resources such as coal and for manufactured goods like Kentucky bourbon, to once again be transported by rail, road, and river to markets around the rest of the country. Kentucky's formal, genteel society, centered largely in the vicinities of Louisville and Lexington, was alive and breathing as well. A sense of normalcy was seeping back into the Bluegrass Region after two decades of misery.

With the Deep South, once the primary market of Kentucky distillers, still economically softened from the pummeling sustained in the Civil War, David M. and his distilling peers turned their attention to the developing western tier states for business. These vast territories located west of the Mississippi River were thought, by Kentucky's most active and aggressive distillers, to be potentially prime bourbon whiskey markets. Barrels of Old Tub started traveling west, following the sun, as railroad lines began fanning out from Louisville, Cincinnati, St. Louis, and Chicago. In 1870, a mere 1,017 miles of track existed within Kentucky. By 1890, that total had climbed to 3,000 miles. With tens of thousands of miles of telegraph lines reestablished from coast to coast and from Canada to Mexico from 1866 to 1882, ordering more barrels of Old Tub by wire from, say, a brokerage house in Omaha, Nebraska, or Springfield, Illinois, or Grand Junction, Colorado, was becoming a regular occurrence during the course of the Bardstown work week.

The fabled American West was opened and then settled largely by bands of men. These hardened prospectors, cattlemen, trappers, hunters, miners, merchants, cartographers, surveyors, and soldiers demanded a drink of substance from barkeepers, restaurateurs, and shop owners. As mining villages and railroad towns started dotting the western landscape, slapdash taverns, inns, and saloons mushroomed and began readily supplying bourbon whiskey from Kentucky. Other more primitive, wholly inferior spirits that were, with great generosity, called "whiskey" were also seen popping up in the West. Basically, there were two types of frontier whiskey: the cheap, harsh-tasting rotgut frequently distilled by disreputable people in the warehouses of western fringe towns and the more expensive authentic whiskey made by Kentucky's coterie of renowned bourbon distillers located largely in Nelson, Anderson, Spencer, Woodford, Fayette, Franklin, Washington, and Bullitt counties.

When bartenders were instructed by gruff, thirsty patrons to "Give me some of your good stuff" to celebrate a good day of prospecting or of laying railroad track or of surveying for the railroad, they wanted Kentucky bourbon whiskey. Bourbon whiskey was the ideal libation for the remote, parched, and often stifling areas of the West since it traveled overland far better than either beer or wine, both of which could and did easily spoil en route, arriving at their destination putrid and undrinkable. It is no understatement to say that authentic bourbon whiskey proved to be the alcoholic drink that lubricated the West during its most storied period in the last quarter of the nineteenth century. Old Tub graced the dancehalls, casinos, brothels, hotel bars, restaurants, and saloons of Wild West towns like Dodge City, Amarillo, and Santa Fe as plentifully as it did the exclusive private clubs and fashionable parlors of San Francisco and Denver. By the time that David M. Beam was pondering semiretirement in 1887, Old Tub was a standard fixture in a high percentage of the towns and burghs west of the Mississippi. Old Tub Bourbon Whiskey had helped, in its own way, to loosen up the West.

Realizing that Jim, his energetic, smart, and engaging third son, possessed the necessary intellectual and physical qualities to potentially guide the family whiskey business well into the twentieth century, David M. at the age of 55 turned many of the everyday operations of Old Tub over to him in 1888. Jim was not, however, handed a golden pass, bestowed by the grace of inheritance. Like his grandfather David Beam had done with his own father, Jim was expected to learn all facets of the business, vital and menial—checking in the corn, rye, and barley shipments; the mashing, fermenting, and distilling procedures; the supply ordering; the staff scheduling; the ins and outs of shipping on the L&N;

the careful preparation of the yeast culture; inspecting the aging barrels on delivery; cleaning the stills and vats; creating the "mash bill," that is, the exact proportions of the three grains used in the mash. Determined that Jim was to earn his commission in the same way that he himself had done, David M. most likely had Jim, broom in hand, sweeping out Old Tub at weekends.

Though only twenty-four, Jim Beam was perfectly suited in temperament and natural ability for this escalation of responsibility and, in turn, wisely began grooming his younger brother Park as an Old Tub distiller. Four years later in 1892, thoroughly convinced that he had made the correct selection, David M. fully retired prior to his sixtieth birthday. In the process, he officially handed over the keys and secret recipes of the family business to Jim who was becoming known within the circle of his closest friends as "Big B."

With this smooth, generational, father-to-son transition the first century of the Beam family legend was almost completed. The dream first conceived by Jacob Beam in the 1780s in the wilds of untamed Washington County, Kentucky, stayed alive for another generation.

Launching the Second Beam Century

Annual sales of Old Tub Bourbon Whiskey were deep into the hundreds of barrels by the time the Panic of 1893, a knee-jerk stock market sell-off on June 27, took place, setting off three years of severe national depression. Even in the gloom of rigidly pinched economic times, the horizons of Kentucky bourbon whiskey kept expanding across the United States in the years right before the turn of the twentieth century. Two years before Henry Ford built his first car in 1896, Jim Beam decided to reorganize the family business. He changed the company name and invited his brother-in-law, Albert Hart, the husband of his sister Nannie, to participate as a partner. Albert Hart and Nannie B. Beam married in 1888 in the company of Bardstown's elite.

With the blessing of his father, Jim Beam legally renamed D.M. Beam & Company, Beam & Hart Distillery, though the distillery plant itself was still commonly called Old Tub. Jim remained master distiller and manager; Park stayed on as distiller; and Albert Hart ran shipping, grain contracting, and inspection and distribution. The Harts were a long-established and respected farming family in the Bluegrass Region and were, in fact, among the first homesteaders in Kentucky. Jim and his brother-in-law, who was two years older than he was, decided to keep the name "Old Tub" on their popular bourbon so as not to confuse the buying public. At first, Jim and Albert were making only one style of bourbon whiskey. *The Nelson County Register of 1896* reports in detail that "The distillery of Beam & Hart is situated about two miles from Bardstown on the Springfield branch of the L&N railroad. . . . The distillery is on the headwaters of Froman's creek, one noted for its unbounded capacity of pure water. The capacity of the house is 150 bushels per day. Mr. Hart is an expert judge of fine grain. . . . Mr. Beam does his own distilling, and his product is not to be excelled by anyone."

Beam & Hart owned and operated four warehouses, three large and one small, with a storage capacity of 10,000 barrels, a remarkable total for the day. But this depicts how popular a whiskey Old Tub was during the decade of the 1890s. Albert was also the manager of the warehouses, which *The Nelson County Register of 1896* describe as being ". . . splendidly constructed and ventilated."

Sales of Old Tub were brisk in the mid-1890s as more markets opened up especially in the West as dusty settlements and lonely outposts evolved into thriving villages and towns. The marketplace in the Deep South was also starting to rebound as the region's cities, in particular, Atlanta, Mobile, New Orleans, Baton Rouge, Little Rock, and Nashville, were showing signs of significant economic and civic improvement. With Old Tub Distillery still situated next to the L&N, Beam & Hart was one of the railroad's foremost commercial clients.

Other intriguing insights into the personalities of Jim Beam and Albert Hart were freely offered by the endlessly fascinating, if prosaic, *The Nelson County Register of 1896*. The *Register* characterized Jim Beam as being "full of energy . . . no one is more popular in this community than he. He is unmarried, and enjoys the comforts of his life at his country residence, where he entertains with lavish hands." Of Albert Hart the *Register* opined, "Like Mr. Beam, he is an unusually handsome man, robust and healthy. He attends to his duties like clock-work, and has a reputation for veracity and politeness. . . ." If one solitary thing could be said about Jim Beam it was that he liked to entertain his friends. Even after he retired, elegant soirees at Big B's large house on "Distiller's Row" in Bardstown were the hottest tickets in Nelson County.

Jim Beam, probably feeling parental pressure from David M. to sire an heir before he turned forty, did finally marry in 1897 at the age of 33. Mary Catherine Montgomery (1876–1962), Jim's junior by 12 years, caught Big B's eye and in short order he proposed. Jim and Mary Beam had three children, T. Jeremiah, Mildred, and Margaret, and were married for over a half-century. David M. was particularly proud when his grandson T. Jeremiah Beam, known as Jere (pronounced "Jerry") was born in 1900.

One year after marrying the vivacious and articulate Mary Montgomery, Jim decided for reasons that remain unclear to reorganize his company once again. This time, however, he brought in two non-Kentuckians with deep pockets, Thomas Dennehy and Jeremiah S. Kenny, to be his partners. Clear Springs Distillery Company of Bardstown was the name of the new entity. Jim Beam's official titles were president and master distiller. Chicagoans Dennehy and Kenny were listed as co-owners. Piecing together bits and bobs of sketchy information as well as hearsay and dollops of family gossip, it can be deduced that things hadn't worked out enormously well with Albert Hart. It is also likely that Jim had big plans that would require substantial infusions of investment capital, which the Beams and the financial institutions of Kentucky were still sorely lacking. Consequently, he looked to friends in the huge city 300 miles to the north that was the unchallenged commercial, financial, industrial, transportation, and communications heart of the central United States, the queen city of the Great Lakes, Chicago.

Jim Beam was an ambitious man of immense pride, ability, and wit who, some people speculate, didn't want to be known throughout distilling history only for one very good bourbon whiskey by the name of Old Tub. He wanted to stretch his legs as an innovative distiller and entrepreneur by developing new and different brands, based on different combinations of mash bills and strains of yeast. That is not to claim in the least that Jim didn't want to remain true to his great-grandfather's recipe or his father's wish that he continue the family distilling legacy. He did, which is why he continued to make Old Tub in the manner of the three generations that preceded him. But Jim Beam was a different cut of Beam.

Two of Jim's finest qualities by all existing accounts were his unquenchable curiosity and his personal quest for being the best at anything that he did. In an era of innovation and technological advancement, Jim Beam wanted the family business to grow in strength by growing in harmony with the times. New brands could, in his mind, accomplish those goals. But new brand development even then consumed lots of money through trail and error and bringing new brands to the retail shops and general merchandise emporiums. Soon after Clear Springs Distillery Company was formed, three new Beam-generated brands of bourbon came onto the marketplace, Clear Springs, Jefferson Club, and Pebbleford. Of these whiskeys, Pebbleford is still talked about today within the distilling community and by bourbon historians as being one of the finest bourbon whiskeys ever produced in the state of Kentucky, probably in North America. Regrettably for all admirers of fine whiskey, Pebbleford, alas, no longer exists.

As the nineteenth century dissolved into the twentieth century, Jim Beam, his Kentucky distilling peers, and all the nation's distillers, winemakers, and brewers were about to come face-to-face with the most formidable foe they had ever as an industry encountered. The dreaded demon wasn't war or other armed conflict. It wasn't economic skittishness or even the international market downturn as the world stood jittery on the threshold of a new century. It wasn't drought or other natural disasters. The unrelenting menace was the grassroots temperance movement, symbolized primarily by the Women's Christian Temperance Union (WCTU) and their poster child, the nearly six-foot tall, 175-pound female form of a fanatical Christian who publicly claimed to have conversations with Jesus. The name of that woman, strangely a Garrard County, Kentucky, native, would forever come to typify mindless and reactionary intolerance. That axe-wielding woman was Carry Nation.

Talking with the Lord

Carry Amelia Moore Gloyd Nation (1846–1911) was the anti-alcohol equivalent of John Brown, the fanatical abolitionist whose similar self-professed "divine mission" and subsequent public displays of rash violence in the 1850s helped ignite the Civil War. Nation, the WCTU, and their followers didn't want responsible, moderate usage of alcohol by legal age adults. Their one-pointed goal was state-by-state or, preferably, federally legislated prohibition, the total ban on any alcoholic beverages being produced or consumed within the established boundaries of the United States of America. Armed with her trademark axe and followed by scrabbling scores of sympathetic women, Nation's sensational physical attacks on taverns and saloons in the state of Kansas dramatized her deranged ambitions to a nation that was spellbound by her audacity and fervor.

On the lecture circuit throughout the Midwest, Nation was a powerful and compelling presence as she spoke to standing-room-only crowds in town halls, churches, and hotel ballrooms. She claimed to the gasps of her listeners that her first husband Dr. Charles Gloyd died horribly because of excessive drinking and, as such, was rotting face down in a drunkard's plot. She likewise asserted that she had regular chinwags with Jesus who in no uncertain terms anointed her as his personal antialcohol emissary. She posited with complete conviction to rapt, mostly female audiences that saloonkeepers had made secret pacts with Satan and the dark denizens of hell.

Indeed, Carry Nation was cunningly masterful at playing the Satan-and-the-fires-of-hell card to her audiences. Addressing a gathering of Topeka, Kansas, merchants and businessmen in February of 1901, Nation raved from the lectern, "Your master, the devil, has you under his thumb, and you poor scullions do just what he wants you to do and he makes you believe that there is no escape . . . I came to rescue you as well as those you are murdering . . . We invite you to join us in the destruction of the machinery hell has set up here on Earth to literally devour humanity. . . ."

Persuasively and passionately presented, this type of diatribe was admittedly potent, meaningful stuff to people whose lives had been adversely affected by family or friends who had trouble with inebriation or were simply spending too much time propping up the bar at their corner saloon. It is an undeniable fact that ordinary Americans of the late nineteenth century, in particular, men, consumed more beverage alcohol per capita than we do today. As they had been since colonial times, bars, taverns, and saloons were the acknowledged meetinghouses of America. In 1900, the magic boxes of radio and television had yet to be invented to lure home the parched gentleman who at the end of his workday desired an amiable chat with his cronies over a few shots of whiskey and a game of poker. Men spent much time in taverns during this period and their wives, sisters, mothers, aunts, fiancées, and cousins hated it and were frustrated by it. Carry Nation, therefore, had a broad and accepting audience in virtually every town and city she visited.

But, Carry Nation's delusions were frightening in their scope. Eyewitness reports state that as Nation would viciously chop her way through one saloon after another she could be heard wailing above the crash of glass and wood "Jesus, my Lord and Savior, let me do your will!" Some years after her first husband perished, she married David Nation only to be divorced by him due to her ultra-radical views of people enjoying any variety of sensory pleasure. An equal opportunity zealot, Nation abhorred smoking and chewing tobacco; preached vehemently against the evil nature of sexual pleasure even within the bonds of marriage; despised liberal, modern-thinking writers and artists, not to mention progressive politicians like Theodore Roosevelt; but most of all, Nation's bailiwick was the eventual legal forbidding of alcoholic beverages.

To aid Nation's, the WCTU's, and the entire temperance movement's cause, the United States was swept up in a tidal wave of fire-and-brimstone Puritanism and religious fundamentalism in the late nineteenth century. Americans seemed to be spending all their spare time either in taverns or in churches. Nine years after Carry Nation's death by stroke in 1911, the Eighteenth Amendment, the Volstead Act, was ratified by the states and enacted by Congress, commencing 14 years of legal Prohibition and almost a decade and a half of unremitting hardship and calamity for distilling families like the Beams and the other Kentucky bourbon clans.

The seeds of the temperance movement had, however, been planted in American soil 57 years before the baby girl named Carry Amelia Moore was born in Kentucky. According to *Whiskey: An American Pictorial History* (1978, p. 109) by Oscar Getz, the first recorded organized temperance group appeared in 1789 in Litchfield, Connecticut, about a year after Jacob and Mary Beam had entered Kentucky through the Cumberland Gap to homestead in Washington County. Through the 1820s, 1830s, and 1840s more vociferous, well-oiled groups, like the Sober Society of Allentown, New Jersey, the Union Temperance Society of Saratoga County, New York, the multistate Sons of Temperance, the Independent Order of Good Templars, the Washingtonians of Baltimore, Maryland, and the New York State Temperance Society, were gathering members, momentum, funding, and political clout within the halls of state legislatures and the meeting rooms of newspapers.

In 1833, the Congressional Temperance Society formed in the District of Columbia, establishing a firm foothold for the movement at the very seat of federal power. By 1842, the Congressional Temperance Society reorganized their main platform, altering it now to champion total abstinence from the stand of moderation it had previously adopted when the group was formed nine years earlier. The prohibitionist sharks, determined to bring the beverage alcohol industry to heel, were sensing blood and alcohol in the water. "Temperance" became a euphemism, a sort of secret word by the 1850s for "prohibition" among the various, far-flung societies, groups, and organizations opposed to drinking.

The all-consuming black hole of the American Civil War temporarily diverted the country's attention away from the temperance debate until 1869 when the National Prohibition Party was formed. The WCTU, in the meantime, feted their own inception five years later in 1874. Though they would eventually cast her out, Carry Nation was the WCTU's frontline standard-bearer in the early years. By the time that Jim Beam was personally distilling Old Tub and Albert Hart was inspecting incoming grain shipments at the Beam & Hart Distillery, the Anti-Saloon League entered the fray. The Anti-Saloon League united the various antialcohol organizations into one powerful, if strident, voice.

To make matters even tenser for America's alcoholic beverage industry, scores of Christian churches nationwide willingly became the collaborators of the temperance movement, preaching abstinence and threatening eternal damnation to any poor soul who consumed alcohol. One wonders if David M., Jim, and Park Beam had to quietly sit in their church on Sunday mornings and listen to their pastor lambasting the production and consumption of whiskey. Alcohol, in the jaundiced view of the Prohibitionists, was eroding away the family structure of America. Along with the commonplace pillaging and outright destruction of taverns and saloons around the nation, songs, plays, marches, and demonstrations hailing prohibition and the divine virtues of temperance flourished both in major cities and average-size towns by 1910. Editorials from conservative newspapers and church-funded periodical publications called for swift, decisive, and stiff federal action. Thousands of ordinary people carrying antialcohol placards and signs on city streets were hard to ignore. Many politicians, eyeing their own seats in state legislatures or the House or the Senate, seats that were much coveted by pro-prohibition opponents, caved in under the tremendous pressure of the temperance movement. The whiskey had escaped the bottle and nothing could put it back. The Law of the Land had to buckle under the strain of protest onslaught.

Two years after Carry Nation's demise, David M. Beam died in 1913 at the age of eighty. That year was pivotal for Jim Beam in other ways as well. His son and heir apparent, T. Jeremiah, the fifth generation, began earning his stripes at Clear Springs Distillery at the age of thirteen. Jim made sure to teach T. Jeremiah the ropes just as David M. had tutored him. Thinking of expansion even under the cloud of possible federally imposed prohibition, Jim purchased another Nelson County distilling plant, F.G. Walker, for $13,000 that had come up for sale due to bankruptcy. The distillery was renowned for two good bourbons, Queen of Nelson and F.G. Walker. The distillery equipment was top-notch and the warehouse capacity of 20,000 barrels was enticing. Jim assumed the position of president of F.G. Walker in addition to his responsibilities at Clear Springs. The Beam family business was taking on the appearance of a modest empire. Others wondered if Jim wasn't overexpanding at a time when the distilling industry was about to engage in battle with a tough challenger. Jim's decision to purchase F.G. Walker would pay off years later in an unexpected way.

What Straight Bourbon Whiskey Is by Law

Federal law dictates what exactly a straight bourbon whiskey is and regulates how it is made. First and foremost, only whiskeys made within the United States meeting the federally mandated criteria may be called "bourbon whiskey." In other words, no whiskeys produced outside the United States may legally be labeled as bourbon whiskey. Though the majority of America's bourbons are made in the State of Kentucky, bourbon whiskeys can be the product of any of the 50 states. Virginia is a major bourbon producing state (Virginia Gentleman Bourbon Whiskey). Bourbons have been made in Pennsylvania, Indiana, and Illinois.

To be commercially traded as a bourbon, by law, the grain content of the mash must be comprised of a minimum of 51 percent corn; the distillate must not be distilled at higher than 160-proof, or 80 percent alcohol by volume; matured at no higher than 125-proof; the new spirit must be matured for at least two years in new, charred, white oak barrels and bottled at a minimum of 80-proof. The law does not stipulate that the barrels must be constructed from American oak, as is widely thought. As "straight whiskey," bourbon cannot have any flavor or appearance enhancements added. Straight bourbon whiskey is a completely natural alcoholic beverage.

Whiskey distilling in the years preceding the First World War was a major "impact" industry in Kentucky. In Kentucky as a whole, bourbon whiskey distillers produced slightly less than 28 million gallons in 1900. Thirteen years later in 1913, that total had jumped to almost 43 million gallons of bourbon. Within the city limits of Louisville, 35 distilleries were operating at maximum capacity in the years right before the assassination of Austrian Archduke Franz Ferdinand, marking the start of the First World War. The bourbon whiskey business contributed mightily to the state's tax base. Then came two more disasters to be dealt with by the Beams and the bourbon whiskey community, the war in Europe and national Prohibition.

Closing Down and Making Do

In 1916, Jim Beam, admired throughout the distilling trade as a genuine and skilled custodian of this ancient art, was elected president of the Kentucky Distillers Association (KDA). It is reported that prior to his installment as the KDA president, he silently wept at the thought that David M. would never know of his honor. But like the inventories of premium Kentucky bourbon whiskey, the good news was about to run out.

The Eighteenth Amendment to the United States Constitution was submitted to the individual states for ratification on December 18, 1917. Thirty-six states were required for ratification. It was ratified the following January 16, 1918 when the state of Nevada supported it. (Curious when one thinks of all the imbibing that occurs in 2003 in that state.) Prohibition, as legislated by the Volstead Act, officially began at 12:01 A.M. on Saturday, January 17, 1920. That fateful year Jim Beam was fifty-six years old. T. Jeremiah Beam was twenty. According to *The Story of America* by Allen Weinstein and David Rubel (2002, p. 469), the amendment banned "the manufacture, sale, or transportation of intoxicating liquors." The temperance movement, flush with triumph, couched their victory declarations in terms stating that it was every American's "patriotic duty" and "God's will" to abide by the law.

Yet, ironically, in the wave of religious fundamentalism that clutched the nation by the throat during the period of 1850 to 1920 some states had already flirted with the concept of going "dry," at least on the surface. Maine went dry in 1846, Vermont in 1852, New Hampshire and Massachusetts in 1855, New York for a brief span in 1854. So, what was the point of the Volstead Act other than religious fundamentalists imposing their radical views on others through their political muscle? In retrospect, the Congressional enactment of Prohibition marked the beginning of the end, at least temporarily, for the pre-First World War evangelical movement as average citizens, who had been stunned into silence by the vitriol of the prohibitionists, started rebelling in ways that made the temperance movement shudder. Ordinary Americans, by the tens of thousands, privately rejected the spirit of the Volstead Act and continued drinking distilled spirits all through Prohibition . . . in bathrooms, alleyways, coat closets, basements, barns, and, of course, in the countless illicit drinking dens known as *speakeasies.*

Before Prohibition, New York City boasted approximately 16,000 taverns, bars, and saloons that served alcohol. During Prohibition, the number of New York City speakeasies that illegally and furtively poured homemade bathtub gin and smuggled-in Scotch whisky was reportedly more than 32,000. As history has clearly depicted, Prohibition was the primary culprit that gave rise to organized crime. Previously uncooperative and local-turf gangs in Chicago, New York, and Detroit, became highly efficient and coordinated regional bootlegging operations, supplying illicit liquor to speakeasies and anyone willing to part with some cash. Underworld gangs who, in part, were indirectly created by the religious fundamentalists through their misguided fanaticism made fortunes from smuggling rings that surreptitiously snuck in copious amounts of whiskey, brandy, and gin from Canada and Mexico, as well as from unguarded coastlines. The common phrase "the real McCoy," a testament to something's or someone's authenticity, originated during the Prohibition Era based on the declaration that the whiskey smuggled to the States by a ship captain by the name of McCoy was, in fact, real Scotch whisky.

While the nation's legitimate distillers sold their distilleries, mothballed their plants, or out of desperation started other types of businesses, moonshiners around the country went on a distilling rampage, producing harsh, frequently dangerous, neutral spirits made of toxic wood alcohol and other dubious compounds that could cause blindness and other maladies such as "Jake Leg," the immediate, sometimes permanent paralysis of one side of the body from drinking bad or contaminated moonshine. Typical Prohibition Era moonshine was anywhere from a day to a month old. Shiners colored their white sugar distillate, or "hooch," with charcoal, fruit juice, burnt peaches, or caramel "to give it some age," or at least the appearance of a little maturity.

"White lightening" sold for $1 for a half-pint on the streets of Bardstown; $2 if the supply was short and demand was long. The citizens of north-central Kentucky knew who the local moonshiners were because they drove around in the flashiest cars and wore the best clothes. Little action by law enforcement, however, was taken against the moonshiners because they were viewed as trying to make a living during tough economic times. Most Kentuckians were staunchly anti-Prohibition and anti-federal government. Eyewitness accounts claim that during Prohibition, Bardstown had three hardly disguised saloons on Main Street and one in the back room of a hotel.

Not only were the nation's legitimate distillers financially hurting. The U.S. government itself, one of the perpetrators of the Prohibition scheme, was a sorrowful loser. It is estimated that the Federal Treasury missed out on $500 million a year on excise duties, formerly levied on distillers and their spirits. Over 14 years of Prohibition, that total sum factors out to roughly $7 billion in lost revenues. Other estimates, perhaps including the costs of greater law enforcement due to the rise in organized and local crime, claim the revenue loss at more than $11 billion. The coffers of the individual states, counties, and municipalities didn't fare much better. For a nation dealing with, first, the trauma of the First World War, then with the stock market crash, and subsequent Great Depression of the early 1930s, this was not an auspicious or timely occurrence.

On a lighter note, the absurdity of Prohibition provided plenty of fodder for America's humorists, editorial page writers, and satirists. One of the all-time best wisecracks came from W. C. Fields, who said in 1934 after the official repeal of the Eighteenth Amendment, "Once during Prohibition I was forced to live on nothing but food and water."

For Jim and T. Jeremiah Beam and other Kentucky distillers, the Prohibition Era was a professional and financial debacle and a personal tragedy. Gary and Mardee Haidin Regan recount in *The Book of Bourbon and Other Fine American Whiskeys* (1995, p. 75), "Six distilleries were given permits to sell medicinal whiskey during Prohibition . . . and these companies were allowed to store whiskey and sell it to licensed druggists, who in turn could mete it out to customers who had a doctor's prescription." Jim Beam's two distilleries, Clear Springs and F.G. Walker, were not among the six distilleries allowed by permit to produce whiskey. Staring disaster straight in the eye, Jim Beam decided to sell Clear Springs to a trio of businessmen, Garfield Barnes, Lambert Willett, and W. O. Stiles, before the bell of Prohibition tolled. The Regans went on later to conclude in *The Book of Bourbon* (1995, p. 76), "The Volstead Act all but destroyed many of the legitimate whiskey distilleries. Most of them were dismantled, and of the 17 plants operating in Kentucky prior to Prohibition, only seven were making whiskey in 1935."

Kentucky towns, such as Tyrone in Anderson County, that were built around a thriving distillery became disenfranchised ghost towns, their buildings unprotected against pillagers. The book *A New History of Kentucky* by Lowell H. Harrison and James C. Klotter (1997, p. 304) relates that the city of Louisville "lost an estimated eight thousand positions when its distilleries closed, and the state lost 5 percent of its jobs."

Before Prohibition, there was a Nelson County saying when someone was feeling a little more flush with cash than usual. They were described as being "as rich as Jim Beam." During the 14 years of Prohibition, Jim Beam tried his hand at three different businesses to keep the family fortunes afloat. His innate skill at being a first-rate distiller, entrepreneur, and marketer unfortunately did not translate well into other lines of work. Not one of Jim's nondistilling ventures during Prohibition resulted in success. The Sunlight Mining Company and Sunbeam Quarries Company in Kentucky did as badly as Jim's attempt at citrus farming in Florida.

During the latter years of Prohibition, the Beams were financially strapped. One eyewitness by the name of Jack Stiles, a Bardstown neighbor of the Beams, told the story through an oral history of Nelson County compiled by the Kentucky Historical Society in Frankfort of Jim Beam buying groceries one day in the late 1920s and having only $5 in his pocket. He had picked up more than $5 worth of supplies and with some embarrassment had to return the items he couldn't afford. "The Beams were broke," said Stiles on the audio tape that was recorded in 1989. Another acquaintance of the Beam family, Thomas Moore McGinnis, who participated in the Nelson County oral history project related how the old saying of "rich as Jim Beam" stopped being a colloquialism during Prohibition due to the fact that "Everybody in town seemed richer than Jim Beam."

Another family friend, John W. Muir, related through the Kentucky Historical Society project how pleasant and affable a man Jim Beam was, even though he and his family had fallen on hard times due directly to Prohibition. Said Muir of the legendary Jim Beam, "I knew James Beauregard Beam well. Though I was much younger than him, he'd sit and talk with me on Sunday mornings. It was an older man, younger man friendship. I'll always remember him fondly."

Remarkably, Prohibition marked the only time from 1795 to the present day that the Beams did not distill whiskey in Kentucky.

Picking Yourself Up, Brushing Yourself Off, and Starting All Over Again

The "Noble Experiment," as it was haughtily labeled by its self-righteous supporters, was a costly folly and utter failure that gravely injured the fragile national economy and teetering state economies as less tax revenues were collected and law enforcement costs sky-rocketed due to higher crime rates. Prohibition also devastated the legitimate, time-honored American distilling industry that, like any thriving industry, wasn't without blemish, scoundrels, or scandal but was hardly deserving of a total shutdown and public castigation. In the final analysis, Prohibition, doomed to failure from the start, was a national embarrassment and disgrace that depicted Americans as being backward, intolerant, and petty. But those truths didn't miti-gate the immediate everyday needs of Kentucky's ravaged distilling community.

In the 1932 American presidential election, candidates Her-bert Hoover of the Republicans, the bland incumbent on whose watch the Great Depression had commenced, and challenger Franklin Delano Roosevelt of the Democrats, the flashy, articulate governor of New York State, had very little separating them in terms of crucial issues except for one pivotal point. Aware of the disgrun-tled state of the general populace, the Democratic party wanted badly to push Congress to immediately repeal the Volstead Act and reinstate the legal consumption of all beverage alcohol. Deep-seated problems, both national and local in nature, were manifold. The enormous revenue shortfall, due to Prohibition, in the United States Treasury was fueling the Depression because there were no funds available for public work projects; organized crime lords like Al Capone were, thanks to Prohibition, running rampant from coast-to-coast stretching the budgets of local governments; states were squawking because of tax shortfalls; and public opinion polls were clearly showing that the vast majority of American adults had en-dured enough of the limitations of Prohibition and wanted to get back to drinking without having to look over their shoulder.

Public figures, most notably industrialist John D. Rockefeller, who had originally supported Prohibition reversed their positions after seeing the ruinous result of its enactment and were urging their friends in government to do whatever they could to conclude the Prohibition Era. With these circumstances and factors leaning in his favor, the Democratic ticket of Roosevelt-Nance defeated the Republican ticket of Hoover-Curtis in November of 1932 by a comfortable margin of over seven million votes. With FDR sitting in the Oval Office, doubtless cigarette in hand, the Volstead Act was repealed for beer and wine on March 19 of 1933, at his vigorous urging. As more and more states began ratifying the Act's repeal, distilled spirits were released from the yoke of Prohibition later on that year. It is said that the new president, the nation's thirty-second, celebrated the repeal of the Eighteenth Amendment by the enactment of the Twenty-First Amendment by making a pitcher of his notoriously horrible martinis, the ones made with a teaspoon of olive brine that White House guests and staff were expected to glug down appreciatively for almost a dozen years under the beaming gaze of the president. By December of 1933, the Noble Experiment was at long last pronounced dead.

In Bardstown, Jim Beam still spry, enthusiastic, and energetic at age sixty-nine looked at son T. Jeremiah, Jim's younger brother Park and his sons Earl and Carl, Jim's nephews, and uttered one sentence, "Boys, time for us to get back to work." During Prohibition, Jim's ill-fated Sunbeam Quarries Company had operated near an old distillery site, the Old Murphy Barber Distillery, in Clermont in neighboring Bullitt County. Murphy Barber, conveniently located on the L&N Railroad's Springfield extension line, had been a working distillery from 1891 to 1918. Cane Spring was the fine old bourbon produced there prior to Prohibition. Jim and T. Jeremiah had purchased the property during Prohibition for the purpose of quarrying on the site. Having sold Clear Spring Distillery in Bardstown on the eve of Prohibition, Jim, Park, and T. Jeremiah at least had the distilling equipment from the F.G. Walker Distillery in storage with which to begin rebuilding a family distilling business.

To properly break ground, however, the Beams, whose cash reserves had been severely depleted during the shutdown, needed infusions of investment capital. To that end, Jim struck a deal with a trio of Chicago investors by the names of Phillip Blum, Oliver Jacobson, and Harry Homel after they had expressed interest in underwriting any new ventures fronted by the famous Jim Beam. The deal was simple: for $5,000 apiece Blum, Homel, and Jacobson would own the company outright in one-third shares and Jim and T. Jeremiah would operate it. All agreed to move ahead.

On August, 14, 1934, the James B. Beam Distilling Company was incorporated. Brothers Earl Beam and Carl Beam, who was known to all, friend or foe alike, as "Shucks," stayed on with Jim and T. Jeremiah, helping especially with the fermenting and distilling. Prior to construction and immediately after Prohibition was repealed, Jim Beam set out to develop a new culture of yeast for the fermentation part of the production process. He did so successfully. That same culture is used in 2003.

Astonishingly in the late autumn of 1934, Jim, at age seventy, and T. Jeremiah, at age thirty-four, along with Earl and Carl Beam, T. Jeremiah's cousins, took only 120 days to finish their new distillery. Preferring to begin from scratch, they razed all but one of the existing, dilapidated Murphy Barber buildings. Because of money concerns, most of the construction was personally done by father, son, and nephews. Jim showed up every day and at the minimum supervised every aspect of the resurrection. Construction on the 660-bushel per day plant was far enough along by early March of 1935 that the Beams could start the mashing process in preparation for fermentation and distillation. The plan tinkered on by both Jim and T. Jeremiah was to temporarily continue with the established Old Tub brand. Then, Jim discovered that he no longer owned the rights to the name "Old Tub." Therefore the name of the frontline bourbon had to be gradually phased out and eventually changed. Colonel James B. Beam, the predecessor of Jim Beam Kentucky Straight Bourbon Whiskey, was born.

On March 25, 1935, the new James B. Beam Distilling Company in Clermont (Bullitt County), Kentucky, hung its shingle and hosted an open house for the local community and the Louisville press. Kentucky journalist Thomas E. Basham attended and reported on the event the next month in "Distilleries of Old Kentucky," recalling, "In this new plant, as through his long, historic distilling career, Colonel Jim continues to make a strictly '96-hour,' Nelson County Sour Mash Bourbon, only. On the first 'run' day . . . when asked by a visitor what he thought his yield would be, he replied, 'I am not interested, Sir, in how much, but how good a whiskey I can get out of a bushel.' "

Jim Beam's gentlemanly aura as a competent master distiller, or as he frequently understated it a "practical distiller," of fine bourbon whiskey was no fabrication, no affectation, and certainly no figment of a public relations manager's vivid imagination. The courtly demeanor was who Jim Beam was. While he would be the first to admit over a dram of shimmering, topaz-colored bourbon that he left a lot to be desired as a Florida citrus grove farmer, a rock quarry owner, and a coalmine operator, there was no disputing his talent, his unique genius as a master distiller of high-quality straight bourbon whiskey. The Old Tub Sour Mash name gave way by the late 1930s, first to "Colonel James B. Beam," then to "Jim Beam Kentucky Straight Bourbon Whiskey," the name that remains today for the flagship brand. The safeguarded family grain recipe was identical to the one first created by Jacob Beam in the 1780s and 1790s. Jim Beam's signature, James B. Beam, was placed prominently on each front label. It still adorns the label.

When the James B. Beam Distilling Company and other distilleries reopened in the mid-1930s, there was a critical shortage of good quality bourbon whiskey in the United States. The nature of whiskey production is such that quality straight, or unblended, bourbon whiskey doesn't appear overnight. Whiskey making at its highest level is a long-term affair. Production needed to begin quickly and stay running until enough fermented and distilled stocks could be aged for at least two years in oak barrels. Straight bourbon whiskey, by law, must be matured for at least 24 months in new oak barrels that have been charred on the inside.

But the roster of serious dilemmas facing Kentucky's family distillers included more than getting distilleries operating again from mothballed conditions. They also had to come to grips with the fact that in the decade and a half since Prohibition had dawned and died American drinkers had become accustomed to other varieties of whiskey, in particular imported Scotch and Canadian whiskies, as well as so-called "white" spirits, especially gin. While straight bourbon whiskey had relished the enviable position of being the most popular spirit in pre-Prohibition America, the cold reality was that a new generation of drinkers spawned in the 1920s and 1930s had to be introduced to Kentucky's pride and joy almost as though it was a new distilled spirit entry. That required time, money, and effort. Many of the smaller, less prosperous post-Prohibition distillers, acknowledging that the task at hand was too daunting and expensive, sold out to larger companies. This launched the era of consolidation and merger within the American distilling industry that exists to the present day.

Two of the wealthier concerns of the post-Prohibition period proved to be Schenley and National Distillers. Schenley absorbed noted distilleries such as George T. Stagg and James E. Pepper, thereby controlling quality brands like Ancient Age Bourbon Whiskey and James E. Pepper Bourbon Whiskey. They later bought out the rights to the other well-known brands and distilleries, specifically I.W. Harper Bourbon Whiskey, Cascade Distillery in Tennessee, and Old Charter Bourbon Whiskey. National Distillers owned venerable bourbon whiskey brands including Old Taylor, Old Crow, and Old Grand Dad. National also bought a famous distillery and brand of straight rye whiskey, Old Overholt. By the mid-1930s, National Distillers represented and controlled approximately half of the whiskey trade in the United States. It is worth pointing this out at this juncture because down the road in the 1980s National Distillers and James B. Beam Distilling Company would strike a deal that would significantly impact not just the two companies but the entire North American distilling industry.

The slate of other prominent post-Prohibition whiskey impact players included Brown-Forman (Early Times, Old Forester bourbon brands), Frankfort Distilleries (Four Roses brand), Austin Nichols (Wild Turkey brand), Glenmore Distilleries (Kentucky Tavern brand), Stitzel-Weller (Old Fitzgerald brand), Barton Distillery (Ten High, Kentucky Gentleman, Very Old Barton brands), and Heaven Hill Distillery (Bourbon Falls, Heaven Hill brands). While absorption of several brands under one roof threatened to dilute their profile, it was also the sole way at the time for these superb brands to survive. Members of the Beam family, all blood relations to Jim Beam, and descendents of Jacob Beam, were critical to the early success of more than a few of these companies and brands.

What the Angels Are Said to Be Drinking in Kentucky

Once the new spirit is placed in oak barrels for maturation of at least two years, the whiskey undergoes biochemical changes during this aging period. This is due both to direct contact with the oak and to oxidation due to the porous nature of the oak. With porosity comes evaporation, especially in the summer months when north-central Kentucky's average day is balmy and humid. Estimates as to the annual rate of evaporation loss run from 2 percent to 4 percent per barrel. That's a lot of perfumy alcohol in warehouses that house tens of thousands of aging barrels. The whiskeymen refer to the flowery smelling evaporation loss as the "angel's share."

By 1940, the positive news of the availability of increased bourbon whiskey stocks was being overshadowed by talk of yet another world war looming across the Atlantic Ocean in Europe. Even if they weren't breaking records, however, sales of straight bourbon whiskey were on a slow rise by the spring of 1941. Consolidation had, to some degree, worked in the favor of the whiskey business.

The marshalling of resources had largely been successful in salvaging an industry on the brink. Unfortunately, a new, inferior breed of American whiskey, blended whiskey, or brown spirits that were comprised mainly of tasteless neutral grain spirits and a small percentage of good quality straight whiskey, was gaining in popularity. Consumer confusion over the fundamental difference between blended and straight whiskey muddied the water for the distillers of higher end whiskey. Yet the key importance of brand recognition held sway over the more discerning imbibers. Valued brand names of Jim Beam, I.W. Harper, Old Crow, Old Forester, Old Grand Dad, W.L. Weller, Old Charter, and others withstood the challenge from within their own industry . . . sometimes their own company.

The events that occurred at Pearl Harbor in Hawaii on Sunday, December 7, 1941, would go a long way to excavate more pot holes, some gapingly deep ditches, in the winding road to recovery for Kentucky's—and America's—distilling industry.

Continuing in the Face of Another World War

In 1941, Harry Homel and Oliver Jacobson sold their shares in the James B. Beam Distilling Company to Harry Blum, Phillip Blum's son, for around $1 million, making the Blums the sole proprietors. The internal sale was instigated from the outside when Schenley made an offer to buy the well-run and profitable James B. Beam Distilling Company. Negotiations turned sour and were terminated when Blum found out that Schenley had agreed to retain the services of Homel and Jacobson, but not Blum. Though Blum wouldn't have wanted to go over to Schenley anyway, he was offended enough to quash the deal and purchase the one-third interests of his partners.

While Jim Beam with some reluctance transferred the bulk of the day-to-day operations of James B. Beam Distilling Company to

T. Jeremiah and Park's boys by the early 1940s, he remained the primal force behind the scenes, needing by nature to keep his hand stirring the pot. Jim's brother Park retired from James B. Beam Distilling Company in 1943, passing the distilling torch to his able sons Earl and Carl. Most accounts imply that Jim sorely missed Park when he left to consult at Shawhan Distillery.

One commonly told story describes Jim's concern with the protection of the all-important family recipe for yeast and the unique strain that he himself developed in 1934. Yeast, if you recall, is the biochemical trigger for the fermentation of the grain mash. Each individual yeast culture imparts a singular flavor to the whiskey and is therefore deemed to be of vital importance to distillers. Even a minor variation in the culture could alter the taste of the bourbon whiskey. Always concerned that a disaster might befall the distillery after it shut down for the workweek, Jim would assiduously take home a portion of the yeast culture in a sealed jar to protect it from any unforeseen weekend calamity. Every Friday evening like clockwork Big B would be observed by his neighbors and friends driving his black Cadillac from Clermont to his big home on Distillers Row in Bardstown, the jar of yeast nestled safely in the front passenger seat beside him.

That simple tale as well as any illustrates the enduring character of Jim Beam even in his twilight years: attentive to detail, personally immersed in the grand as well as the mundane, and, most of all, fully mindful of the Beam family legacy. Perhaps the horror of Prohibition or the advancement of age had made Jim an especially cautious septuagenarian. What is clear is that Jim Beam like his father, grandfather, and great-grandfather took nothing in life for granted.

War had been brought to America's doorstep and the distilling industry was expected to do its part in the national war effort. The distillers of Kentucky pitched in by producing industrial alcohol, a fundamental compound required for a myriad of wartime necessities. In *The Book of Bourbon and Other Fine American Whiskeys* (1995, p. 84), authors Gary and Mardee Haidin Regan document the variety of wartime goods in which industrial alcohol was a critical element. Wrote the Regans, "It's interesting to note just how much the whiskey business helped the war effort . . . In the manufacture of rubber, antifreeze, tetraethyllead (used in the production of aviation gasoline), rayon for parachutes and ether, among other things." Those "other things" included the making of Jeeps (23 gallons for every jeep); 19¾ gallons of alcohol for every 16-inch naval shell; and one gallon for every 64 hand grenades or two 155mm Howitzer shells.

Other Kentucky-based industries followed suit. The company that produced Louisville Slugger baseball bats, for example, retooled its equipment to make rifle stocks. Coalmines worked longer shifts to produce more coal for the factories devoted to the war effort.

The downside to this patriotic activity was that just when the Kentucky bourbon whiskey industry had been about to regain its footing in the marketplace, production of grain spirits for the creation of whiskey was curtailed due to the war. As a result, whiskey inventories again declined as one year of war became two and two turned into three and three years evolved into four years. By the formal end of hostilities in 1945, the stocks of Kentucky straight bourbon whiskey were perilously low, industrywide once again. There was a dearth of good quality whiskey around the nation. To make matters worse, returning GIs were heard singing the praises of the Scotch whisky that they had been exposed to when stationed in the United Kingdom.

In 1944, Jim Beam quietly retired from James B. Beam Distilling Company. T. Jeremiah, Earl, and Carl Beam, along with the Blum family weathered the remainder of the war at Clermont and came out swinging in 1945, gearing up for all-out production. In early spring of 1947, Earl decided to depart the James B. Beam Distilling Company to pursue the master distiller post at Heaven Hill Distillery of Bardstown when Joe L. and Harry Beam stepped down. Carl "Shucks" Beam was, in short order, named master distiller at James B. Beam by his cousin, T. Jeremiah. Carrying on with James B.

The Jim Beam Distillery at Clermont, Kentucky. *Courtesy of Jim Beam Brands Co.*

Left to right: Carl Beam, David Beam, Baker Beam, Booker Noe and T. Jeremiah Beam in the 1960s. *Courtesy of Jim Beam Brands Co.*

Left to right: Carl Beam, T. Jeremiah Beam, Booker Noe and Baker Beam in the early 1970s. *Courtesy of Jim Beam Brands Co.*

Masters chat. Master Distiller Emeritus Booker Noe talks with his successor Master Distiller Jerry Dalton. *Courtesy of Jim Beam Brands Co.*

The Clermont, Kentucky home of T. Jeremiah Beam is listed in the National Registry of Historic Places. *Courtesy of Jim Beam Brands Co.*

Jim Beam standing in front of his office after the repeal of Prohibition. *Courtesy of Jim Beam Brands Co.*

Jim Beam with his assistant distiller Bill Douglas prior to Prohibition. *Courtesy of Jim Beam Brands Co.*

Master Distiller Emeritus Booker Noe in one of Jim Beam's rackhouses. *Courtesy of Jim Beam Brands Co.*

Jim Beam in the late 1930s in Clermont. *Courtesy of Jim Beam Brands Co.*

Aging barrels are stored in tiers, nine rows high at Jim Beam. *Courtesy of Jim Beam Brands Co.*

By law, the interior of bourbon barrels must be charred to specification. *Courtesy of Jim Beam Brands Co.*

Booker and Fred Noe check many barrels before deciding on which will produce Booker's Bourbon. *Courtesy of Jim Beam Brands Co.*

Booker Noe, T. Jeremiah Beam and Carl Beam in 1965. *Courtesy of Jim Beam Brands Co.*

The sense of smell is the key sense for whiskey-men like Fred Noe. *Courtesy of Jim Beam Brands Co.*

Beam Distilling Company were T. Jeremiah Beam, Carl Beam, and Harry Blum. All hoped for a postwar boom in business activity. Jim Beam was now eighty-two and was still, on occasion, seen ferrying the yeast culture home from Clermont on Friday nights.

On early Christmas morning 1947, James Beauregard Beam, the fourth generation of Beam distillers, prominent Bardstown and north-central Kentucky citizen, patriarch of the Beam family, and the most famous whiskey distiller of his time, died in his Distiller's Row home at the age of eighty-three. Jim was found by his wife, Mary, at around 6:00 A.M. The coroner concluded that Jim had been dead for about two hours when Mary entered the room. Cause of death was listed as a hemorrhage. Jim had been retired for about three years and had been known to suffer from heart problems, but was considered to be in overall good health for a gentleman his age. Just a few months before he passed away, Jim and Mary had celebrated their fiftieth wedding anniversary.

The peerless king of Kentucky distilling, Jim Beam was survived by his wife Mary, son T. Jeremiah, and daughters Mildred Beam and Margaret Noe. Margaret's son Frederick Booker Noe, Jim Beam's grandson, was eighteen when he attended his grandfather's funeral service at the Bardstown Baptist Church on a cold morning between Christmas and New Year's Day. Booker's uncle T. Jeremiah at the urging of Jim had already started keeping his eye on his tall nephew. With Jim Beam now deceased and T. Jeremiah Beam forty-seven years old, the next generation had to be considered, groomed, and put to the test. After all the welfare and preservation of the family business had to be placed above all other considerations.

T. Jeremiah and Carl Beam: Jim Beam Bourbon Steps onto the World Stage

STILL IN THE MURKY shadows of the Second World War, the world, shredded by conflict and political upheaval, set course in the late 1940s on a deliberate if fitful healing process that would impact every continent, each nation. The United States, Europe, and the rest of the world took a collective deep breath before shakily embarking on the paths to infrastructural restoration, bridging radical political viewpoints, resuming global trade with the signing of sweeping international accords, fostering new strategic alliances, and slow but steady economic recovery.

The inhabitants of the blue planet were primed for sweeping socioeconomic, class, and political reforms. In San Francisco, representatives of 50 countries signed the landmark charter in 1945 that created the United Nations. The United States' $12 billion aid package, known popularly as the Marshall Plan, helped stimulate the economies of Western Europe between 1947 and 1951. Feeling the pressure created by overextension, the British and the French abandoned many of their colonial interests. Teeming with immigrants from Russia and Europe, Israel became an independent state in May of 1948. The Soviet Union under the bloodthirsty regime of Joseph Stalin spread its influence deep into Central and Eastern Europe. In response to Stalin's military adventures, the NATO alliance was formed between the United States and nations of Western Europe. The Communists took power in China and in the northern provinces of Korea. Anti-communist feelings pulsed through the American psyche, which was still feeling snake-bitten and jumpy after the surprise attack at Pearl Harbor.

Economic stimulants, free markets, and global trade, many political leaders of the day felt, were the key elements to reconstruction in the areas of the world hit hardest by the war. In the midst of recovery from widespread hostilities around the globe, international politics, though, continued to be driven, often by force, by ideological and territorial affiliations. Consequently, the arena of international politics was still a seething, bubbling lava flow in the late 1940s and early 1950s. The slightest provocation from such things as unannounced military maneuvers too snugly close to a disputed border or an unconscious diplomatic slight could prove to be the match to ignite a crisis.

By contrast, back home in North America relative tranquility permeated the 48-member strong United States. In a stunning upset that thwarted political pundits, newspaper editors, and pollsters alike, incumbent Harry S. Truman defeated Thomas E. Dewey by 2.1 million votes in the national election of November 1948. Truman remained in the White House for another four years, nursing his glasses of Kentucky straight bourbon whiskey splashed with an ounce or two of ginger ale. In May of 1948, jockey Eddie Arcaro rode the marvelous thoroughbred Citation to victory at the Kentucky

Derby at Churchill Downs in Louisville. A young, polite professional golfer by the name of Sam Snead stole the hearts of galleries coast-to-coast with his sweet, fluid swing. Baseball's mighty New York Yankees cruised regularly into the post-War World Series, including 1947 plus their remarkable strings of consecutive appearances from 1949 to 1953 and from 1955 to 1958. Television transplanted radio as the electronic medium of choice across America. The blurry, grainy, black-and-white images, captured live, of TV's trailblazing personalities, such as Milton Berle, Sid Caesar, Lucille Ball, and Jackie Gleason, were the talk of the at-work nation.

Coca-Cola, the foremost soft drink of America, had a new, formidable, and aggressive rival in Pepsi Cola. Shiny, steel-paneled *diners,* complete with blaring jukeboxes, greasy hamburgers and giddy bobbysoxers, popped up across roadside America, sometimes nearby the motor hotels that were called *motels.* Newly constructed neighborhoods, like Levittown on Long Island, New York, spilled out from the edges of major cities forming the initial commutable villages and hamlets called *suburbs.* Men worked at day jobs that were described as being either white collar or blue collar then mowed their matchbox-sized lawns on Saturdays; women as a matter of course toiled at home seven days and nights a week; and the children of these couples attended schools that always seemed located right around the corner. Everyday life returned to normal in America, but in many ways it was better than the economically sour pre-war years. The population's sense of optimism was unbridled and infectious, inspiring a genuine growth economy. The America of the late 1940s and 1950s was, for lack of a better word, settled.

The orderly calm that pervaded the nation was starkly mirrored in how its legal-age citizens dealt with beverage alcohol. Throughout much of the reckless, often profligate pre-WWII decades spanning from 1890 through the 1930s, the consumption of alcohol both in mixed drinks and neat, meaning unadulterated, was conducted largely outside the home in poorly lighted bars, taverns, saloons, and, during the Prohibition years, in speakeasies. The nesting instinct, the urgent need for domesticity and conformity that overwhelmed average Americans after the Second World War played itself out most graphically through the invention of the in-home "cocktail party." This benign metropolitan and suburban phenomenon occurred at the so-called "happy hour," the after work/before dinner 120-minute period between 5:00 P.M. and 7:00 P.M. in which distilled spirits, especially straight bourbon whiskey (Jim Beam, Old Grand-Dad, Old Crow), blended Scotch whisky (Cutty Sark, J&B Rare, Johnnie Walker Red), blended American and blended Canadian whiskeys (Seagram 7 Crown, Seagram V.O., Canadian Club), gin (Gilbey's, Gordon's, Fleischmann), and the up-and-coming clear spirit, vodka (Smirnoff), were the featured, even trendy, libations.

But while the times were fundamentally good, the times likewise had their flaws and even their casualties. The social atmosphere of the 1950s glorified the perfunctory cocktail party and the fabled three-martini lunch. The bittersweet aftereffects on many of their proponents were depicted with searing accuracy in John Cheever's short stories, many of which appeared in the *New Yorker*, others in *Esquire*. *The Swimmer*, one of Cheever's and the period's most insightful pieces of short fiction about suburban life, tells the story of Neddy Merrill, a failed man on the brink who drinks and swims his way home through the backyard swimming pools of his neighbors. The story was even made into a movie starring Burt Lancaster.

Of the straight and narrow, button-down post-WWII period journalist William Grimes, the current restaurant critic of the *New York Times*, wrote in his book *Straight Up or On the Rocks: A Cultural History of American Drink* (2001, p. 117), "The sanitized version of middle-class life that defined the 1950s, or served as its official myth, can be seen in the nation's drinking habits . . . The appetite for novelty that had launched a thousand drinks of the golden age and the Roaring twenties disappeared. The man in the grey flannel suit drank a dry martini, a gin and tonic, a Scotch and soda—safe choices that put you in solidly with the right people."

Statistics from the time show that those urban and suburban gentlemen and ladies also tipped many an old-fashioned glass filled with topaz-colored Kentucky straight bourbon whiskey. In the mid-1940s, Kentucky distillers were responsible for producing between 65 percent and 70 percent of all spirits made in the United States. But while beverage alcohol consumption may not have had the sheen or the panache of the preceding decades, drinking on a per capita basis was heading north. Drinking within the confines of home in the company of friends meant drinking more because that kind of imbibing environment was safer and comfortably private. Americans emerged from the Second World War with a raging thirst, one that they preferred to quench at home. With all its proclivities, vapid cocktails, and mundane lives, the most dominant, dynamic, and strangely memorable decade of the American Century, the fantastic 1950s, was switched "On."

And, a largely consolidated American distilling industry geared up to meet the evolving consumer demands that were fueled by the bright prospects of a fresh era of peace and across-the-board prosperity.

Changes at James B. Beam Distilling Company

Three years before his death, Jim Beam, by that point the near mythical, fourth-generation Kentucky distiller, handed the reins of the family business to his son T. Jeremiah Beam, nephew Carl Beam, and the Blum family of Chicago. Feeling secure that the fifth and sixth generations of Beams had what it took to guide the business, Jim went quietly into retirement in Bardstown with his wife Mary Catherine. In 1946, T. Jeremiah officially took the helm of James B. Beam Distilling Company as president and treasurer.

Two years later in 1948, a year after Jim Beam's death, Harry Blum assumed the role of president to allow T. Jeremiah more time to properly oversee the distillery, aging warehouses, and bottling plant and to work more closely with master distiller Carl Beam.

T. Jeremiah, while not a master distiller of bourbon whiskey by trade, was a respected and well-traveled bourbon ambassador who liked to talk to people about his father, Jim Beam Bourbon, and the Kentucky whiskey industry in general. The duties of company president, a job frequently mired in organizational minutia, paperwork, and staff meetings, didn't suit T. Jeremiah's out-going, freewheeling personality. In addition, Blum happened to be the major shareholder of the company.

In early July of 1949, the other irreplaceable member of the fourth generation of bourbon whiskey distilling Beams died in Bardstown. Six years after retiring from the James B. Beam Distilling Company, Jim Beam's younger brother, able partner, and trusted confidante Park succumbed at the age of eighty to a convergence of lingering illnesses. His obituary in the *Courier-Journal* stated, "He had been in declining health for several years." William Park Beam, youngest son of David M. and Margaret Beam, husband of Mary Sue and the father of five children, had been widely respected within the bourbon industry. At the time of Park's death, two of his sons, Earl and Carl, were master distillers at Heaven Hill Distillery and James B. Beam Distilling Company, respectively. Other Kentucky whiskeymen viewed Park as a gifted distiller and the man who, in stride with his older brother, had contributed substantially both before and following Prohibition to the continuing success of the family business, Old Tub Bourbon and later Jim Beam Bourbon.

In the revitalized marketplace, distilled spirits sales, impacted heavily by domestic and foreign consumption, rose substantially year after year in the late 1940s and early 1950s. Spirits of a different nature, emotional, ran high in Clermont, Kentucky as under T. Jeremiah Beam and Harry Blum's watch Jim Beam Kentucky

Straight Bourbon Whiskey once again whetted adult whistles from Seattle to Miami, from Bangor to San Diego. The late 1940s was also a time for promising and steady growth in the export market as 12-bottle, 9-liter cases of Jim Beam Bourbon were shipped across the Atlantic Ocean on U.S. Navy supply vessels to the homesick American servicemen who were stationed at bases in Germany, the Benelux countries (Belgium, the Netherlands, and Luxembourg), and the United Kingdom. European and British shopkeepers, pub owners, and restaurateurs were keenly aware that the American GIs stationed in their countries frequently requested a whiskey made at home.

To appeal to this huge, enthusiastic, and free-spending audience, British and European merchants began ordering and stocking Jim Beam Bourbon in their establishments. Largely through the far-reaching channels of the Armed Forces, Americans were implementing the Marshall Plan and acting in concert with NATO forces at air, sea, and land installations. The grain whiskey first developed in the 1790s by German descendent, master distiller, and Kentuckian Jacob Beam touched the soil a century and a half later that was the ancestral home to all of the Beams. The Jim Beam around-the-world phenomenon was born and nothing would ever be the same again for the James B. Beam Distilling Company or the Beam family.

In Clermont, the Beam plant was bursting at the seams by the end of 1950 as heavy production kept the distillery buzzing night and day. The enormous annual sales increases of Jim Beam Bourbon posted in 1950 and 1951 forced T. Jeremiah and Blum to consider without delay the expansion option as well as the addition of key staff. In 1950, as was virtually preordained since before Jim Beam's funeral, T. Jeremiah contacted his nephew Frederick Booker Noe II, the son of T. Jeremiah's sister Margaret Beam Noe and her husband Frederick Booker Noe I, to offer him a position at the understaffed Clermont distillery. Booker had just turned twenty-one. Tall at 6' 4", educated at the University of Kentucky, naturally enthusiastic, and, most important of all, a grandson of Jim Beam, affable Booker was the perfect and only selection to become the apprentice to Beam master distiller Carl Beam.

An astounding, unprecedented 30 percent rise in sales of Jim Beam from 1952 to 1953 made it abundantly clear to T. Jeremiah, Blum, and the Beam board of directors that the Clermont plant could no longer on its own sustain the type of activity that was expected of it. Failure to act decisively would hurt growth on both the national and the nascent international fronts. Swift and sure action had to be taken.

In November of 1953, the James B. Beam Distilling Company purchased a flat 450-acre site situated near the sleepy burgh of Boston in Nelson County, south of Clermont, that had on it a mothballed distillery complex know formerly as Churchill Downs Distillery. JBB Plant #2 at Boston soon became a full-fledged distillery with accompanying warehouse storage capacity of 60,000 barrels. The pristine, limestone water source was nearby Wilson Creek. The branch water was collected in a concrete reservoir constructed specifically for that purpose. By mid-year of 1954, JBB Plant #2 at Boston was operating at full capacity. Shortly after the Boston plant opened, Booker was named distiller of Plant #2 by his uncle T. Jeremiah. With Baker and David Beam assisting their father Carl at Clermont and Booker in charge of the Boston plant, the sixth generation of Beams was now fully engaged in the family business.

Case sales of Jim Beam Bourbon and several other fine straight bourbon whiskeys rose steadily through the remaining years of the 1950s as the nation, Great Britain, and continental Europe consumed copious quantities of the American distilled spirit. The world's fascination with anything perceived as having an American origin from television programming, especially westerns, to sweet soft drinks, clothes, popular music, movies, and automobiles had become insatiable. The economic achievements of America in the 1950s were generated in part from the country's ability to market itself and its culture as well as its goods and services to other nations. The United

States stood as a lighthouse of freedom, opportunity, technological and scientific innovation, and self-expression. Few transportable commodities reflected the customary American values of rugged honesty, individuality, and wholesomeness more than straight bourbon whiskey from Kentucky, in particular, Jim Beam Kentucky Straight Bourbon Whiskey.

Think of it from the perspective of someone residing outside the United States in the 1950s, someone who perhaps didn't enjoy the freedoms that Americans took for granted or maybe didn't dwell in as nice a house or community as America was depicted as having just about everywhere. Bourbon whiskey was made in the heartland state of Kentucky; it was made up mostly of golden corn, the quintessential indigenous New World grain; the whiskey was matured in barrels constructed of sturdy American white oak from forests located in Missouri and Indiana; and, last, bourbon whiskey was produced by generations of unassuming, polite men of few words.

Even if that person hadn't thought that deeply about the imagery, Jim Beam Kentucky Straight Bourbon Whiskey was nevertheless unpretentiously packaged in the same clear glass, square-shaped bottle as it is today. Anyone at home or abroad could with ease gauge the warm honey brown color and purity of the product. The bright white label announcing "Jim Beam" in black, slightly rounded type, clear lettering, and uncomplicated language is the same nowadays as is was in the 1950s. "Sour Mash." "40% Alc/Vol (80 Proof)." Jim Beam's signature, James B. Beam, resting beneath the words "None genuine without my signature" supplied a powerful message of authenticity to admirers of whiskey or of America. Jim Beam was the American bourbon whiskey to have, not only in Springfield, Missouri, or Springfield, Massachusetts, but likewise in Bonn, Germany; Toulouse, France; Naples, Italy; or Manchester, England.

Clinging to generations-old traditions with a hard and fast grip during this explosive era of growth was paramount to T. Jeremiah. In his role as the designated custodian of the Beam family legacy,

T. Jeremiah, along with Carl and Booker, assumed personal responsibility for many of the fundamental duties in the distilleries, warehouses, and bottling plants. T. Jeremiah reportedly feared that in
the face of booming business everyday procedures might suffer due
to cutting corners or a lack of concentration. T. Jeremiah, Carl,
and Booker instilled in their coworkers the importance of the seemingly rudimentary things like making certain that the jug yeast
culture originally developed by Jim Beam after Prohibition was reli-
giously used for every new batch of fermented mash, every day of
the year, without fail. The lesson of prudence that his father unin-
tentionally taught by taking care to transport home in his black
Cadillac a jar of jug yeast every Friday night from the Clermont distillery wasn't lost on T. Jeremiah. All of which conveniently segues
to a couple of the best stories that illustrate the circumspect, communicative, and inclusive nature of T. Jeremiah.

When pressed by a visiting reporter once in the mid-1960s
about why he still insisted on using only the family yeast culture
recipe rather than less costly and less labor-intensive cultures,
T. Jeremiah courteously replied first in technical terms about the
importance of maintaining proper acid accumulations, pH levels,
and peak alkalinity. Noticing the glazed-over expression on the
face of the newspaperman, T. Jeremiah patiently tried the tack
about the need for consistency from one batch of whiskey to the
next, that the customer paying his or her hard-earned money for
Jim Beam Bourbon deserved to be satisfied, bottle after bottle,
time after time, and that even the slightest change in the yeast culture could noticeably alter the taste of Jim Beam Bourbon. Realizing that the reporter still had the identical blank look on his face,
T. Jeremiah finally said with the courtly smile of a true Kentucky
gentleman, "Let's just say we think it makes a better Bourbon,
huh?" Message received.

One of T. Jeremiah's major strengths was his natural facility
with communication. His approach to business was to keep the
Beam employees at all levels informed about the issues that affected

the company as a whole. In the 1950s and 1960s, the strapped-for-cash state of Kentucky raised excise taxes several times on whiskey production, irking the bourbon whiskeymen who already felt unfairly penalized by state and federal duties. For instance, the state of Indiana's storage tax on distilled spirits was $10 a barrel while Kentucky's was $28 per barrel. In response, some Kentucky distillers began to relocate their storage warehouses in neighboring states, like Indiana, to save money. At one point in the early 1960s, Louisville's respected daily newspaper run by the Bingham family, the *Courier-Journal*, ran an editorial defining the distilled spirits tax levy issues and calling for the Court of Appeals to reevaluate the lop-sided tax structure on distilled spirits in Kentucky. Unfortunately, the *Courier-Journal* editorial that urged the court "to cut or repeal outright the production tax" ran on a Saturday, a traditionally soft readership day for newspapers.

T. Jeremiah, aware that it was likely that most of the 300 Beam employees hadn't seen the editorial, issued a memo the following Monday morning along with a copy of the *Courier-Journal* opinion piece to each and every Beam employee for their perusal. The memo was titled, MEMO TO ALL MEMBERS OF THE BEAM FAMILY. In the company memo, T. Jeremiah said in part "This editorial covers all the latest facts which have *now developed with the passage of time* since the production tax was doubled in 1956. Not only those of us at BEAM but everyone in the Distilling Industry can help keep the industry from being forced out of Kentucky into other states by using our individual influence to insure that those legislators in the new legislature will rescind this unfair (to Kentucky) production tax." The memo was signed "Sincerely, T. Jeremiah Beam, Senior Vice President."

Under T. Jeremiah's steady guidance a sense of purpose, almost of mission, spread through the company all through the 1950s as volume uniformly grew and Jim Beam Bourbon started to overtake competitors. A hand written flow chart for the James B. Beam Distilling Company plant organization, dated July 1, 1958, shows "T. J. Beam, Senior Vice-Pres" in the uppermost box. To the left and down from T. J. Beam is the Master Distiller box with the name "Carl Beam" scratched in it. Connected by a descending line is the "Distiller Booker Noe" box directly below that of Carl Beam. Though the family no longer owned the company, the company was still their domain.

Speaking of Carl "Shucks" Beam, Carl's place in the Beam hierarchy is one of the few confounding matters in the Beam saga. Carl, son of Park, nephew of Jim, and cousin of T. Jeremiah, is the one Beam inextricably linked to Jim Beam Bourbon from the end of Prohibition to the early 1970s yet who is today inexplicably the most overlooked twentieth-century family member. The focus for the fifth generation is squarely placed on T. Jeremiah Beam, son of Jim Beam.

Carl's value to the company while he was employed by Beam appears by all accounts to have been fully acknowledged and duly rewarded both by T. Jeremiah and Harry Blum. In November of 1959, in fact, the position of vice-president was added to Carl's existing title of master distiller. Even more odd is the undeniable fact that Carl was typically and prominently featured as a Beam front man in Jim Beam Bourbon print ads that ran in the mid-1960s. One American Gothic-like ad from 1965 shows Carl standing next to his wife Edna in what appears to be an old-fashioned general store. The direct headline succinctly reads "A secret recipe. Part of the Beam family art for 175 Autumns." Carl was featured in other print ad campaigns of the day that highlighted two generations of Beams.

Carl and Edna Beam lived in a house located on the Clermont plant property and as a result Carl could be stumbled across at the distillery at any time of day or night for close to 40 years. Quiet, reserved, and sometimes described as being "earthy" perhaps because of his hobby of growing monstrously large gourds, Carl was the masterful tutor of the Beam's family's sixth generation, his own sons Baker and David, and of Booker Noe. Self-effacing and kind,

Shucks was every bit as much as Jim and T. Jeremiah Beam a main-spring component of the Beam distilleries from the repeal of Prohibition up until the time of his retirement in 1974.

Maybe in the end, Carl's low-key personality and unaffected demeanor made him less interesting than his more extroverted cousins. Or perhaps it had to do with the reality that he was only Jim Beam's nephew and not his son and direct heir. Whatever the case, Carl's steadfast distilling genius was one of the prime catalysts that catapulted Jim Beam Bourbon forward as a foremost brand of American whiskey, making it an international icon well before his tenure at Beam was concluded.

Taking the Biggest Leap of All in 1967

In October of 1959, Chicago millionaire and James B. Beam Distilling Company principal stockholder Harry Blum decided to step down as president at the age of sixty-five. At the request of the Beams and the board, he stayed on in the less demanding but still influential post of board chairman. Blum understandably wanted to spend more time with his family in Chicago, his hometown, as well as at a home in Florida. Replacing Blum as president was forty-year-old Everett Kovler, formerly the Beam executive vice-president. Kovler, who was married to Blum's daughter Marjorie, had been hired by Blum and T. Jeremiah in 1946 and had excelled with skill and diplomacy through different departments including marketing, advertising, and sales. In 1960, Booker Noe was appointed to be master distiller at Plant #2 in Boston by T. Jeremiah and Kovler. Carl remained as master distiller and vice president at Clermont, the flagship plant, assisted by his son Baker.

The company prospered as sales continued to skyrocket off the charts. Records from the early 1960s show that the James B. Beam Distilling Company employed 300 people year round and 500 people at peak seasonal periods. The payroll at the time approached

$1.5 million. At the Clermont plant, seven bottling lines were busy most of the year. The production totals of both Beam distilleries taken together produced 125,000 barrels of bourbon whiskey in both 1962 and 1963. The company, though, wasn't the sole beneficiary of its success. In 1962, the company paid a total of $48 million in federal, state, and county tax levies. The Bullitt County treasury pulled in $174,626 of it while Nelson County benefited by $135,376.

Go Tell It on the Mountain: Maturing Bourbon Whiskey

Part of the Beam legacy is how they have always naturally, meaning without much human intervention, matured their bourbon whiskeys. As is mandated by the federal government all straight bourbon whiskey must be aged for a minimum of 24 months in new oak barrels that have been charred on the interior. If a whiskey ages in barrel for 23 months and then is removed, it cannot legally be labeled as straight bourbon whiskey. There exist no legal stipulations, however, on the type of warehousing to be employed, meaning open or closed, temperature-controlled or natural, hilltop or valley floor.

Proper warehousing of the aging barrels is a key element of the production process, one that greatly influences the final product. It is in the maturation stage where the raw grain spirit actually transforms itself into smooth, drinkable bourbon whiskey by the biochemical interaction with the oak and oxygen. Some distillers prefer temperature-controlled warehouses, or *rackhouses* as they are typically called in Kentucky, wherein the whiskey ages at a steady, consistent rate over its maturation period. The Beams, on the other hand, by family tradition left their rackhouses at the mercy of Kentucky's climate that is typically very balmy and humid in the summer and frosty but not arctic in the winter. Many of the Beam rackhouses rest on hill-tops where they get the most wind as well as the most sun and heat and the least humidity.

The *Austin Statesman* reported in detail in 1965 on why the Beams age their bourbons the way they do. "Millions of dollars have been spent by large whiskey distillers over the years to find some substitute for 'time'—a chemical, electrical, or mechanical means to speed the process—to no avail. The Beams are content to let the mystery of what actually happens and why within the barrels remain unsolved. They are convinced that a true Bourbon must be naturally aged . . . Their aging storehouses are unheated—faced north to south to receive the fullest exposure to the sun. Painted in dark colors to absorb the heat." The belief on the part of the Beams is that by allowing the bourbon whiskey to mature in harmony with atmospheric and seasonal conditions the end result will be better because it is less manipulated.

The barrels located in the top tiers of the Beam rackhouses age quicker because it is hotter up there in the warm weather months than it is at ground level. Maturing of distilled spirits accelerates in warm conditions as the spirit literally expands, invading the oak barrel. Barrels are rotated at different height levels within the rackhouses so that they can mature evenly as well as naturally. This is a costly process due to the amount of continual labor involved.

Jim Beam Kentucky Straight Bourbon Whiskey is aged for four years in oak barrels. Over the span of four years, including Kentucky's steamy summers when evaporation loss is high, each 50-gallon barrel loses about 20 percent of its content due to evaporation. Continued the report of the *Austin Statesman*, "The very extremes of weather avoided by others (meaning, other distillers) for reasons of cost—are to the Beams—essential for the 'working' of the maturing bourbon."

As senior vice president, T. Jeremiah ran a tight ship in Clermont and Boston, but provided a positive working environment in which local people evidently flourished. A good indication that illustrated the degree of employee loyalty and satisfaction was how long employees tended to stay with James B. Beam. A Louisville *Courier-Journal* newspaper article from May of 1963 covered a company dinner in Louisville hosted by T. Jeremiah Beam and Harry Blum where employees with 10 years or more of service were feted. Said the *Courier-Journal* "Longevity of service is a tradition in the Bourbon Industry in general, and the Beam company in particular. Of the total of 214 employees who have been with Beam for 10 years or longer, 15 have completed 25 years' service, 22 have 20 years, 46 have 15 years, and 131 have 10 years. Approximately 40 percent of all of Beam's employees have been with the company for 10 years or longer."

On June 2, 1965, the one-millionth barrel of Jim Beam Bourbon since the repeal of prohibition was filled. There was no question but that by the mid-1960s The James B. Beam Distilling Company juggernaut, guided by T. Jeremiah and Carl, Booker and Everett Kovler, was rolling . . . powerfully so.

But, to be sure, the whole bourbon industry was experiencing unprecedented growth. From 1949 to 1966, bourbon whiskey sales in the United States alone rose by an extraordinary 239 percent, with the biggest spikes in terms of annual percentage coming in 1950, 1953, 1959, and 1964. More statistics released in 1969 from The Bourbon Institute (now the Distilled Spirits Council of the United States or DISCUS), a trade organization supported by the bourbon whiskey industry and headquartered in New York City, showed a steady climb in bourbon whiskey sales from 1958 to 1968, going from around 25 million cases a year to 32 million cases. During this dynamic period, straight bourbon whiskey overtook blended whiskeys as the liquor category frontrunner. The report stated, "Over the last 10 year period, Bourbon sales enjoyed its greatest period of growth. In 1962, Bourbon moved into first place in national popularity—a position it has held ever since. In this period, Bourbon also maintained a steady lead of 16 million cases over the most popular import." That most popular import at that time was Scotch whisky.

Time Line: What Else Was Happening the Year That Bourbon Was Made the "Native U.S. Spirit"

March 28, 1964: Anchorage, Alaska flattened by major earthquake.

April 1964: Arnold Palmer wins his final Masters Tournament at Augusta National.

May 2, 1964: Jockey Bill Hartack rides Northern Dancer to victory in the Kentucky Derby.

May 4, 1964: The Senate passes the resolution naming bourbon whiskey as "distinctive" to the United States of America.

May 27, 1964: United States reports that it will begin sending military planes to Laos.

June 22, 1964: Three civil rights workers disappear in Mississippi.

July 2, 1964: President Johnson signs civil rights bill.

July 30, 1964: The congressional bill creating Medicare is signed into law by President Johnson.

August 4, 1964: Bodies of three missing civil rights workers located. Twenty-one white men eventually are arrested.

August 7, 1964: Tonkin Gulf resolution is passed, legally sanctioning action by the president in Vietnam.

August 11, 1964: War on Poverty bill okayed by Congress. The bill also approves funding for VISTA, a domestic peace corps, anti-poverty funding, and the Job Corps.

September 27, 1964: Report from the Warren Commission concludes that Lee Harvey Oswald acted alone in the assassination of President John F. Kennedy.

October 1964: The St. Louis Cardinals beat the New York Yankees in the World Series four games to three. St. Louis pitcher Bob Gibson is voted the Most Valuable Player of the series.

October 4, 1964: Federal grand jury convicts 7 of the 21 white men accused of killing of three civil rights workers in Mississippi.

November 3, 1964: Lyndon Johnson defeats Barry Goldwater and is elected to second term as president.

In early May of 1964, bourbon whiskey got an unexpected public relations boost from a previously antagonistic source—the Congress of the United States. A resolution passed both houses stating that bourbon whiskey was a "distinctive product of the United States" and that authentic bourbon whiskey could, therefore, only be produced in America. After the insult of and strife caused by the Eighteenth Amendment, this governmental recognition of bourbon whiskey's status in the fabric of the country provided cold comfort to the former distilling families who had forever lost a livelihood due directly to Prohibition. On the whole, the distilling industry, especially that element which was still centered in Kentucky, cordially embraced the resolution. Many people within the bourbon whiskey industry understandably looked upon it as a vindication of their unique craft.

Other interesting trends from the same decade included the solid advances made by vodka, which rose from 5.5 million cases to just over 14 million. This was a harbinger of things to come when the odorless, tasteless, and characterless white spirit that blended so insidiously well with anything would handily vanquish all distilled spirit competitors including bourbon whiskey. Vodka's eventual dominance in distilled spirits created a chilly, shaken, and stirred, but brave new world especially in the 1970s and 1980s when wines and white spirits were deemed classy and "in" and brown spirits were déclassé and "out."

But, for the moment, bourbon whiskey in the halcyon days of the 1960s was the undisputed king of distilled spirits and Jim Beam Bourbon was the monarch's crown prince, at home and abroad. It was internationally recognized and distributed and effectively operated by the fifth and sixth generations of the same founding family. What an attractive catch the James B. Beam Distilling Company must have been in the watchful eyes of other companies, suitors really, that were in the hunt for prime and profitable acquisitions. The *Courier-Journal*, northern Kentucky's most read newspaper of the period, published a major, multipage article on Kentucky's bourbon industry in its Sunday magazine on March 27, 1966. In it the writers exposed that 45 licensed whiskey distilleries in 17 counties were flourishing. There was no question that Kentucky's bourbon industry and its top distilleries were riding high.

By 1966, though, Chicago millionaire and philanthropist Harry Blum had had enough of the liquor industry and so he retired from being board chairman. It was clear that Blum and Kovler wanted out of literally all their ties to the liquor trade, even the family's ownership of the prized James B. Beam Distilling Company. Some observers, in fact, believed that Blum's son-in-law had been actively but quietly courting potential buyers almost from the moment he became president. In the late autumn of 1966, Blum and Kovler privately informed T. Jeremiah that they were on the verge of selling the company established by their fathers Jim Beam and Phillip Blum to a sound and major consumer products firm, American Brands, Incorporated. There is no record of T. Jeremiah's reaction.

At the time American Brands, which was headquartered in New Jersey, owned Motts Apple Products and Jergens Lotion. With increasing negative publicity swirling around smoking and litigation against several tobacco companies looming, the company decided to change directions by divesting itself of its tobacco holdings. The James B. Beam Distilling Company, an attractive cash-producing entity, would become a wholly owned subsidiary of American Brands. The deal that transferred ownership from the Blum family to American Brands was completed in December of 1966. Enlarging their hold in a more benign consumer arena, American Brands also bought Sunshine Biscuits.

Strangely, that same year the Blums became the victims of a highly publicized extortion scheme perpetrated by a Miami, Florida hoodlum, Frederick G. Clyde, who threatened to harm members of the Blum family unless they paid him handsomely. The Blums paid out the sum of $100,000 to Clyde. Though the FBI arrested Clyde and returned the money, the trauma of the plot took its toll on Harry Blum and his family.

The management team of American Brands was keenly aware of the vital importance of both the Beam family legacy and the mere physical presence of the Beams at the facilities in Kentucky. Only a dolt couldn't see that the Beams were the oil in the company engine. American Brands hadn't become successful by being foolish or rash in their decisions. The James B. Beam Distilling Company was the acknowledged champion of the American whiskey industry. As such, American Brands astutely convinced T. Jeremiah to stay on as senior vice president in charge of production. Carl and Baker remained as master distiller and distiller, respectively, at Clermont and Booker continued on as master distiller at Boston. The key members of the Beam family kept the plants producing at record levels well into the early 1970s.

Industrywide, the good times continued for Kentucky's whiskey-men. In 1970, the Bourbon Institute (BI) reported that straight bourbon whiskey was still the number one distilled spirit in the U.S. marketplace, accounting for a whopping 84.2 million gallons sold. The BI statistics also revealed that bourbon whiskey was being exported to 102 nations, with West Germany being the frontrunner. Doubtless, the huge U.S. military deployment in West Germany helped these figures, but other countries were likewise seeing large gains for bourbon whiskey sales from 1969 to 1970. Australia was up 54 percent in just one year due largely to GIs who were on leave from their tours of duty in Vietnam. Mexico was up 42 percent; United Kingdom was up 48 percent; France was up 22 percent; and New Zealand was up an astounding 334 percent. How long could this go on?

American Brands, realizing what a golden opportunity had come its way, decided to invest heavily in their new property. From 1967 to 1975, they spent $17 million upgrading both Beam plants in order to produce, mature, bottle, and ship Jim Beam Bourbon across the United States and to, by 1975, 139 nations and all U.S. military bases. Under the guidance of T. Jeremiah, Carl, Baker, and Booker, the James B. Beam Distilling Company's payroll rose from 300 to 500 full-time employees and 700 during peak periods.

Then came the purchases of other vacant properties. American Brands bought Limestone Springs Distillery in Bullitt County in 1970, solely for warehouse space. In 1973, the old distillery complex then called Glencoe was purchased. This historic Nelson County plant was likewise referred to by the locals as the Bardstown Distillery but was originally named Clear Springs Distillery by Jim Beam himself in 1898 when he and two partners opened it. The old Clear Springs site was obtained for its 52,524-barrel storage capacity. T. Jeremiah was reportedly amused no end by the irony of how the Clear Springs property, initially developed by his father, ended up in the Beam distillery portfolio after three-quarters of a century.

The buying spree continued in 1974 when the company bought the mothballed Bardstown plant known as Waterfill & Frazier. This entity, like the old Clear Springs plant, also had a previous Beam family connection. This particular link came from the Prohibition era when Joseph L. Beam, Jim Beam's cousin, and his son Harry Beam took control of Waterfill & Frazier during the mandatory national shutdown. They dismantled the equipment, transported it in pieces to Juarez, Mexico, reassembled the fermenters and stills, and started distilling whiskey south of the border. This project, spear-headed by Joseph L. and Harry, was claimed by family members to be underwritten by a mysterious female entrepreneur. That shadowy arrangement lost its luster after around three years and once Prohibition was on the road to being repealed, the Beams headed back to Kentucky to start up Heaven Hill Distillery.

That year also featured one of the weirdest natural events in modern Kentucky bourbon industry history. On a stormy, dark, and oppressively humid springtime Wednesday, April 3, 1974, to be precise, a tornado dancing out of the northwest peeled the exterior metal walls and roof off a massive, six-story aging warehouse at the Beam-owned old Churchill plant at Boston, leaving behind the skeleton-like wooden tiers of racked oak barrels exposed to the elements. Eyewitnesses reported that barrels of whiskey were flying through the air like pebbles as the twister with sudden fury hop-scotched through the complex, narrowly missing the distillery building as well as other aging warehouses. Over 5,200 barrels of Jim Beam Bourbon were destroyed. Remarkably, there were no injuries; just shocked observers. Booker, who oversaw the facility, had the barrels of maturing bourbon carefully removed, the damaged warehouse demolished, and another warehouse erected.

The Beams: Cadillacmen

Another side of T. Jeremiah Beam, something he learned from his father Jim Beam and his uncles, was his fervent love of and endless fascination with Cadillac automobiles. Looked upon as the ultimate American made car, Cadillacs were the symbol of prestige, taste, and success. In an article from February of 1972 in the *Kentucky Standard*, a Bardstown publication, that originally appeared in the *Insider*, the magazine for Cadillac owners, T. Jeremiah claims to have had his initial ride in a Cadillac when he was three. By 1910, at the age of ten T. Jeremiah was frequently seen being driven around by his uncle Tom Beam in a

1909 Cadillac, owned by his uncle. T. Jeremiah himself learned to drive in the winter of 1910.

"The following spring my father bought the first four-door car delivered in Louisville, a 1911 Cadillac touring car. For some time, I was the only member of the family that drove," said T. Jeremiah. "When the self-starter and electric lights came out we had to have these innovations, so my dad bought two 1913 models, a touring car and a roadster which served us until 1915, when we got a V-8 and then another 1916, both touring cars."

T. Jeremiah went on to own an impressive number of Cadillacs because as he put it "I never had the urge or any desire to own a foreign car, since I think the Cadillac is superior to anything in the world. Through the years I have had 24 or 25 Cadillacs."

By the time that revelers rang in 1975 with Auld Lang Syne, the James B. Beam Distilling Company had enough quality, dry warehouse square footage in which to age roughly 850,000 barrels of bourbon whiskey. Equipment improvements at the Boston plant made it an ultra-modern distillery that by itself processed 6,000 bushels per day rather than 5,400. In comparison, company records from almost 40 years earlier, dated March 26, 1936, show that the James B. Beam Distilling Company at Clermont averaged 669 bushels per day in 1935, or approximately 11 percent of what just Plant #2 at Boston was producing. In even more stark contrast, the Beam & Hart Distillery in the 1890s had a daily capacity of a mere 150 bushels and enough storage space for 10,000 barrels, a lofty total for its period.

By the summer of 1975, all new milling, mashing, and fermenting equipment was installed at both Beam distilling plants, including enormous stainless steel fermenting tanks. The changes reaped benefits from the start as production volume could finally meet demand without straining the personnel, space and machinery of the company. American Brands had in eight years time taken a major Kentucky bourbon whiskey distillery and out of it created an American mega-distillery.

Special limited edition "novelty" bottlings of Jim Beam bourbons packaged in ornate china decanters were first offered publicly in 1955 and had by the late 1960s become a thriving side business for the James B. Beam Distilling Company. At its peak in the early 1970s, there were more than 100 Jim Beam decanter collector's clubs dotted around the country. Members would swap or buy Beam decanters from other members. Some editions sold for as much as $2,000 a piece, a princely sum for the day. Over a span of two decades, hundreds of different china decanter editions were created. The special limited editions became such a wildly successful phenomenon that the company ended up buying the glass manufacturer, Regal China of Antioch, Illinois.

The special limited edition program, though, took a bizarre turn when counterfeiters, based in southern Ohio, started placing fake Jim Beam decanters in the marketplace, duping club members. This embarrassing deception prompted Jim Beam officials to take quick and decisive action. The prosecutor's office in Warren County, Ohio, tracked down the counterfeiters in Lebanon, Ohio. Reported the *Courier-Journal* of the scandal, "The chief investigator for the Warren County (Ohio) prosecutor's office, George Dorcheff, who was largely responsible for retrieving the fake bottles and their molds, estimated their value at more than $250,000."

The story went on to explain that the special editions' popularity stemmed from a confluence of reasons: their extremely limited numbers, the idiosyncracies of each mold, and the history that supported the creation of every edition. Decanters came in a variety of shapes, like foxes, birds, or banks. Other editions in the forms of elephants and donkeys appeared after presidential elections. During that period, it seemed that however Jim Beam Bourbon was presented, it sold well.

With the ambitious facility expansion came the versatility to take on the making and bottling of other types of products, so in the mid-1970s, the James B. Beam Distilling Company began bottling imported Scotch whiskies, like Bell's and Spey Royal, as well as brands of Canadian whiskies, German wines, Mexican tequilas, liqueurs, domestic vodkas, and Italian vermouths. In 1975, the company purchased Taylor Food Products of Los Angeles, California. Taylor Foods manufactured liquid nonalcoholic cocktail mixes under the Mr. & Mrs. T. brand name. Their Bloody Mary mix was the top-selling brand of its type in the nation. Guests being given a tour of the Clermont plant could by 1975 observe Jim Beam Bourbon being bottled on five or six lines while Mr. & Mrs. T.'s mixes were packaged on another two or three lines. The Clermont plant now boasted 11 bottling lines.

Along the way, Harry Blum whose financial and managerial contributions to the pre-American Brands Incorporated era are frequently overlooked, died in October of 1971 at the age of seventy-seven. T. Jeremiah retired in 1973 and became a consultant to James B. Beam Distilling Company, assisting his nephews whenever they required his experience. T. Jeremiah, leaving no heir, died four years later in 1977 at the age of seventy-seven. Carl Beam's retirement in 1974 opened the door for his son Baker to assume the role of master distiller at Clermont. Baker worked closely with his cousin Booker, the company master distiller who oversaw all distilling at both plants. In 1984, Carl, the forgotten member of the Beam clan passed away at the age of seventy-three.

The fifth generation of T. Jeremiah Beam and Carl "Shucks" Beam had artfully carried and indeed greatly embellished the Beam family banner by navigating the company through the choppy waters brought on by significant production growth both nationally and internationally and a major change in ownership. T. Jeremiah and Carl had survived these things all while safeguarding the fundamental quality of their charge, Jim Beam Bourbon.

Now, the sixth generation's time had come.

Booker Noe:
Big Man, Small Batch

THE HIGH-FLYING BOOM days of bourbon whiskey began to level off as the decade of the 1970s took hold. The unprecedented 20-year run of bourbon whiskey from 1950 to 1970 had been enjoyed with relish by the Kentucky bourbon industry, the James B. Beam Distilling Company, in particular, and by millions of American and international consumers. But dark thunderheads of social change permeated the skies and those tempestuous storms directed drinking trends. The pecking order of America's distilled spirits category was about to be critically impacted by a trio of distinct and occasionally crisscrossing factors.

First, the marked shift in the nation's frame of mind from the chauvinistic, swaggering confidence of the post-World War II period to a more tentative, self-doubting posture was kindled by grassroots unrest. The general mood of the country was adumbrated and divided by a confluence of emotionally taxing events and issues that adversely affected the buying habits of consumers. These mounting catalysts included more than five years of bitter, sometimes bloody, dissent over the war in Vietnam; the changing mores concerning the roles of family, women in the workplace, a woman's right to abort or keep an unborn child, and sexuality as a whole; the legislative, judicial, and street corner battles that forced the nation to confront genuine civil rights for everyone; cold-blooded assassinations of high-profile political and civil rights leaders; the publishing in June of 1971 by the *New York Times* of the Pentagon Papers; the badly bungled burglary in 1972 of the Democratic National Headquarters by Republican zealots that instigated the Watergate scandal and the eventual resignation of the thirty-seventh president, Richard M. Nixon; and the questions of a vocal, educated, articulate, and defiant youth movement that vigorously depicted the largely conservative viewpoints of their parents and grandparents as passé, plastic, and as representing the antiquated establishment.

Second, a significant sea change in consumer buying habits followed in the wake of the natural but, in this situation, volatile eclipsing of one generation by its successor. Compared to the bright, calm, and properly groomed America of 1946 to 1966, the brooding and unshaven America of 1967 to 1977 was somber, cynical, and at times violent. The natural connection between generations was strained by unusually powerful and frequently self-inflicted and senseless static. In the worst, now comical, moments of miscommunication and division it turned into rifts between the fans of Patti Paige versus those of Bob Dylan, lovers of sleek Cadillacs versus owners of hand-painted VW vans, and wearers of dark blue three-piece wool suits and brown wing-tip shoes versus admirers of tie-dyed tee shirts, blue jeans, and leather sandals.

Traditional eating and drinking habits were hardly immune from the figurative wounds inflicted by nonconformist, anti-tradition opinion. Bourbon whiskey, blended whiskey, and Scotch whisky had securely been the 80- to 100-proof (meaning 40 to 50 percent alcohol by volume since "proof" in America is arrived at by multiplying alcohol by volume times two) grain-based elixirs of the postwar generation. Now, with every passing year, these spirits were inching their way up on the roster of unflattering emblems of an out-of-touch generation. In the view of their children, the World War II generation was an age group that had reached its zenith in the 20-year span following World War II, but now was on the wane. Bourbon whiskey's case sale statistical peaks had been reached from 1964 to 1970. By 1972 and 1973, those years were being referred to in the past tense as category benchmarks by spirits industry observers. By 1974 to 1975, Kentucky's bourbon whiskey industry as a whole was concerned about the softening of whiskey consumption and, consequently, the general sluggishness with a few exceptions of inventory depletions compared to the previous decade.

Third, bourbon whiskey's lead position in spirits sales in the United States gradually eroded due to the relentless rise of another variety of distilled spirit. Bourbon whiskey's mighty juggernaut, thought during the 1960s to be unstoppable for many years to come, was in serious danger of being derailed this time not by temperance fanatics, excise taxes, or the restrictions of war but by one of its own kind. A competing grain-based distilled spirit, innocently clear in appearance, eminently mixable and easily made, was the culprit. The limpid 80-proof (40 percent alcohol by volume) offender purposely eschewed barrel aging, so production of it was by its nature fast, voluminous, and furious. Adding insult to injury during the time of the Cold War, the primary enemy of America's native spirit, bourbon whiskey, had a Russian name, vodka. The word *vodka* means "small water" and is the diminutive of *zhizenennia voda,* which translates to "water of life."

Vodka: Without a Trace

The U.S. government classifies and defines the natures of all alcoholic beverages so they can figure out how to both regulate and serve duty on them. Here's how the Bureau of Alcohol, Tobacco, and Firearms defined vodka in Subpart C. Section 5.22,

Item 1 of the U.S. Standards of Identity for Distilled Spirits: ". . . a neutral spirits, so distilled, or so treated after distillation with charcoal and other materials as to be without distinctive character, aroma, taste, or color."

Far more than other clear distillates such as rum and gin, vodka was something of a chameleon. Gin and rum owned obvious aromatic and flavor attributes; gin was herbal, rum was sweet. Even in cocktails traces of their virtues could be discerned by savvy palates. Vodka, on the other hand, was by definition "characterless." With little facility, vodka could be cleverly disguised in myriad mixed drinks like the Bloody Mary, Vodka Gimlet, Screwdriver, Vodka-tini, and Moscow Mule. As such, vodkas applications were seemingly infinite for anyone not wanting to be seen by friends, working compatriots, or mates as a lush, a boozer, or a rummy.

Just as bad, vodka was heartily endorsed by an internationally admired fictional icon of the day by the name of James Bond. Vodka's most serious direct threat to bourbon whiskey, though, was that it was the diametrically opposed counterpunch to the spirit of Kentucky. Vodka was transparent, ethereal in the nose, and blandly dry tasting; bourbon whiskey was amber-colored, grainy sweet to the sense of smell, and richly flavorful in the mouth. Bourbon whiskey was perceived by the emerging Baby Boomer generation and refugees of the post-World War II crowd as being a clunky remnant, a stale left over from the 1960s and 1970s while vodka was touted as being *au courant*, internationally produced, and recognized, even svelte.

William Grimes, author of *Straight Up or On the Rocks: A Cultural History of American Drink* (2001, p. 120), succinctly captured what happened to vodka over the past half a century in seven sentences. Wrote Grimes in his revised edition, "The real growth lay ahead. Vodka had made a ripple, not a wave. But in the early 1950s that changed. From perhaps 40,000 cases in 1950, sales leaped to 1.1

million cases in 1954, then increased fourfold the following year, when the word 'vodkatini' entered the language. In 1967, vodka eclipsed gin in popularity. Nine years later, overtaking whiskey, it became the leading spirit consumed in the United States. And so it remains today."

The meteoric ascent first of domestic vodka brands, such as Smirnoff during the 1950s, and then later of foreign brands, like Stolichnaya, Finlandia, and Absolut, from the mid-1960s through the mid-1980s caused veteran whiskeymen, like Booker Noe, master distiller of Jim Beam Bourbon and other distillers, to shake their heads in wonder and disbelief. How could Americans who had always appreciated distinct, bold characteristics in their beverages fall heavily for a distilled spirit that is by its very legal definition as laid out by the Bureau of Alcohol, Tobacco, and Firearms odorless and tasteless? How, the whiskeymen wondered to each other and to members of the press, could American consumers become enamored of a neutral grain spirit in the purest sense of the word?

Jim Beam's grandson, Booker Noe, the sixth generation in the Beam bourbon whiskey story, had an opinion and was willing to offer it. Booker was in 1974 afforded the chance to air his views about the surging vodka tide when journalist Eleanor Randolph interviewed him at his home in Bardstown. Randolph's story first appeared in the *Chicago Tribune* and later in other publications. The title of Randolph's article, "Bourbon Folks Don't Mix with Vodka Crowd," more than alluded to the hard feelings and bewilderment that existed especially from one side. Besides being a noteworthy chronicle of the era's shifting trends as vodka was about to overtake bourbon whiskey as America's most popular distilled spirit, the article likewise provides a crisp, albeit brief, character study of Booker in his forties as he wrestled with the vodka/bourbon conundrum. Booker is seen as a sincere, fiercely prideful man who is seemingly incapable of being anything but totally candid, come what may, take it or leave it.

While his views of vodka have perhaps mellowed over the years, Booker's frank opinions in 1974 left little doubt as to his stance at the time. Starting out her interview, Randolph asked Booker what he thought of vodka. She quoted Booker as saying, "'How can anybody drink this stuff?' the husky bourbon distiller was asking from his front porch swing. 'Put it in orange juice and it tastes like orange juice,' the voice boomed out into the quiet Kentucky afternoon."

Randolph then recounted, "Noe, who is known throughout the state as a man with an unerring nose for well-aged bourbon, is mostly good natured. But this afternoon he was spitting out his words like the old wads of Red Man chewing tobacco they still favor out in the hills a few miles away. 'It don't taste and it don't smell,' he said finally." Randolph related further on how at the time, specifically 1974, Kentucky accounted for more than 70 percent of the nation's bourbon whiskey output. Kentucky produced around 59 million gallons of bourbon whiskey annually. Randolph herself, not Booker, not any of the other distillers she quoted, described vodka as being "the worst thing to hit bourbon country since Prohibition."

Booker in his well-practiced role of perfect host and Kentucky gentleman invited Randolph to make herself comfortable while he fetched her some bourbon. Observed Randolph, "Noe lumbered into the kitchen and pulled an old orange decanter from the shelf. Carefully, he removed the plug and gestured for his guest to stay a few feet away. 'Smell that,' he said softly. Even across the room, the odor was unmistakable, the gentle scent of yeast and corn that ages mysteriously into 14-year-old bourbon. Noe poured two glasses slowly, then added water to his guest's share . . . 'Taste that,' he offered . . . Noe took a sip and kept his eyes closed as though he were in church. That,' he said reverently, 'is good bourbon.'"

A salient point about Eleanor Randolph's prophetic article, however, comes later on when she discussed how marketing "consultants and advertising men in synthetic suits with their portable

computers and thick packets of data sheets" from New York and
Chicago "descended" on Kentucky in an attempt to persuade the
whiskeymen that tastes had changed and that they should for their
own welfare get with the program. Wrote Randolph in the fictional
voice of the advertising men, "Taste is out, they explain softly. People don't smoke as many Chesterfields as they used to, they say as
an example . . . The same is true of whiskey. Americans don't like
anything that perks up their tastebuds."

To the Kentuckians who produced America's premier distilled
spirit, a statement like this was tantamount to heresy. Their entire
modus operandi for close to two centuries had revolved around providing distinctive aroma and taste. Perhaps, however, the most
telling statement in Randolph's *Chicago Tribune* article that sum-
marizes the period of the late 1960s and early 1970s came from an
unidentified investment analyst who spoke at the annual Wine and
Spirits Wholesalers of America (WSWA) Convention in Miami in
1973. Said the analyst as quoted by Randolph, "It is our belief that
people drink to be socially acceptable and for effect, not for the
taste of distilled spirits. . . ."

To be fair to the period's consultants, marketing gurus, and advertising experts, they were just doing their jobs by being matter-
of-factly correct in their assessments. But more to the point, at
what hollow place had America's legal-age consuming public arrived in light of the fact that the national preference was leaning
toward what was fundamentally a vapid, bang-it-out distilled spirit
rather than a distinctive, finely crafted beverage? Were the aging
post-World War II drinkers looking to be hipsters and the young
adults of the Baby Boomer generation really basing their beverage
alcohol choices on *how* they thought other people would view them
rather than on *what* they really desired to imbibe? Statistics on
drinking trends substantiate the assessments that the nation was
turning its back on many of the drinking habits that were popular
in the 1950s and 1960s. The analyst addressing the WSWA convention in 1973 may have seen the immediate future.

The cultural emptiness that many people believe was rife in America during the 1970s and 1980s depicts how much national character may have been maimed or traumatized in the alley fight between the generations in the late 1960s. The storied emergence of a fey alcoholic beverage like vodka accurately mirrored how deep the divisions and the wounds had been and how ultimately mediocrity rose from the ashes of such potent social turbulence. The famous hamburger joint commercial where the little old lady with the gravelly voice demands to know "Where's the beef?" appropriately characterized consumer America in the 1970s and 1980s. With vodka now out-pacing bourbon whiskey in the swinging disco era, thoughtful consumers could be imagined asking after tasting their first vodka, "Where's the flavor?"

Reported Randolph of Booker's further views on vodka's flavor profile, "If it tastes like anything, it tastes like one of those soft drinks with cyclamates in it,' Noe said, still smiling." That's vintage Booker. But while he was at the time attempting to put a gently teasing spin on the situation, Booker and other prominent members of Kentucky's bourbon whisky elite, including American Brands, were gravely concerned about the future of America's distinctive native whiskey. In some ways, their apprehension was unwarranted. America was a huge, expanding marketplace with diverse tastes and ample room for lots of spirit types. It's tough and disappointing, however, to be knocked off the top rung on the ladder. But, face it. Would the Congress of the United States of America at any time in the future pass a resolution praising the inherent virtues and uniqueness of vodka like they had on behalf of bourbon whiskey? Of course not.

Nevertheless, after experiencing two and a half decades of sustained, pulsating growth both at home and abroad many of Kentucky's fabled whiskeymen braced for yet more uncertain times as the public's fickle taste preferences were poised to shift and gyrate once again. This time, to their eventual relief, the change in tack would end up benefiting the makers of bourbon whiskey.

The Wine and Food Revolution Cometh

Despite vodka's surging preeminence, not all the beverage alcohol revolutions of the 1970s and 1980s were judged as being detrimental, at least in the final analysis, to straight bourbon whiskey. Along with the perceived retreat from the so-called "brown spirits," such as whiskey and brandy, fine wine became a Baby Boomer generation fixation, an authentic consuming passion. The reasons were multiple: America's native wines had markedly improved; Australia's cheap and cheerful wines invaded the United States and quickly established beachheads; and the aura of Europe's exalted wines somewhat softened, becoming less intimidating to average punters. The lemming-like movement to "light," "low alcohol," and "white," in particular from the early-1970s to the mid-1980s, heralded in some regard the ready acceptance of fine wine as a viable daily or, at least, relatively frequent beverage choice.

Americans, long looked upon by the British and the Europeans with justification as a gustatorialy immature and challenged society, were starting to recognize and appreciate the subtle joys of better foods and more sophisticated alcoholic beverages. The teaming of wine and food by the early 1980s under the guidance of gifted stateside chefs like Julia Child, Alice Waters, Jacques Pepin, Wolfgang Puck, and others as well as forward-thinking California winemakers, especially Robert Mondavi, advanced the cause of culinary interest within the general public by leaps and bounds. Restaurant chefs and California winemakers were by 1984 to 1985 gaining celebrity status. Suddenly, it was hip to be food-and-wine savvy by the time one reached the ripe old age of thirty.

The schools of wine education that opened in major and medium-sized cities pioneered by respected authorities like Harriet Lembeck, Patrick Fegan, Mary Ewing-Mulligan, and Kevin Zraly taught interested consumers the fundamentals about wine and often how it related to and enhanced different kinds of cuisine. American consumer publications on wine, led early on by Marvin

Shanken's the *Wine Spectator,* Joshua Greene's *Wine & Spirits Magazine,* and Robert Parker's the *Wine Advocate,* helped to cultivate and expand the culinary consciousness of North American consumers. International travel, both privately and professionally, likewise opened up new worlds of sensory treats to Americans. In the realm of business, the wine and food cultured executive was looked on as a valuable asset as commercial and trade horizons reached new heights on a global scale in the 1980s.

But more than anything else, the wine and food revolution's most enduring contribution from the late 1970s and 1980s was the launching of the practical education of the collective American palate. For the first time in the nation's relatively short history, widespread openness to and interest in the mechanics and possibilities of the sensory pleasures found in the food and alcoholic beverage fields was showing more vitality than just a muffled pulse. The unleashing of the evolving American culture, with its innate sense of enterprise, curiosity and its unbounded ability, on discovering the nuances of finer living would reach the distillers of Kentucky in unexpected ways . . . in time.

Troubles brought about by flagging whiskey sales in general hounded some sectors of the distilling community of Kentucky in the early 1980s. Stories of job lay-offs and plant closings regularly appeared in state newspapers. Joseph E. Seagram & Sons, for example, shut down their Louisville distillery in 1983 and dismissed 400 people in the process. Other distilleries were cutting back, as well, in production and full-time employees. According to statistics from the Kentucky Distillers Association, Kentucky distillers were still selling around 50 million gallons of bourbon whiskey in 1983, or roughly three-quarters of the country's total whiskey output. Some Kentucky distilleries, like James B. Beam Distilling Company, Heaven Hill, and Brown-Forman, diversified by producing other kinds of beverage alcohol to meet the prevailing tastes and to supplement their bourbon whiskey sales.

In the face of skittish sales forecasts, all was not doom and gloom for bourbon whiskey distillers in 1983 to 1984 as several brands of American whiskey such as Kentucky Tavern Bourbon Whiskey, Jim Beam Bourbon Whiskey, Maker's Mark Bourbon Whisky, and Jack Daniel's Tennessee Whiskey actually posted healthy gains. The James B. Beam Distilling Company, in fact, reported that sales of Jim Beam Bourbon passed the 4 million case mark that year. In his capacity as master distiller, Booker continued to increase production levels at both the Clermont and Boston plants to meet the demand for Jim Beam Bourbon. Going against the grain, Jim Beam Bourbon posted record sales for four consecutive years in the early 1980s. The export market continued to flourish for Jim Beam Bourbon as Europe's continued interest in American goods and its image of individualism and wide-open spaces helped to offset slower sales at home. Another fast-emerging overseas market for Jim Beam Bourbon was Australia.

At home, the wine and food revolution was shifting from second to third gear as the growing American middle class aspired to more rewarding eating and drinking experiences. The enjoyment of life's finer consumer products was no longer the exclusive playground of the super-wealthy. Emerging from a recession by 1984 to 1985, the American economy showed signs of growth. Inflation decreased, employment increased, as did the value of the dollar against other currencies. The Cold War grew less contentious as the Soviet Union, led by Mikhail Gorbachev, appeared more open to the concept of political reform. An air of global optimism, politically and economically, was slowly building.

Along with the wine and food explosion came another beverage alcohol wave as the call for greater quality in all consumable goods grew. Scotland's whisky distillers sensed the upward track of America's collective taste and the yearnings for new and exciting experiences that were, the Scots hoped, likely to follow. Consequently, they began exporting the highly distinctive, idiosyncratic, and more expensive category of Scotch whiskies, the single malts, across the Atlantic. The calculated move made complete sense. The United States had since World War II been a fertile market for blended Scotch whisky, the other, lighter style of Scotch. Blended

Scotch brand names like Johnnie Walker, J&B, Cutty Sark, Black & White, and Dewar's, so fashionable to Americans in the 1950s and 1960s, had maintained a relatively strong profile in North America even in the midst of the 1970s to 1980s spirits slowdown. The next potential craze by the newly taste-sensitive and increasingly affluent American public just might be in high-end brown spirits. No fools, the Scots.

On top of that, there was in the middle years of the 1980s an ironic, told-you-so burst of nostalgia for, of all decades, the maligned 1950s. The Baby Boomers who had revolted against the sins of their fathers during their teenage years did an unexpected about-face. The strains of parenthood, the daily grind of a real job, and the boredom of having to make house payments, in other words, the identical banal things their parents confronted 25 years earlier, compelled the Boomers to reconsider that maybe dad wasn't such a bad guy after all. Maybe even, by ordering a glass of Glenlivet 12 Year Old Single Malt Scotch in a restaurant bar, they would impress the old man after he had ordered the Cutty Sark. The vacant, soulless atmosphere of the 1980s probably contributed to the social discomfort.

By the late 1980s, the Baby Boomers were beginning to demand greater intensity and higher quality in all the alcoholic beverages that were consumed. Having advanced the ability to appreciate the finer aspects of good wine and savory, well-prepared food throughout the post-Vietnam War era, adventurous American consumers from their late twenties to early forties were determined to expand their sensory horizons. One sure-fire way to accomplish this was to introduce more challenging types of alcoholic beverages to their palates. Fortified wines, like sherry but especially vintage port, and distilled spirits, most commonly whiskeys and French brandies, presented without question more formidable tests for the senses. In what can only be thought to be either an embarrassing display of brazen contradiction or maybe the simple crossing over into adulthood, many Baby Boomers were turning into weekend aficionados of top-notch, pricey "brown" spirits.

Single malt Scotch whiskies, like The Macallan, Laphroaig, Balvenie, and Glenmorangie, and XO-level cognacs from French brandy producers such as Hine, Delamain, and A. de Fussigny constituted the "new-found" brown spirit discoveries favored by the finicky, if pampered, Boomers. On the home front in 1984, the Ancient Age Distillery of Frankfort, Kentucky, known today as Buffalo Trace Distillery, caused a quiet sensation of its own when it released Blanton's Single Barrel Bourbon. Blanton's was the nation's first super-premium straight bourbon whiskey to be offered since Prohibition's repeal in 1933. Matured in a single charred oak barrel, Blanton's was the first widely distributed example of what America's bourbon whiskey distillers could do in direct response to the robust single malts of the Scots. Blanton's Single Barrel Bourbon proceeded to be a modest consumer and media hit. Ancient Age Distillery had, however, introduced a new era and a new high-priced category for bourbon whiskey distillers.

But, something else of a homegrown nature was about to occur in Kentucky that in the late 1980s would add another golden arrow to the domestic whiskey quiver. An even newer super-premium category of straight bourbon whiskey, one fitting for the times, was not so much about to be born as it was merely reborn. Or, so its originator tells it. The era of Small Batch Bourbon Whiskey was about to begin.

Booker's Bourbon

Booker Noe was in charge of the Boston plant for a little under 40 years. To some keen observers, the whiskeys that were produced at Plant #2 in Boston under Booker's watch were the cream of Jim Beam. Friends, business associates, and members of the press who visited Booker at Boston would often be taken into the aging rackhouses by Booker to sample some bourbon whiskey right out of the barrel. Knowing the status of the whiskey in seemingly every barrel was one of Booker's primary tasks.

One of the most mysterious elements that constitutes being a great master distiller, one skill that could never be taught in books, is possessing the delicate combination of knowledge, sensitivity, and experience to realize when a whiskey had reached its peak inside the barrel and when, therefore, it needed to be extracted for bottling. Few Kentucky master distillers, in fact, probably only Jimmy Russell at Wild Turkey, Bill Samuels at Maker's Mark, Parker Beam at Heaven Hill, Lincoln Henderson at Early Times, and Elmer T. Lee at Ancient Age, Booker's contemporaries, understood and applied the process as thoroughly as Booker.

As the Jim Beam Company master distiller overseeing all whiskey production, Booker had access for four decades—and still does even in retirement—to all the best bourbon whiskeys maturing in all the rackhouses owned and operated by Beam. No one on either side of the Atlantic has ever figured out precisely why, but barrels of maturing whiskey age differently, frequently markedly so. Even whiskeys from the identical distillation, pumped into barrels the same day, resting next to one another in the same warehouse will for unknown reasons react individually to the wood, the climate, and the air. As one of his perks, Booker would choose, on occasion, a particularly fine set of barrels of perfectly aged bourbon whiskey and bottle the fresh whiskey directly from the small numbers of selected barrels, leaving it uncut, meaning undiluted, and unfiltered. Booker referred informally and simply to this special secret bourbon as "Booker's Bourbon." It was Booker's own private stock, the special handpicked whiskey he drank throughout the year.

The Secret to Booker's Bourbon: It's the "Center Cut"

Booker Noe takes particular pains—and delight—in describing what it is that makes his blue-ribbon Booker's Bourbon so unique. Here's how Booker makes his private stock.

"Well, you see, Booker's comes out of eight warehouses . . . old nine-storey rackhouses built by my grandfather . . . hold

20,000 barrels each. So, you strip away the outside walls and you see nine-stories, three barrels high per storey. That's 27 tiers of barrels sitting there. No temperature controlling in these warehouses, no sir. When it's hot outside, the top floors bake . . . I mean, sometimes up to 120 degrees. A man can't stand the heat up there for any length of time in July, August. But the bottom stories, the very bottom tier stays cool, 70, maybe 80 degrees at the hottest 'cause it's more humid, it's damper down there.

"What I'm hunting for are the barrels in the center rows, the fifth and sixth stories. The 'center cut' is what I call them. After seven, eight years or so, the alcohol level is a little bit higher, maybe 126 or 127-proof, in the center cut than when it went into the barrel at exactly 125-proof . . . which is low by just about everybody's standards in Kentucky. Hell, most of them distill at 135, 140, sometimes 145-proof. Lower the proof at distillation, the more robust the flavor. Anyway, I have them take out 50, maybe 100 barrels at a lick for every new bottling of Booker's. Slice those barrels right out of the core tiers of the warehouse. That's why it's called 'small batch' . . . for the limited number of barrels. The best barrels."

Why does Booker think this is the choicest warehouse area for Booker's?

"I select from these central areas because I know from experience that the whiskeys in the seven to eight year range will be oaky and vanilla-like, robust but smooth. Not too much tannin, but lots of texture. Too much tannin will have it taste too dry, overdone. I like Booker's to be on the sweeter side. Hell, think of the center cut from a watermelon, that sweetest part. Center cut's what it all about for Booker's."

For all intents and purposes, Booker's Bourbon was a throwback to another era. Being uncut and unfiltered meant that Booker's Bourbon packed a considerable wallop. Its alcohol strength ranged from 60 percent to 64 percent by volume, well above what was considered the typical range. While resting undiluted in the oak barrel, bourbon whiskeys normally range in alcohol strength anywhere from 58 percent to 72 percent. Keep in mind that virtually all contemporary bourbon whiskeys, including Jim Beam Bourbon, are extracted from scores of barrels at a single time, filtered to remove impurities, mixed together, and reduced with water to bring the alcoholic strength down to 40 percent to 43 percent by volume. These steps make the whiskey more immediately palatable for the overwhelming majority of consumers who like the undemanding smoothness of Kentucky bourbon whiskey. These procedures are performed by all Kentucky bourbon whiskey distillers to ensure uniformity of flavor and consistent quality from bottling to bottling.

Booker's Bourbon, by contrast, was an anachronism because in the late eighteenth and early nineteenth centuries, no Kentucky distillers reduced the natural barrel strength or filtered their whiskeys. Virtually all early distillers sold their powerful, aromatic, and flavorful whiskeys either directly from the barrel or by the entire barrel. Frontier drinkers downed their whiskeys unfiltered and uncut because that was the manner in which they had become accustomed to consuming it. The most they might do was to add an ounce or two of water.

Booker employed his private stock as a late afternoon delight for visitors to the Boston distillery. He would tell the visitors to meet him at his office after they had been given a distillery tour and he would treat them to something "really special." National sales manager of Jim Beam Brands in the 1980s Michael Donohoe remembered in a taped interview that on a field trip to Bardstown in 1984 he had been exposed to Booker's Bourbon for the first time. Described Donohoe of his maiden voyage, "I took a sip and said to Booker, 'This isn't Jim Beam. What is it?' Booker said, 'Hell, Mike, it's just a special individual batch from a special place in the rackhouse.'" Donohoe didn't forget the visit.

In 1987, Barry Berish, the then chief executive officer and president of Jim Beam Brands, headquartered in Deerfield, Illinois, asked his staff managers to come up with an unusual gift for the

holidays for the company's key distributors, accounts, and liquor retailers. Berish wanted something unique, a memorable present that
got away from the usual basket of liquor. Donohoe remembered
Booker's private stock of bourbon and called him to see if Booker
could provide three to four hundred bottles for the holidays.

Recalled Donohoe of his phone call to Booker, "I asked Booker
to send his best bourbon. Booker said, 'You want my best bourbon,
it's not 90 or 95 proof, you know. It's higher than that 'cause it's
right out of the barrel.' He said that the supply wasn't a problem but
that he'd want to bottle it in a different type of bottle than Jim
Beam's customary square bottle. It just so happened that he had
about a thousand old Chablis bottles stored in a warehouse. He used
those. I also asked Booker to hand write a label and attach it to the
bottle just so everyone would know that it was his private stock."

The gifts of Booker's Bourbon were delivered late in 1987
around the country. The favorable, almost frenzied, feedback that
Jim Beam executives got back from the recipients of Booker's Bourbon snowballed into an avalanche. The Beam sales staff was, in the
subsequent weeks and months, continually hounded by suppliers,
restaurateurs, bartenders, and liquor merchants. "Why isn't this stuff
available for me to sell to my patrons?" they were asked. Beam decision makers, specifically Donohoe and Berish, informed Booker that
the response to Booker's Bourbon had been overwhelmingly positive.

In early 1988, Beam planners, acknowledging the successes of
Blanton's Single Barrel Bourbon and Scotland's single malt
Scotches, were looking to break into the super-premium league but
with a fine product that was neither single barrel bourbon nor
single malt Scotch. Rather than buying an old brand or going
through long months of research and development on a new brand
of spirit, the Beam team kept coming back to their own master distiller and his high-octane private stock bourbon whiskey. Would
there be enough high-grade whiskey to distribute nationwide, even
on a limited basis? Booker reported back that there was. With
Booker's consent and crucial participation to personally choose the

barrels, the decision was made to present Booker's Bourbon on a very limited scale to a wider audience. The first release happened in 1988 and totaled one thousand six-bottle cases. Booker's Bourbon proved to be an immediate sensation.

By 1989, it was evident to the Jim Beam Brands managers in Deerfield, Illinois, that they had very possibly come up with the high-margin super-premium winner that they had been looking for. Importantly, it appeared that Booker's Bourbon would not detract at all from their frontline brand, Jim Beam Bourbon, but even complement it. The members of the press who dealt with wine, food, and lifestyle matters started to show interest in the peculiar bourbon. Booker, larger than life and refreshingly frank, became the object of press mentions and short features. The Beam staff urged Booker to come to Chicago to host a tasting for a few selected merchants and members of the press. Who better to talk about Booker's Bourbon and Jim Beam Bourbon than Jim Beam's grandson?

Michael Donohoe is now chief executive officer and president of Future Brands, a partnership between Jim Beam Brands Worldwide and the Absolut Spirits Company. Donohoe was present at that public inaugural tasting. Of the reaction from the invited guests to the no-nonsense, yet amiable and erudite Booker who speaks in a customary drawl of Bluegrass Kentucky, Donohoe said, "At our first public tasting, Booker got up and talked about his private stock and the guy sitting next to me, Fred Rosen of Sam's Warehouse, said to me, 'Is he an actor?' I said, 'No. That's Booker. He's our master distiller.' And Fred Rosen says to me kind of stunned, 'I can't believe it. This guy's unbelievable.' After all the tastings we conducted with Booker, I didn't meet one person, one connoisseur who didn't respect him for his knowledge about whiskey and distilling."

Booker's credentials to audiences of all varieties were centered mainly on the fact that he was a genuine Kentucky master distiller as much as that he was the grandson of Jim Beam. Booker actually produced and personally chose the bourbon that the people were sampling. There was no question from the audience about making bourbon whiskey that Booker, in his polite but authoritative country manner, couldn't answer in the frankest, clearest terms. When Booker, who rarely prepared for the tastings, supplemented his answers with off-the-cuff stories about how he cured hams in the distillery mash cookers, how his wife Annis and their close family friend Marilyn "Toogie" Dick made the best ham and biscuit sandwiches you ever tasted, how he played "jug" in a local bluegrass band, how he fly fished in any kind of weather, and how Annis baked hams at home making certain not to blow the door off their oven especially after *that one incident*, the audiences were beguiled, amused, and were hard pressed to let Booker return to his hotel room before the stroke of midnight.

Booker's Bourbon and Booker himself caused a tidal wave of media interest in bourbon, small batch, Jim Beam the man, and super-premium whiskey, in general. How a company follows an unqualified success like Booker's Bourbon was the relevant question facing the Jim Beam Brands marketing people. The question was answered, first, by stepping back to assess all the goodwill chalked up by Booker and, second, by carefully gauging the company's existing whiskey assets. Jim Beam was the largest selling bourbon whiskey in the world and owned the biggest stocks of bourbon in America. If there were over 850,000 barrels of maturing bourbon in 66 rackhouses, wasn't it likely that Booker and his team could ferret out even more outstanding barrels in order to expand the attractive theme of "small batch bourbon" to include one, two, maybe even three more super-premium offerings? And, assuming that was feasible, what if this high-ticket assemblage was marketed together as, say, The Small Batch Bourbon Collection? It was decided internally at Jim Beam Brands in 1991 that the concept of an exclusive collection had legs and was sustainable in an increasingly sophisticated marketplace.

In 1992, Booker's Bourbon, by then a runaway hit, was joined by three more small batch bourbons, each selected and developed by

Booker. They were Knob Creek, named after the stream that burbled past Abraham Lincoln's boyhood Kentucky home and packaged in a squat, old-fashioned, apothecary-like bottle; Basil Hayden's, which employed a bourbon recipe credited to fabled eighteenth-century master distiller Basil Hayden that dates back to 1796 and was bottled in a tall, clear, high-shouldered bottle; and Baker's, which honored the style of bourbon championed by Booker's cousin Baker Beam when he was distiller at Clermont in the 1950s and 1960s and was bottled in a sloping, transparent wine bottle.

Booker's Bourbon is typically aged for from six to eight years, depending on Booker's selection of the barrels, and ranges between 120 and 127 in proof. Knob Creek is nine years old and 100-proof (50 percent alcohol by volume). Baker's is always offered at seven years old and 107-proof (53.5 percent) and Basil Hayden's is eight years old and a mild 80-proof (40 percent).

How to get the word out about The Small Batch Bourbon Collection? Road trip, starring F. Booker Noe. By the time The Small Batch Bourbon Collection national tour was in full throttle in 1992 and 1993, Booker had become bourbon whiskey's media sensation. The Jim Beam Brands marketing machine went into action. It often happened that event space originally booked for 200 people had to be changed the day before the event in order to accommodate the 400 to 500 people who requested entrance. Booker Noe coming to town was the distilled spirits equivalent of the Rolling Stones arriving to do a gig.

Commented Michael Donohoe on the triumph of Booker's Bourbon and its subsequent imitators, "Bourbon was in the doldrums in the late 1980s. No question about it. Booker's Bourbon was a small success at the time. But in this industry, any time you have success, there will be followers. And that's what happened. Basically, we were all thinking the same thing at the time in the back rooms. But we at Beam were fortunate because nobody had a Booker Noe. It was Noe that brought Booker's to the forefront. He was the one who made it happen."

Kathleen DiBenedetto, current group product director for all super premium products at Jim Beam Brands Worldwide, doesn't believe that Booker's Bourbon was developed in reaction to anything that other distillers were putting into the 1980s marketplace. As much as anything, DiBenedetto makes the case, it was spawned from Noe himself "relishing his roots; Booker enjoying whiskey the way it used to be. It's not so much about trying to do something different for difference's sake, but actually about something he felt people should experience. The uniqueness of bourbon straight out of the barrel (is something that today) nobody could enjoy. It was his singular pleasure; it was Jim Beam's singular pleasure. It was the way everybody at the turn of the last century used to drink bourbon. We had lost that. By the end of the twentieth century, this was no longer available . . . Booker doesn't respond to trends. He does what he thinks he should do."

Just last year, Booker commented about the small batch bourbon phenomenon, saying in his customary form of understatement, "I didn't think it would come along so well and so fast, tell you the truth. It was a matter, I guess, hell, of just getting out and letting people try it."

Booker Noe, Sixth Generation, Unfiltered and Uncut

Spending time in Bardstown with Jim Beam's grandson Booker Noe and his family is akin to time-warping back to a magical era when America was painted in sepia-tinted pictures. Corny as it sounds, those images are of general stores with wood-plank floors, fireflies trapped in mason jars, wooden school desks with ink wells, men and women all wearing hats, and of barefoot boys ambling down a vacant dirt road to the local fishing pond on a late June afternoon, dragonflies hovering above it. My wife and I entered the big, sturdy brick home on North Third Street, the old home of Jim

Beam to the intoxicating aroma of not bourbon whiskey but of ham and homemade biscuit sandwiches. An unseen clock chimed the hour, welcoming us.

The present-day Noes of Bardstown, Booker, Annis, and their son Fred and his family, are the link, the flesh-and-blood lifeline to the generations of Beams who have since 1795 made straight bourbon whiskey as well or better than anyone else in Kentucky. Booker retired in the early 1990s, becoming master distiller emeritus and official Beam spokesman for the bourbon whiskeys. Until recently, he could still be found walking around the aging warehouses sniffing the maturing bourbon whiskeys to gauge solely by his acute olfactory sense which ones will be extra special.

"Aw hell, I remember it like it was yesterday," bellowed Booker, all 6 foot, 4 inches and 360 pounds of him on a light day as we camped in his and Annis' sitting room in Bardstown, the same room that his grandfather Jim Beam used to sit, entertain and silently observe all who were present. Born in 1929 to Margaret Beam Noe, Jim Beam's daughter, and Frederick Booker Noe, Frederick Booker Noe II had left big impressions his whole life. Why stop now?

"My first recollection of bourbon is when my grandfather took me to the distillery at Clermont . . . must have been 1938, maybe 1939, I was about ten years old, I guess. I recall going up stairs, the steps up to look down into the fermenting vats . . . wooden tanks back then whereas today they're all stainless steel."

Booker paused as he pondered.

"I remember the smell. I remember sniffing the grain smell. Grandfather showed me the fermentation. It was belching gas and moving. Like it was alive. The motion of it was rolling from one side to the other, belching gas, and I recall thinking it was going to spill over the sides." Booker laughed at the completely reasonable conclusion of a young boy, his first time seeing, smelling, hearing the family distillery.

While audiotapes commissioned by the Kentucky Historical Society of Bardstown of Jim Beam's contemporaries described

Prohibition, Jim Beam and what he was like, Booker remembers his legendary grandfather in the fondest of terms but in a different way. After all, this was the man who along with Booker's uncle T. Jeremiah Beam selected him to carry the family mantle. While some written accounts had painted Jim Beam as being something of an extrovert and bon vivant, Booker narrated a different story, described a different man than otherwise characterized.

"Grandfather was a quiet type of person. He wasn't a blowhard. We'd come here to this house for the holidays. He always wore a shirt and tie around the house. Liked a diamond stickpin in his tie. He would sit quietly. He did a lot of observing. Some relatives, like George Beam, grandfather's nephew, and his wife, thought he was a stuffed shirt. But then, hell, they were missionaries in Greece," recalled Booker, nodding his head.

Booker moved into the big house with his grandmother after his grandfather's death in 1947. Booker was eighteen. "I do remember my grandmother saying 'Jim almost runs us out of the house with that yeast.' Of course, grandfather made the yeast culture right here in the kitchen and it would smell, well, hell, kind of sulphury . . . almost, can I say it, like a privy." He whispered *privy*, making sure that Annis and Toogie wouldn't hear the coarse word.

Booker related that his uncle T. Jeremiah gave him the family yeast culture formula prior to his death in 1977. Booker, in the role of master distiller, created the culture in the North Third Street house for years. Cautious like his grandfather, Booker said, "I kept it here in the deep-freeze 'cause you never know."

So, if Jim Beam was in truth a "quiet type," what about Booker's uncle T. Jeremiah Beam, the fifth generation? "Ohhh-ohhh," said Booker, shaking his head side-to-side, "He was more of a party guy than grandfather. Jeremiah was what known as a 'ball man.' He loved every type of ball game there was. Old Carl Beam used to tell a joke. Carl would ask 'Where's Jere Beam?' Then he'd answer, 'Find the biggest ball game in the country and that's where Jere Beam is.'"

"That's an exaggeration, though, isn't it?"

"Exaggeration?" boomed Booker. "Hell, when grandfather died on December 25, 1947, Jere was on his way to the Sugar Bowl. Hell, the state police had to stop him, pull him over on the side of the road to tell him his father'd died."

Prohibition ended in 1933 when Booker was four years old. But he does remember the stories told to him by his uncle and cousins about the wild and difficult years of shutdown. "There were 75 to 100 distilleries within a 25-mile radius of Bardstown before Prohibition. They all closed. Only a few reopened after repeal. Grandfather wanted to get his son into the business so that he could pass the tradition of whiskey making on. It took a lot of effort at the age of seventy to start over. Jere had done a lot of partying at school and hadn't gotten to know the distilling business, so he started from scratch."

During Prohibition, Booker retold stories he had heard from Earl, his cousin, of how big, black cars with Illinois license plates would be seen driving at night through Bardstown, hauling away the stockpiled whiskey and taking it back to Chicago. There was money to be made in bootleg whiskey, after all. "Ol' Al Capone liked bourbon whiskey, I heard, 'til it ran out" cracked Booker. When the whiskey stocks were finally depleted, the big black cars with Illinois plates ceased making their nocturnal visits to north-central Kentucky.

Booker started working for James B. Beam Distilling Company in 1950 at the age of twenty-one. "I just went to work. Hands on. There were no classes. I learned how to do everything all at once. Worked in the yeast room. Managed the boilers that generated the steam for the stills."

Who were his tutors, his biggest influences in the science and art of bourbon whiskey distilling?

"Well, there was my uncle Jere and Carl, his cousin, and Park Beam. I just went right into the manufacturing part of the business. Learned something from each of them."

During his apprenticeship, Booker remained at the Clermont plant for more than three years. Then when the second plant at nearby Boston became operational in 1954, he was named distiller there. Booker stayed at Boston making bourbon whiskey for the better part of forty years. "In 1950, at Clermont, we converted 8,000 bushels of grain a week to 40,000 gallons of spirit. That was per week," said Booker.

The common conversion ratio for bushels of grain to fresh distillate is one-to-five, meaning for every bushel of grain fermented and distilled the modern Kentucky bourbon distiller gets five gallons of raw spirit. That harsh spirit will become bourbon whiskey following the legal minimum of two years in charred oak barrels. Distillers from the late eighteenth century and early nineteenth century had a conversion ratio more in the neighborhood of a one-to-two and a half or, on good days when all the equipment was properly working, one-to-three. Drawing the comparison over a half-century, Booker said, "Today when both plants are working full-out, we produce 90,000 gallons of spirit in a day."

Through the 1950s the number one selling straight bourbon whiskey was Old Crow Kentucky Straight Bourbon Whiskey. "Old Crow and Jim Beam were like this (Booker brandished two massive digits stuck together to illustrate his point). Then, in the late 1960s, maybe 1970 Jim Beam pulled ahead and that's been it ever since." Today, Jim Beam Brands Worldwide owns the Old Crow brand.

Booker was named master distiller of the James B. Beam Distilling Company in 1960. During Booker's stellar four-decades-long tenure as master distiller, he upped production to meet the demand a dozen times. Under his guidance, Jim Beam Bourbon achieved true international status and well-deserved fame as a world-class brand. Asked to sum up his five decades of being intimately involved with the bourbon whiskey industry, the family business, Jim Beam Bourbon and the creator of Booker's Bourbon, Booker in the tradition of his grandfather modestly replied, "It's been a good ride. Hell, been a good ride."

Photo Finish: Horseracing and Thoroughbreds in Kentucky

Kentuckians boast that they are famous for many fine things that reflect the genteel nature of the land that they have inhabited since the late eigtheenth century. Thoroughbred horses and racing, like bourbon whiskey, have a long and storied history in the Bluegrass State. As new settlements mushroomed in the 1780s and 1790s, horses played an indispensable role in the region's founding, acting not only as the single-most important mode of transportation but also in the clearing and tilling of fields, the hauling of supplies and the grinding of grain. In Lowell H. Harrison and James C. Klotter's book A *New History of Kentucky* (1997, pp. 136 –137) the authors make plain the essential need for horses through, if nothing else, their astounding prevalence, writing, "Ninety-two percent of the taxpayers in 1800 owned a horse; the average owner had 3.2 animals."

Horse breeding became a respected and thriving trade in Kentucky with the recognition of the Commonwealth's unusually superb natural resources of fertile soil, mineral-rich water and gentle terrain in the vicinity of Lexington. Additionally, the introduction of English-bred horses in the 1790s helped launch the industry. Originally, it's thought that fleeter horses were bred to run races in the streets Lexington, which eventually banned the practice. The Kentucky Jockey Club, founded in 1797 in Lexington, developed rules for racing by the early nineteenth century that were subsequently adhered to at tracks around the state by the mid-1800s. The opening in 1832 in Louisville of the Oakland Race Course identified north-central Kentucky as the epicenter of horseracing in the United States.

But breeding as much as racing became a symbol of north-central Kentucky life as vast farms, occupying thousands of acres of prime grassland, were established for the sole purpose of creating faster and faster runners and trotters. The fame of pioneering Kentucky horse farms and their stock, such as Woodburn Farm and Cabell's Dale, spread throughout the nation and to Europe and Great Britain. Today, horse breeding in the Bluegrass is a multimillion dollar industry that rivals whiskey-making in prominence and stature.

F. Booker Noe II wouldn't ever acknowledge it, much less say it, but his grandfather and uncle could not have chosen a more worthy successor, one who could have better embodied the pure essence of whiskey making in Kentucky.

Other Beams:
Behind Every Good
Bourbon Whiskey

WHEN VIEWED FROM THE promontory of genealogical charts and other amassed documentation, the Beam family tree casts an image not unlike a towering American oak. The analogy, it could be argued, applies on a figurative basis not so much because bourbon whiskey is matured in this native hardwood but more because the comparison is easily made. The sturdy, Byzantine, and occasionally knotty nature of the Beam family translates well to the mass and strength of an established domestic oak's trunk and the complexity of its branch network. The Beam Oak then, as it turns out, is an imposing two-century-and-counting, still vigorous, gnarly mammoth, complete with ham-thick primary limbs that support Schwarzenegger-like arms that themselves fork into a wiry mesh of whip-like tendrils ready to sprout new leaves and, more importantly, acorns.

The family trees of the other great Kentucky-based distilling families—the Moores, Samuels, Wathens, Dants, Peppers, Mat-tinglys, Ripys, Boones, Pogues, Browns, Cumminses, Bixlers, and Medleys all come to mind—likewise inhabit an exclusive, ancient, heartland woods. Each tribe proudly and rightly boasts of rich multigenerational whiskey-making activity within the Common-wealth, many three generations, some four generations, and a select few five generations of sterling service. Allowing for much deserved respect to be bestowed on all these Kentucky whiskey families, they would all be the first to acknowledge the manifold achievements and the distilling mastery of the ubiquitous Beams.

The preceding chapters have accounted for six generations of one branch of the industrious Beam descendents, Beam-Noe, a line that began with the late eighteenth-century marriage of Jacob and Mary Myers Beam. The Beam-Noe branch, which on a worldwide basis is the most famous limb of the Beam Oak, has propagated the Old Tub, Jim Beam Bourbon, Beam's Choice Bourbon, Jim Beam Black Bourbon, Booker's Bourbon, and The Small Batch Bourbon Collection brands. But other prominent branches originating from the identical trunk have guided the fortunes of an astounding num-ber of other bourbon whiskey distilleries in Kentucky as well as dis-tillery operations in other states and even in other countries. It would be a careless and impolite omission not to cite these other important Beam family members of bourbon whiskey distilling lore. Shining a broader spotlight on the Beam clan as a whole only lends more insight, credibility, and perspective to the American distill-ing achievement that is Jim Beam Bourbon.

Jo Ann Beam, a gregarious, vibrant, and genealogically smitten member of the sixth generation, is responsible for the title of this chapter. She is the daughter of Harry Beam who was the second master distiller of Heaven Hill Distillery in Bardstown and a grandchild of Joseph L. Beam who was himself a great-grandson of Jacob Beam. Jo Ann Beam was employed at the Jim Beam facility at Clermont for nearly four decades. "There's a saying in Kentucky that goes, 'Behind every good bourbon whiskey, you'll find a Beam,'" she related in an interview conducted at the Oscar Getz Museum of Whiskey History in Bardstown in October of 2002. That adage sums up what many people in the bourbon whiskey industry, mostly non-Beams, have espoused for at least a century. Many people residing far beyond Kentucky but who have commercial ties to the bourbon industry still believe it to this day.

Marshalling all the research material collected, analyzed, and organized for *American Still Life* regarding the Beams, and marking as the starting point Jacob Beam's selling of his first barrel of whiskey in 1795, the following conclusions strikingly illustrate the Beams' trade-wide impact:

1. Over the past 208-year (1795 to 2003) period spanning seven generations, there have been, at the minimum, 30 master distillers and distillers descended from Jacob Beam who have worked in the American distilling industry.

2. At least 30 North American distillery enterprises, some admittedly having multiple names over the years but nonetheless individual business undertakings, in three countries, the United States, Canada, and Mexico, have employed Beams either as distillers, master distillers, or as consulting distillers.

3. The whiskey-making influence of the Beams has influenced a conservatively estimated 40 different brands of North American whiskey, the majority being bourbon whiskey. That figure of whiskey brands is likely higher given that some long-defunct brands entered the marketplace and within a decade or less died, thereby, fading in the memory banks and in the often incomplete and convoluted records of the American whiskey business.

From this vantage point, it is little wonder why the Beams have evolved into the Royal Family of American bourbon whiskey distilling, with Jim Beam Bourbon at present occupying the foremost position. As such, because of their accomplishments, the Beam family owns an enchanted aura that, while the Beams don't seek it, attracts a good portion of the public attention garnered by the bourbon industry. Yet, while the direct DNA link that connects Jacob Beam, David Beam, David M. Beam, James Beauregard Beam, T. Jeremiah Beam, Booker Noe II, and Fred Noe created the branch of the Beam Oak from which sprang Jim Beam Bourbon, other whiskey-making branches with intriguing tales have spiced the history of America's native libation. The following brief histories more often than not overlap with the Jim Beam Bourbon story due to the frequently tight familial relationships between the scores of Beam uncles, cousins, fathers, and sons.

Early Times, Good Times, Sad Times

One of Jim Beam's most illustrious uncles was John Henry Beam (1839–1915). Commonly known as Jack, John H. was born in 1839 in Mooresville, Kentucky. He was the kid brother of Jim Beam's father David M. Beam, the son of David Beam and the grandson of Jacob Beam. In his teenage years, specifically the 1850s, Jack worked alongside his brother David M. in the family's Old Tub Distillery in Washington County. Their father David Beam died young at the age of fifty in 1852. David M., Jack's senior by six years, took command of Old Tub soon after their father's demise and in a few years' time relocated the family business to Bardstown in Nelson County to take advantage of the Louisville & Nashville Railroad's Springfield branch. Leaving no room for confusion as to who sat in the captain's chair, David M. renamed the family distilling operation D.M. Beam Distillery.

Jack aspired to carve out his own niche in the distilling trade. After his brother departed for neighboring Nelson County, Jack decided to remain in Washington County to keep the Old Tub facility running and to sharpen his own distilling skills. Jack turned twenty-one in 1860. Comprehending the wisdom exhibited by his older brother, later that year Jack moved the remnants of Old Tub to Early Times Station in Nelson County, a site that rested right on the L&N Springfield branch. Jack christened both his distillery and his bourbon whiskey "Early Times."

A lean operation with a tidy 50-bushel capacity, Early Times Distillery gained fame very quickly for its superior bourbon whiskey. The Louisville-based distributor of Jack's popular Early Times Bourbon was Pearce, Hurt & Company. Along with brother David M.'s Old Tub, Early Times was one of the few nationally distributed whiskeys by the 1870s. Jack married Maria Nall in 1864. They had a son Edward D. nine years later in February of 1873. By the early 1880s, Jack was producing a trio of well-received bourbon whiskey brands, Early Times, Jack Beam, and A.G. Nall, so named presumably for one of his wife's relatives. Early Times, in particular, had a very high content of corn, 77 to 79 percent, in its mashbill, making it sweet, light, and very palatable in an age of hearty, some might say, bruising whiskeys.

To meet the soaring demand head-on, especially as the American West opened up to settlement, Jack doubled the bushel-per-day capacity of Early Times Distillery to 100 bushels by 1882. By the mid- to late-1880s, the nationwide economic slowdown panicked some Kentucky distillers. Whispers of a national economic collapse were rife. A handful of distillers made rash decisions as they sought to protect their investment and equity during the potentially turbulent times. Jack, it was thought at the time, foolishly and prematurely surrendered title and ownership of the distillery he had built to his distributors, Pearce, Hurt & Company. One of the Pearce, Hurt & Company principals, B. H. Hunt, assumed the post of president of Early Times Distillery while Jack descended the corporate ladder to vice president and master distiller.

By the early 1890s, both tragedy and triumph impacted the private and professional lives of Jack Beam. On the personal side, Jack's first wife Maria died in 1890. To offset his mourning, Jack became consumed with work. On the business side, sales of Early Times Bourbon sailed off the charts, making his decision to divest appear all the more ill-advised. To deal with rampaging sales B. H. Hunt and Jack decided to once again enlarge the plant's capacity. Jack turned over his day-to-day distilling duties to H. T. Cravens, a respected distiller, so that he could focus on the company's aggressive expansion plan. In stages the distillery increased in size fourfold to 400 bushels per day by the mid-1890s. One of Jack's innovations applied during the expansion of Early Times was the implementation of heated warehousing. A trailblazing concept that is employed over a century on by some Kentucky distillers, climate-controlled rackhouses allow the maturing whiskeys to age at a more even, steady rate than those whiskeys resting in unregulated rackhouses, where temperature fluctuations affect the rate of aging in fits and starts.

By 1880 to 1881, Jack's son Edward D., his only child by first wife Maria Nall, was getting more involved with the business as an apprentice distiller. Edward, a quick study, was then named distillery general manager of Early Times in 1894. Edward not only managed Early Times Distillery, he likewise bred racehorses, Kentucky's other primary industry of the era. His horses were sired by the finest studs of the period.

Despite relinquishing his proprietary stake in Early Times in the mid-1880s, Jack's personal wealth nonetheless increased steadily as the success of Early Times skyrocketed all through the 1890s. As a man of relatively healthy means and regional renown, Jack's social stature was assured within the community of north-central Kentucky. The Nelson County Record of 1896 described Jack as being "one of the best men in the county, from every point of view." The article also talked about his stately, rambling Nelson County residence, saying, "He resides on one of the finest blue grass farms in Kentucky, which contains 1,000 acres."

In October of 1896, Jack remarried, taking Margaret Thompson as his second wife. His second marriage, though, lasted only seven years since in 1903 Margaret died. In the meantime, Early Times

Bourbon continued to expand its market presence in the United States and North America. In April of 1913 at the age of seventy-four, Jack married again. Vivacious and significantly younger than Jack, Anna Figg Brown of Nelson County became his third wife. Then the floor that underpinned Jack's life caved in. In March of 1915, Jack's only son, Edward died at the age of forty-two. Jack, no longer active at Early Times Distillery, was bereft with grief. Unable to recover emotionally from the loss of his son, Jack died two months later in May of 1915 from, as his obituary earnestly reported, ". . . infirmities due to age, and after every effort known to medical science had been resorted to in order to prolong his life." Nothing, medically speaking, could have prolonged Jack's life.

In the vacuum suddenly created by the close back-to-back deaths of Jack and Edward, Jack's nephew John W. Shaunty with some trepidation stepped into the role of Early Times president. After John Henry Beam died, his original creation, Early Times Bourbon, like so many alcoholic beverages, began to fade in the marketplace by 1916–1917 as the temperance movement and talk of Prohibition dominated the news of the day. In 1918, Shaunty had little choice but to shut down the Early Times Distillery, temporarily ending an era. Staring into the abyss of Prohibition, Shaunty found a buyer, a gentleman by the name of S. L. Guthrie, who in 1920 purchased not only the distillery but also the parcel of Jack's farm that hadn't been willed to Anna Beam. In 1922, the string of Early Times-related deaths continued when John W. Shaunty unexpectedly died.

But the legacies of Jack Beam and his beloved Early Times Bourbon weren't about to drop into oblivion. In the early years of Prohibition, the respected Louisville distiller Brown-Forman bought the whole Early Times inventory from S. L. Guthrie, thousands of barrels that had been quietly maturing in Bardstown rackhouses since the distillery closed. They wisely purchased the Early Times brand name, an acquisition that would pay off handsomely in the decades to come. Brown-Forman, as it turns out, was one of the half dozen distilling companies that were licensed to sell spirits for medicinal purposes throughout Prohibition, making the Early Times purchase viable, even attractive.

Once Prohibition was repealed, Brown-Forman rapidly reestablished Early Times as a prominent national brand of bourbon whiskey through the remainder of the 1930s and the World War II years. The intense brand attention reaped rewards by the early 1950s. Reported Gary Regan and Mardee Haidin Regan in *The Book of Bourbon and Other Fine American Whiskeys* (1995, p. 130), "By 1953, Early Times had become the top-selling bourbon in the country, and because Brown-Forman strongly believed in 'quality whisky at quality prices', it was never offered at a discount." Consequently, Brown-Forman's profit margins from Early Times case sales were high.

The next chapter for Early Times dawned in 1955 when Brown-Forman opened their new Early Times Distillery located in what was at the time the Louisville bedroom community of Shively. Early Times stayed at or near the top of the bourbon whiskey heap in terms of national sales until 1970 when Jim Beam Bourbon finally captured the number one spot. It has kept that spot in its clutches ever since. Early Times, which in 2001 was ranked the number three bourbon behind Jim Beam and Evan Williams in the *Adams Liquor Handbook* (2002, p. 48), is still made at the Shively plant today along with another hallowed name in bourbon whiskey history, Old Forester, the first brand of bourbon whiskey to be offered in mass-produced sealed bottles.

The Brown-Forman distillers currently make Early Times in two distinct versions, one for the domestic audience and one designed specifically for export. For the home market, Early Times Old Style Kentucky Whisky is not by legal standards considered a bourbon whiskey because some of the barrels that it is matured in have been previously used. Early Times Kentucky Straight Bourbon Whisky, on the other hand, which is aged only in new charred oak barrels, fits the full criteria for bourbon whiskey and is made at this point exclusively for foreign markets.

If he were alive, Jack Beam would surely cajole the Brown-Forman distillers into reintroducing Early Times authentic Kentucky Straight Bourbon Whisky to the taste buds of its original fan base, American consumers.

Beam Generations at Heaven Hill

Prohibition, which was enacted in 1920 after the passing of the Eighteenth Amendment through both houses of Congress in 1919, was repealed by the Twenty-first Amendment in late 1933 on the heels of Franklin Delano Roosevelt's election to the presidency and his calls for a "New Deal." In 1935, the year that Jim and T. Jeremiah Beam officially opened the James B. Beam Distillery on the site of the Old Murphy Barber plant in Clermont, Bullitt County, a new whiskey distilling enterprise was established a couple of miles south of Bardstown. It was the Heaven Hill Distillery, erected on the old William Heavenhill farm on Loretto Road, also known as Kentucky Highway 49. The group of investors included the five Shapira brothers, George, Gary, Ed, Mose, and David; Harland F. Mathis; Marion Muir; and R. J. Nolan as well as Joseph L. Beam (1868–1956), the accomplished fourth generation master distiller.

The Shapiras had been involved in the retail clothing business in Kentucky, successfully operating small departments stores prior to and during Prohibition. As Prohibition's days were clearly becoming numbered, the brothers were advised about the potential business opportunities that revolved around the reintroduction of beverage alcohol into the marketplace. They concluded that bourbon whiskey, a local trade with a long social and cultural history and a sound track record of profitability, was on the verge of becoming, once again, an exciting growth industry in Kentucky.

Being retail dry goods merchants, however, the Shapiras needed the expertise peculiar to the whiskey distilling trade that only a trusted, veteran whiskeyman, like Joseph L. Beam, could provide. Beam didn't disappoint his partners as he laid the foundation for what would become one of America's most significant distilling companies, one that would be a perennial rival of Jim Beam, yet always choose to have a Beam as master distiller.

Joseph L., or simply "Joe" as he preferred to be called, was positioned in the middle of his parents' 13 children. His lineage was golden in Nelson County, Kentucky. He was a cousin of Jim Beam, the son of Joseph B. Beam and Mary Ellen Humphrey, the grandson of David Beam, and the great-grandson of Jacob Beam. Distilling was in Joe's genes and he wasted no time in pursuing his bourbon whiskey destiny. His eclectic and varied distilling career spanned nearly six decades. He began as a teenager in the distilling business during the 1880s. Prior to supervising the construction and operation of Heaven Hill Distillery, Joe worked as a young distiller and master distiller at several big-name late nineteenth-century and early twentieth-century whiskey distilleries such as Early Times, J.B. Dant, Tom Moore, Mattingly & Moore, F.G. Walker, Stitzel-Weller, and the Frankfort Distilleries.

In 1894 at the age of twenty-six, Joe married Katherine Leone McGill. Joe and Katherine had nine sons, seven of which would eventually make names in the whiskey distilling industry. Unfazed by the restraints of national Prohibition, the irrepressible Joe and his adventurous youngest son Harry even set up and operated a distillery in Juarez, Mexico, the D & M Distillery. They made whiskey for three years for the mysterious, some reports say infamous, Mary Dowling before returning home to Kentucky before Prohibition ended. Upon resuming life in Nelson County, Joe was elected county jailer for two consecutive terms from 1929 to 1933. Most accounts claim that Joe turned a blind eye to the majority of moonshiners, providing that they weren't obvious in their illegal dealings.

At Heaven Hill Distillery in the mid-1930s, Joe personally supervised all distillery operations and assigned son Harry to the post of distiller by the start of the 1940s. Harry soon became Heaven Hill's second master distiller as Joe gradually cut back his involvement at Heaven Hill to consider other distilling options. In late 1946, Joe and Harry parted company with Heaven Hill Distillery after they, Muir, Nolan, and Mathis were each bought out by the Shapira brothers. As a result of this ownership change, the tantalizing position of Heaven Hill's master distiller became available.

Jim Beam's nephew, Earl Beam (1906–1993), the son of Park Beam, was distiller under his younger brother Carl ("Shucks") at the nearby James B. Beam Distillery. Earl considered taking the job. Parker Beam, Earl's son, told the story in an interview of how his uncle Carl encouraged his older brother to take the job. "He just told my father what a great opportunity it would be for him to take his skills even further," recounted Parker. "Knowing my uncle's sense of humor, he probably also said something to Dad like 'Since I'm not going anywhere soon,' meaning at Jim Beam, of course, 'don't think that you'll be getting my job.'"

In early 1947, Earl succeeded Harry as Heaven Hill's master distiller, the third Beam to hold that position. After selling their interest in the James B. Beam Distilling Company to Harry Blum, Harry Homel and Oliver Jacobson invested in Heaven Hill. Under Earl's steady distilling hand and the sound business leadership of the Shapiras, Homels and Jacobsons Heaven Hill Distillery advanced into the bourbon whiskey business major leagues in the booming 1950s. Heaven Hill Kentucky Straight Bourbon Whiskey was the company's flagship brand at the time. In 1957, under the guidance of Earl, Heaven Hill released Evan Williams Kentucky Straight Bourbon Whiskey, the first in a series of bourbon bottlings through which the distillery honored Kentucky distilling pioneers. Other similar bourbon offerings to follow over the years have included Henry McKenna, Elijah Craig, and J.T.S. Brown.

After working in the trucking business in Atlanta for four years, Parker was hired in 1960 to assist his father as Heaven Hill expanded in size and product line depth. Fifteen years of learning from his father prepared Parker to assume the role of master distiller in 1975, making him the fourth generation of Beam master distillers at Heaven Hill. Of the countless things that Earl taught his son was the importance of the yeast culture and how it influences the taste of the bourbon whiskey. In an interview conducted in the 1970s, Earl talked about the Beams' unique yeast culture, saying, "Our strain of yeast has been in the family for around 175 years. We say it is the same that old Jacob originated long ago. By adding our last batch to a new batch, and keeping everything very clean, the strain has not changed in all that time. Just to show you how jealous a man is with his yeast strain, I tried once to get a stock of Beam yeast from my brother Carl over at Jim Beam's and he wouldn't let me have it."

Though Earl and his brother Carl were neighborhood and national competitors, they enjoyed an unusually close sibling bond, according to Parker. "I remember well going with my father when he was still employed at Jim Beam. I spent many hours at Carl's house, playing with my cousins Baker and David. The fact that Earl and Carl were competing master distillers at two of the largest, most competitive companies never overshadowed that they were, first and foremost, family. After all, they had worked side-by-side for years at Jim Beam. I still can envision my uncle Carl helping my father at Heaven Hill with fermentation or standing with a wrench in his hand just going around fixing things at the distillery."

One of the best pieces of advice Earl ever passed along to Parker about being a worthy master distiller was, in Earl's clipped economy of words, "Let your nose be your chemist." In other words, as Parker explained it, let your decisions be dictated not by computer printouts or by what other, less experienced people are telling you but by your own senses. To a distiller, the sense of smell is the most crucial. Continued Parker, "I can tell what's going on in a distillery, good or bad, just by walking around and inhaling the air for a minute or two. Being a good master distiller is really about paying attention all the time, about being on top of all the little things about the distilling process that are ongoing; from the quality of the grain to the purity of the yeast culture to the right mix of grains on the mashbill to the smell of fermentation to the thumping sounds that the stills make to the quality of the oak that makes your barrels. It's all of it. That's why in the old days master distillers almost always lived on the distillery property. It's a total commitment of being on-call seven days a week, putting in 15 to 16 hours a day."

Earl lived to be eighty-seven. He never really officially retired as Parker and Craig Beam, Parker's son, who since 1983 has assisted Parker at Heaven Hill, both recalled. Said Craig of his energetic grandfather, "He just started coming around less by the time he reached his late seventies but he never made an announcement that he was retiring. He was on top of just about everything until the end. Very little escaped him even well into his eighties. He'd sit on his porch and count the distillery's slop trucks as they went by, figure out what was happening, and quiz us about it. I think he kind of semiretired only when he couldn't climb the stairs up to the offices anymore."

Added Parker, "He retired the day he died. He loved being a master distiller, all the daily challenges. It all comes down to pride really. It's a matter of reputation. The quality of the whiskey is ultimately your responsibility as master distiller and nobody else's."

47,000 Gallons of Bourbon per Day

Along with the establishment of the James B. Beam Distilling Company in Clermont and Heaven Hill Distillery in Bardstown, the other monumental Beam family twentieth-century accomplishment that stands in a class of its own is the story of the "Boys," also known in some quarters as the "Brothers" or the "Seven Beams."

During a seven-decade span that ran from around 1910 through to the mid-1980s, seven of the nine sons of Joe L. Beam and Katherine McGill Beam, the Boys, all second cousins of the more renowned Jim Beam, worked as master distillers at some of the era's most prestigious whiskey distilleries, often simultaneously, sometimes as members of the same team.

The Boys' seven-part legacy began with Joseph Elmo Beam (known as "Elmo") who was born in 1895. The line continued on through Henry Milburn Beam who was called "Harry," born 15 years and five brothers later than Elmo in 1910. Sandwiched in between Elmo and Harry were, in order, Roy Marion (Roy), Frederick Otis (Otis), Wilmer Bernard (Wilmer), Desmond Aloyeisus (Desmond), and Charles Everett (Everett). Two other sons, Lloyd Dee and Meveral died as toddlers.

Close to all of his sons but strict as a parent and tutor, Joe was called "Pop" or "Papa" by the Boys their entire lives. He personally taught each one of them the secret formula for the Beam family yeast culture as passed down by Jacob Beam, his great-grandfather, as well as the artistic and commercial sides of distilling. One of the rules of distilling that Joe indelibly ingrained in the minds of his sons was that the making of bourbon whiskey was a business and a responsibility, not a hobby. To Joe and the Boys, distilling was a respected family livelihood and tradition, not a dalliance with which to toy. Further, it was said throughout the family on Joe's side that he drummed into each of his sons that whiskey was produced for sale, not for personal sipping.

Joe's older Boys, Elmo and Roy in particular, became active in distilling prior to World War I and Prohibition, frequently apprenticing under their father as he circulated through several distilleries, both as distiller and consultant. Like all branches of the Beam family, none of the Boys prospered during Prohibition, the 14-year layoff provided courtesy of the federal government. Fish out of water, the Boys tried their hands at other lines of work. Otis made vain attempts at selling life insurance. Others made unsuccessful forays into retailing. Joe and Harry, as was mentioned earlier, distilled whiskey in Mexico while Elmo journeyed all the way to Montana to distill, sliding in under a little known local law that exempted some distilling practices. The Boys were widely dispersed around the continent and miserable during the shutdown and anxiously awaited word of repeal.

Following the legal reinstatement of beverage alcohol production, sales, and consumption in 1933, one would think that the Boys with their pedigree would have been in the position of immediately being hired as distillers in Kentucky and elsewhere. That was not the case, at least, not through 1934. The disemboweled and dismembered distilling industry struggled to collect itself and restore a sense of order and purpose. Matters were exacerbated by the Great Depression, a period in which investment funding was scarce. The Beam family exceptions were Jim and T. Jeremiah who, as depicted in Chapter 4, got off the mark rapidly in 1934 and 1935 by acquiring capital and rebuilding in Clermont with breathtaking dispatch.

By 1935, over a year had passed since the repeal of Prohibition and the Boys were finally being offered distilling jobs both out-of-state and, of course, within their home state of Kentucky. For the most part, they preferred to remain close to home, meaning Nelson County. Distillers, who desperately needed whiskey inventory to reclaim their status, were slowly obtaining the necessary funding for start-ups. Meanwhile, Joe, his youngest son Harry, and others were preparing to launch Heaven Hill Distillery in Bardstown. By 1936, all seven Boys were back in business doing what they did best, distilling bourbon whiskey. A November 1937 report uncovered in the "American Wine and Liquor Journal—Kentucky Section" written by Alfred Wathen Jr. bore witness to the Boys' comeback, noting that on any given workday the Boys could be collectively responsible for the production of 47,000 gallons of bourbon whiskey, assuming that their distilleries were working at full capacity that specific day. By that point, most distilleries were working at flat out speed just to supply the parched marketplace.

Elmo, the eldest of the Boys, was a highly regarded master distiller who enjoyed two tenures with the Samuels family in Loretto, producing both T.W. Samuels and, later in the 1950s, fabled Maker's Mark, today an industry superstar. Everett circulated among a handful of Kentucky distilleries before leaving the Commonwealth in 1950 for Michter's, an illustrious old distillery established in 1753 and located in Schaefferstown, Pennsylvania. Michter's regrettably closed in 1989. During his tenure as the Michter's master distiller, Everett produced, it is worth noting, some of the greatest pot-still bourbon whiskeys ever produced in America. At that career signpost in rural Pennsylvania, the tradition of Joe and the Boys concluded. In the twenty-first century, no descendants from Joseph L. Beam and the Boys are known to be distillers.

Although there aren't as many Beams involved with the contemporary bourbon industry as there were decades ago, their influence is nonetheless still pervasive. The Beams may not have owned all of the distilleries that they were as a family involved with, but those distilleries could not have produced the number of memorable bourbon whiskeys without them. The roster of legendary brands that carried the Beam family thumbprint reads like a list from the bourbon whiskey hall of fame: Jim Beam, Old Tub, Heaven Hill, Early Times, Evan Williams, Yellowstone, Four Roses, Knob Creek, Pebbleford, Elijah Craig, Maker's Mark, Michter's, Eagle Rare, Booker's Bourbon, Very Old Barton, and T.W. Samuels, to name just a handful. After 208 years, the Beam Oak stands as a monument not only to a family whose innate talent and passion for distilling makes them stand alone but likewise to the heritage of one of America's oldest industries.

The Beam Oak Branches:
A Family's Distilling Legacy

(The father is noted within the parentheses.)

Beam/Noe Branch	Distillery	Whiskey Brands
Jacob (Nicolaus)	Old Tub	Old Jake Beam
David (Jacob)	Old Tub	Old Tub
David M. (David)	D.M. Beam	Old Tub
James B. (David M.)	D.M. Beam	Old Tub
	Crystal Spring F.G. Walker	Pebbleford, Jefferson Club
	James B. Beam	Jim Beam, Bonded Beam, Beam's Choice
Park (David M.)	James B. Beam	Jim Beam, Bonded Beam, Beam's Choice
	Willett J.S. Shawhan	Old Bardstown
T. Jeremiah (James B.)	James B. Beam	Jim Beam, Bonded Beam, Carl's Choice
Carl & Earl (Park)	James B. Beam	Jim Beam, Bonded Beam, Carl's Choice
Baker & David (Carl)	James B. Beam	Jim Beam, Bonded Beam, Beam's Choice
Booker Noe (F. Booker Noe I)	James B. Beam	Jim Beam, Beam's Choice, Booker's, Knob Creek, Basil Hayden's, Baker's, Beam Rye
Fred Noe (Booker)	James B. Beam	Knob Creek, Basil Hayden's, Baker's

(continued)

The Beam Oak Branches *(Continued)*

Joseph L. Branch I	Distillery	Brands
Joseph L. (Joseph M.)	Stitzel-Weller	
	Heaven Hill	Heaven Hill
Harry (Joseph L.)	Heaven Hill	Heaven Hill
Earl (Park)	Heaven Hill	Heaven Hill, Evan Williams
Parker (Earl)	Heaven Hill	Heaven Hill, Evan Williams, Henry McKenna, J.W. Dant, Cabin Still, Ezra Brooks, J.T.S. Brown, Elijah Craig
Craig (Parker)	Heaven Hill	Heaven Hill, Evan Williams, Henry McKenna, J.W. Dant, Cabin Still, Ezra Brooks, J.T.S. Brown, Elijah Craig

Other Joseph L. Branches	Distillery	Whiskey Brand(s)
Joseph L. (Joseph M.)	Early Times	Early Times
	Clear Springs	Clear Springs
	Tom Moore	Tom Moore, Dan'l Boone
	F.G. Walker	Queen of Nelson
	D&M (Mexico)	
	Mattingly & Moore	Mattingly & Moore
	Frankfort	Old Baker, Antique, Old Pirate
	Stitzel-Weller	Mondamin Sour Mash, Mammoth Cave
	Heaven Hill	Heaven Hill

The Beam Oak Branches *(Continued)*

Other Joseph L. Branches	Distillery	Whiskey Brand(s)
Wilmer B. (Joseph L.)	Stitzel-Weller	Mondamin Sour Mash, Mammoth Cave
	Burks Springs	Old Happy Hollow
	Old Kentucky	Kentucky Dew, Cherokee Spring
	Taylor & Williams	Yellowstone
Harry M. (Joseph L.)	Heaven Hill	Heaven Hill
	John E. Fitzgerald	Old Fitzgerald
	Sam Clay	Sam Clay
Roy M. (Joseph L.)	Stitzel Bros.	Mammoth Cave
	John E. Fitzgerald	Old Fitzgerald
	Frankfort	Four Roses, Lucky Star, Old Nectar
	Park & Tilford	Woodford
Desmond A. (Joseph L.)	Frankfort	Sir Thomas, Old Oscar Pepper
	Old Kennebec	Old Kennebec, Jim Perkins, Sam Clay
	Julius Kessler	Kessler, Old Lewis Hunter
C. Everett (Joseph L.)	Salmar (OH)	
	Michter's (PA)	Michter's
F. Otis (Joseph L.)	Frankfort	Honey Dew, Paul Jones, Kentucky Triumph
	Buffalo Springs	Old Stamping Ground
J. Elmo (Joseph L.)	Burks Springs	Old Happy Hollow
	T.W. Samuels	T.W. Samuels

(continued)

The Beam Oak Branches *(Continued)*

Other Joseph L. Branches	*Distillery*	*Whiskey Brand(s)*
Jack D. (Roy)	Taylor & Williams	Yellowstone
Charlie L. (Roy)	Julius Kessler	Old Lewis Hunter, Kessler, Benchmark
	Old Prentice	Four Roses
	Frankfort	Eagle Rare
	Park & Tilford	Woodford

Minor Case Branch	*Distillery*	*Brands*
Minor Case (Joseph M.)	F.M. Head	F.M. Head
	Head & Beam	Head & Beam
	M.C. Beam	Old Trump, T.J. Pottinger & Co.
Guy (Minor Case)	Fairfield	Pride of Nelson
	M.C. Beam	Old Trump
	Richwood	Richwood
Jack (Guy)	Barton	Very Old Barton, Kentucky Gentleman, Colonel Lee
Burch (Guy)	Richwood	Richwood

Finding a
Crown for the Jewel

IN THE WAKE OF Harry Blum and Everett Kovler selling the fiscally sound James B. Beam Distilling Company in 1967 to the company then known as American Brands, the focus of the company could have been diverted away from the Beams, away from the traditional north-central Kentucky home of Jim Beam Bourbon. Bourbon whiskey, after all, could be legally produced in any state. Due to Kentucky's tax structure, whiskey making in Kentucky was expensive. In the sometimes choppy currents of management changes, the Beams could have been relegated to distant background positions or dismissed altogether. Other distilling families caught in the crossfire of ownership modifications born of financial or power wrangling had experienced such fates.

However, the management team at American Brands, to their credit, realized in the early days that the period's existing Beam family members, specifically, T. Jeremiah Beam, Carl Beam, Baker

189

Beam, and Booker Noe, epitomized what the then surging Jim Beam Bourbon brand represented in the marketplace. The company's power brokers likewise acknowledged from the outset that the Beams with great skill actually produced Jim Beam Bourbon, personally guiding it through its metamorphic journey from raw material to mash to beer to distillate to barrel to bottle. The legacy of the Beams was exemplified in the amber-hued bourbon that was packaged in the clear, square-cornered bottle. Therefore, the question of whether or not the Beams should remain at their posts to do what they had always done best, talk about the bourbon, make the bourbon, and supervise all production and aging at the Clermont and Boston distilleries was easily answered.

Three years after the purchase by American Brands, Jim Beam Bourbon passed Old Crow Bourbon as the nation's top-selling bourbon whiskey. By 1975, Jim Beam Bourbon was approaching three million cases annually in sales. In fact, Jim Beam Bourbon trailed only Smirnoff Vodka, Canadian Club Blended Whisky, Seagram's V.O. Canadian Whiskey, and Seagram's 7 Crown Blended Whiskey in total case volume in the domestic market. Old Crow, the venerable straight bourbon whiskey brand owned by National Distillers, had imploded, the victim of a lack of the kind of brand support throughout the 1960s that had propelled rival Jim Beam forward in the United States.

But the euphoria was short-lived as American Brands and its subsidiary were destined to face daunting challenges on several fronts. As was covered in Chapter 6, the bourbon whiskey boom that proved to be the lead story of distilled spirits in America in the 1950s, 1960s, and early 1970s came to a screeching halt by 1974–1975. Within a decade after the James B. Beam Distilling Company changed hands, America's bourbon whiskey industry entered a difficult period of attrition and contraction. Bumps in the road in the late 1970s brought on by the effects of changing generational tastes, regional preferences, and the emergence of vodka and wine created a serious American whiskey sales slump in the 1980s.

As preteen and teenage consumers were increasingly reared on sweet-tasting soft drinks, flavored beverages, and sweetened fruit juices, consumerism in the 1970s in the United States and Western Europe took a dramatic turn. A force since before World War II, Coca-Cola and its soda pop competitors significantly influenced the taste impressions of adolescents who grew up during the 1950s and 1960s. As the Baby Boomers evolved into legal-age adult consumers in the 1970s and 1980s, they were understandably seduced and enticed by "light," "white," or "sweetish" alcoholic drinks. These concoctions included Bacardi rum and cola, wine coolers like Bartles & Jaymes, infused fruit-flavored vodkas, and eventually by the early 1990s the avalanche of "designer" cocktails that all worked diligently to mask the taste of alcohol. As a result, the consumption of the more complex, character-driven spirits like Scotch whisky, cognac, brandy, and bourbon whiskey dropped like boulders off a cliff through the 1970s and 1980s. The decline in the enjoyment of the more robust "brown" spirits was in freefall.

Panicked American straight (meaning, unblended) and blended whiskey (straight whiskeys mixed with neutral grain spirits) brand managers throughout the industry made the mistake of lowering their wholesale prices in the hope of attracting this new generation of consumers. Sporadic price slashing in the North American whiskey segment happened from the mid-1970s through the late 1980s. These ill-advised downward pricing moves not only undercut the profit margins of the distillers and their customers, the distributors and retailers, but they likewise cheapened the already fuddy-duddy image of straight bourbon whiskey. Customarily viewed as a quality homegrown product, straight bourbon whiskey was aligned—and maligned—with the cheaper and inferior blended whiskeys.

Lower profit margins predictably dictated that marketing and advertising budgets for the brands were summarily trimmed. Consequently, many long-time straight bourbon whiskey brands like Old Hickory, Old Stagg, Hill & Hill, J.W. Dant, Old Sunny Brook, the aforementioned Old Crow, and Four Roses were cast adrift in the marketplace, suffering the death of a thousand cuts as they gradually faded from back bars and retailers' shelves. In the meantime, other stalwart North American whiskey brands that had before the 1980s been household names such as Seagram's 7 Crown, a blended whiskey, and Seagram's V.O., a Canadian whisky, got unceremoniously bumped from their long-held number one and number two positions by white spirits competitors, specifically Bacardi Silver Rum and Smirnoff Vodka, the vodka made in America but bearing a Russian moniker.

Two high-profile brands of American straight whiskey weathered the tempestuous era of 1975 to 1990 and actually strengthened their market shares against what could be described in understatement as severe market conditions. Those brands were Jim Beam Kentucky Straight Bourbon Whiskey, owned by a subsidiary of American Brands, and Jack Daniel's Old Time No. 7 Tennessee Sour Mash Black Label, purchased in 1956 for $18 million by Brown-Forman Beverages of Louisville, Kentucky. One of the key reasons for the success of these two brands while Jimmy Carter, Ronald Reagan, and George H. W. Bush occupied the White House was that their marketing strategies reached far beyond any kind of regional limitation that hampered or restricted other brands. Jim Beam and Jack Daniel's were supported and treated by their parent companies as genuine national and international brands.

Tom Maas, the present-day vice president of global brand management for Jim Beam Bourbon, spells out the regionality of the liquor business in the United States over the past seven decades this way, "The modern liquor business from 1933 to 2003 was defined largely by the restraints and bootlegging activities that occurred all through Prohibition. When you look at a map of the continental United States, certain types of distilled spirits have traditionally remained popular in specific geographic locations because of illegal activities during Prohibition. The Northeast is, by custom, Scotch whisky territory due for the most part to its proximity to the United Kingdom and to the influx of illicit Scotch during Prohibition.

"The Southwest and Texas are tequila country. The Northern tier that abuts Canada is still Canadian and blended whisky territory and the Southeast and Central parts of the nation heavily favor bourbon whiskey, both because of their proximity to Kentucky and because there was plenty of illegal whiskey available in the midst of Prohibition."

Jim Beam Bourbon in the 1960s, 1970s, and 1980s and Jack Daniel's Tennessee Sour Mash in the 1980s and 1990s moved outside the confines of what were perceived as regional boxes. In the case of Jim Beam Bourbon, brand investing first came in the form of "blanket" print advertising through much of the 1960s and 1970s. Barry Berish, who retired as chairman and chief executive officer of Jim Beam Brands in 1997 and who in his 40-year tenure oversaw many of the brand's national advertising campaigns as well as its incursions into international markets, remembers that at one point print advertisements for Jim Beam Bourbon appeared in 735 daily and weekly newspapers scattered around the United States.

Says Berish, "The growth of Jim Beam throughout the United States was slow but steady through the 1960s and 1970s. Prior to the sale to American Brands in 1967, the Blum-Kovler regime didn't care much about expanding Jim Beam beyond our national boundaries, even though the brand was relatively well established in Germany and Australia due to the presence of the American Armed Forces. Troops who were stationed in Germany throughout the Cold War and GIs who vacationed in Australia during the Vietnam War championed the brand in those consumer markets. Intense focus on international growth, however, didn't start until well after American Brands took over."

This foreign market vacuum allowed Brown-Forman's Jack Daniel's brand of Tennessee straight whiskey to close the gap with Jim Beam in the late 1980s and early 1990s.

As the director of advertising and marketing for Jim Beam Brands during the 1960s and most of the 1970s, Berish utilized T. Jeremiah Beam as a spokesperson for the brand created by his father much in the way that Booker Noe toured the country in the 1990s and Fred Noe, Booker's son, does in 2003. "The Beams tell their story like no one else because they've done it. They've lived it. I took T. Jeremiah wherever I could to show him off. He was remarkably gracious and eloquent in his depictions of his father and the making of bourbon whiskey. T. Jeremiah was typical of the best things of the South and a true gentleman in the Louisville tradition. It was a pleasure traveling with him. The brand couldn't have had a better ambassador at the time."

When Berish ascended within Jim Beam to become executive vice president in 1977 and then chief operating officer in 1980, he and his handpicked management team yearned to first obtain then develop other potentially profitable brands to complement Jim Beam Bourbon for the purpose of creating a multilevel beverage alcohol company. "Jim Beam was essentially still a one-brand company in 1980 and American Brands, for all intents and purposes, acted as Jim Beam's bank," describes Rich Reese, the present chief executive officer and president and successor to Berish.

But Berish met with internal resistance at first from American Brands as he attempted to land other brands through acquisitions. "Some were right in my hand, but I couldn't get the backing to finalize the acquisitions," says Berish today. Frustrated that he and his team weren't being allowed the freedom to proactively cultivate the company's capacity for growth as competitors were expanding their portfolios, Berish took a chance by confronting the parent company. In a story that is fondly but not boastfully passed on by his successors, Berish approached the management team at American Brands, telling them in essence, "You have in your possession a jewel brand in Jim Beam Bourbon. But this jewel needs a crown." Berish went on to argue that if American Brands gave him the chance and the financial backing, he and his team could build the subsidiary company into an impact player in the beverage alcohol business. He concluded by saying, "If that's not what you want, fine. But if that is the case you should perhaps consider getting rid of Jim Beam."

Berish convinced American Brands that the beverage alcohol industry was a long-term proposition that required proper and steadfast brand building from the grassroots level. If afforded the opportunity, Berish believed that the Jim Beam team that he had gathered could foster other brands of beverage alcohol in addition to their star bourbon. Finally, in 1982, Berish was given the green light to purchase Kamora, a brand of coffee liqueur similar to Kahlua that was produced in Mexico, for $3 million. Kamora was a 60 thousand case a year brand that didn't compete with Jim Beam Bourbon. Today, Kamora accounts for more than 200 thousand cases per year.

The expansion road temporarily ended there, at least for five more years. But as Berish would find out, the wait was worth it. In 1987, National Distillers, a mammoth but basically moribund distilling company whose total yearly sales were 12 million cases, came up for sale through public auction. The auction turned into a heated bidding war as several other companies sorely coveted the brands held by National. Brands like Old Grand-Dad Bourbon, Old Crow Bourbon (the former number one selling bourbon) Old Taylor Bourbon, Gilbey's Gin, Gilbey's Vodka, and DeKuyper cordials, had established strong regional presences and provided a wide array of consumer attraction. They were considered "standard" brands, not "premium" brands like Jim Beam and therefore provided lower profit margins. What the brands would bring to a firm the size of Jim Beam would be increased market share, a significantly deeper and more varied product line portfolio, and wider distribution connections. These were highly tempting virtues to a small, Midwestern beverage alcohol company with one big product, a company that perpetually conducted business in the shadows cast by the "big boys" like House of Seagram, Schenley Industries, Heublein, and Hiram Walker.

"We wanted National Distillers badly," admits Berish. Jim Beam got the okay from American Brands to aggressively bid on National Distillers. National accepted the $545 million bid proffered by Berish. The entire deal was completed in less than six weeks. Jim Beam had suddenly been transformed from a two-brand company, Jim Beam and Kamora, into a multibrand entity. The bold National Distillers acquisition, which took the beverage alcohol industry by surprise, tripled the size of the company. The bourbon brands, Old Grand-Dad, Old Crow, and Old Taylor, were neatly folded over into the American whiskey portion of the new company portfolio with Jim Beam Bourbon remaining the flagship.

"David had bought Goliath in 1987," says Michael Donohoe, the chief executive officer of Future Brands LLC, of the National acquisition. "Nobody thought we'd get it because we were small compared to the other bidders." The National Distillers purchase catapulted Jim Beam into the big leagues. Jim Beam was a player.

Then in 1991, Berish and his squad cast their acquisitions net again into the swells of the liquor industry seas. This time they landed seven strong regional brands that were bought from the House of Seagram for $300 million. This sale came about due, in no small part, to the friendship between Berish and Edgar Bronfman Jr. who wanted to change the direction of family-owned Seagram. Bronfman thought that by spinning off standard brands that had strong regional but not necessarily national presence, Seagram could begin concentrating on premium brands with both national and international profiles. This cache of standard brands included Kessler Bourbon, Ronrico rum, Wolfschmidt vodka, and Leroux cordials.

"These former Seagram standard brands today account for $100 million in gross profits for us every year," claims Rich Reese. "But more than anything else at the time they added mass. That was critical because they gave us more clout with distributors. Suddenly, our portfolio was responsible for 20 to 30 percent of distributor inventories rather than only 10 to 20 percent."

The addition of the standard brands helped promote Beam's flagship brand, Jim Beam Bourbon, through the nation's distribution system due primarily to portfolio linkage and the power that market share automatically bestows on the supplier. These two major acquisitions greatly expanded the marketplace presence of the Jim Beam Brands Company through sheer numbers alone. Portfolio clout and product variety opened doors and compelled distributors to listen.

Following the Seagram brands purchase, the Jim Beam Brands marketing team decided in the early 1990s to put national focus on what they determined to be their three cornerstone brands, Jim Beam Bourbon, naturally, DeKuyper cordials, and Kamora coffee liqueur. With the gradual marketplace acceptance of The Small Batch Bourbon Collection, which debuted in 1992, that collective brand was added to the national marketing push.

With consumer tastes markedly shifting toward pricier brands in all consumer goods fields by the mid-1990s as the global economy soared, the Jim Beam Brands planning team conceived the idea of The Masters' Collection, an elite assemblage of high-end distilled spirits that they hoped would be intriguing both to authentic connoisseurs and to the many thousands of affluent, young, professional wannabe sophisticates. The Masters' Collection included The Small Batch Bourbon Collection, The Dalmore Single Malt Scotch Whisky, Tangle Ridge Blended Canadian Whisky, El Tesoro de Don Felipe Tequila, Chinaco Tequila, and A. de Fussigny Cognacs. In the meantime, Jim Beam Bourbon, the company's core brand, continued its upward march at home and abroad in the first half of the 1990s as it maintained its standing both as the world's number one selling bourbon whiskey and America's top selling straight whiskey.

Ron Kapolnek, Jim Beam Brands Worldwide's current senior vice president and general manager, reflected that when he was hired in 1988 American Brands had informed their subsidiary then known as Jim Beam Brands Company that if they wanted to be considered a "core entity" within the hallways of the parent company, they would have to increase their earnings to $100 million per year. "I'm happy to report that today our earnings have tripled that of core status," says Kapolnek without bravado.

But while the overall performance of Jim Beam Brands Company was more than pleasing to Fortune Brands, one development that revolved around their flagship brand jolted the Jim Beam management team in the mid-1990s—the loss of the number one ranking in the world for American straight whiskey. While Jim Beam Bourbon was and is still the number one selling straight bourbon whiskey in the world by a wide margin, Jack Daniel's Old Time No. 7 Tennessee Sour Mash Whiskey, which is not a bourbon whiskey, captured the top spot as the best-selling American straight whiskey. But Rich Reese, first lieutenant to Barry Berish, had plans to address that thorny issue when on Berish's retirement he assumed control of Jim Beam Brands Company.

Enter Jim Beam Brands Worldwide, Inc.

A year after the departure of Barry Berish, the new chief executive officer and president, Rich Reese, shepherded the concept in 1998 of a truly global enterprise by repositioning Jim Beam Brands Company as a subsidiary of Jim Beam Brands Worldwide, Incorporated, itself a company of Fortune Brands, Incorporated. Just the year prior, parent company American Brands had reinvented itself by becoming Fortune Brands, Incorporated. Internal reorganization and strategic goal readjustments were concepts that were found permeating the air in boardrooms across the world in the mid-1990s. Affecting Reese and JBBWorldwide was the atmosphere of the global beverage alcohol industry that was rife with rumors of mergers, consolidations, and the formations of new strategic partnerships. Guinness and Grand Metropolitan were about to merge thereby creating Diageo, the beverage alcohol industry's most formidable and dominating company. Industry pundits spoke of the squeezing of market share for competing companies because of the formation of Diageo. Other unconfirmed Chinese whispers of radical change swirled around the House of Seagram and its fidgety chairman Edgar Bronfman Jr. Talk of the beverage alcohol trade eventually becoming an industry run by only four, perhaps five, mega-companies danced on the lips of executives and occupied editorial space in the business pages of newspapers, industry newsletters, and web sites.

Reese and his chief lieutenants, Michael Donohoe and Ron Kapolnek, acknowledged that for their company and its brands to continue to prosper they had to begin trolling for suitable partners with which to team for the purpose of expanding their distribution base. Rather than hunt for another takeover prospect that would mean the absorption of yet more brands, Reese, with input from then chairman and chief executive officer of Fortune Brands Thomas Hays, decided to attempt to broaden JBBWorldwide's sales and distribution networks abroad first through a joint venture with other medium-size beverage alcohol firms that could benefit from such a collaboration.

The first such union occurred in July of 1999 with the founding of Maxxium Worldwide B.V., the joint venture between JBBWorldwide, Rémy-Cointreau of France, and Highland Distillers, Ltd. of the United Kingdom. The three equal partners of Maxxium, whose sales and distribution forces focus on almost 60 nations throughout the Americas, Asia, Australasia, and Europe, represented a collection of the world's foremost prestige alcoholic beverages. JBBWorldwide brought Jim Beam Bourbon, Knob Creek Bourbon, and Geyser Peak wines to the deal. Rémy-Cointreau brought Rémy Martin cognac, Piper-Heidsieck champagne, and Cointreau liqueur while Highland Distillers supplied The Famous Grouse Blended Scotch Whisky, Highland Park Single Malt Scotch Whisky, and The Macallan Single Malt Scotch Whisky. Each partner contributed

$110 million to underwrite the launch of the new company that was expected to lower distribution expenses for each of the partners. Maxxium's headquarters were set up in Amsterdam, the Netherlands. One year after the consummation of the Maxxium deal, combined case volume surpassed 16 million cases that accounted for $1.2 billion in sales revenues.

"Before Maxxium we were underrepresented internationally," says Norm Wesley, the present day chief executive officer and president of parent company Fortune Brands. "With that one deal we were able to extend our reach from about twenty countries up to around sixty. The brands are complementary. Each of the partners contributed different distribution assets that could be leveraged. So, if we wanted to grow internationally we had to have all the right resources lined up. It starts with having the right distribution."

With the Maxxium deal in place to help rejuvenate and extend the global market influence of Jim Beam Bourbon, Reese yearned to do the same with sales and distribution on the home front. In May of 2001, Fortune Brands and JBBWorldwide announced their second joint venture. This time, The Absolut Spirits Company, the American subsidiary of Vin & Sprit, the Sweden-based producers of ABSOLUT Vodkas whose worldwide sales exceed seven million cases, was the sole partner. In the agreement, The Absolut Spirits Company paid $270 million for a 49 percent stake in the new company, Future Brands LLC. As part of the Future Brands deal, Vin & Sprit also became an equal partner in Maxxium, thereby strengthening and expanding the influence of that entity. Vin & Sprit also gained a 10 percent share of JBBWorldwide with an option to acquire another 10 percent if they wish.

Michael Donohoe, a key senior member of the Jim Beam Brands management team during the 1980s and 1990s, was named chief executive officer and president of Future Brands. The company was headquartered in the same building as JBBWorldwide in Deerfield, Illinois. Future Brands started in full gallop from the gate as the second largest alcohol distribution company in the United States in terms of volume.

In the opinion of Ron Kapolnek, senior vice president and general manager of JBBWorldwide, the brand building of Jim Beam Bourbon all through the 1990s contributed significantly to the image of the company as a possible partner in strategic joint ventures. Asserts Kapolnek, "Our goal has always been to bolster the image of our core brand, Jim Beam Bourbon. We invested significantly in Jim Beam by managing the bottom line on all our brands and then shifting the cash to the core brand. Recently, we more than doubled our marketing spending behind Jim Beam in the United States. The brand enhancement of Jim Beam surely played a role in establishing the joint ventures."

One of the crucial components to upgrading the image of a brand is to raise its price. During much of the doldrum years of the 1970s, 1980s, and early 1990s, some American distillers continually lowered their bourbon whiskey prices. In the process, they not only damaged their own brands but likewise harmed the bourbon category as a whole. By the mid-1990s, brand building had become the chief priority for distillers such as Jim Beam. It still is.

As one of the nation's most profitable publicly held companies, Thomas J. Flocco, executive vice president and chief operating officer, believes that JBBWorldwide could do even more to increase volume and revenue. "Our goal is to build a world-class marketing organization within JBBWorldwide and to drive both the top line and bottom line." The team plans to accomplish this goal by building the company's core brands through developing "consumer segmentation." In other words, ascertaining through focus group work and qualitative and quantitative research how consumers view brands and why they use them, then creating the marketing strategies to appeal to those traits.

"Our vision," says Flocco, "is to keep increasing Jim Beam's premiumness by steadily raising its bottle price; to triple our advertising for the purpose of bringing new consumers into the circle and to recruit consumers in the 25 to 28 age group to join the franchise; to market to the Hispanic community whose affluence and influence are steadily growing; to reward consumers for buying Jim

Beam in order to build their commitment to the brand; to build a relationship between the consumer and the brand through vehicles like the Internet, our commitment to helping new musicians, like Montgomery Gentry, to develop their talents, as well as through groups like the Kentucky Bourbon Circle whose mailing list numbers in the tens of thousands. And last, by trying to market more at the point of consumption at bars and retail shops. The whole point is to bond the consumer to the Beam brand."

In response to an evolving marketplace, one in which major beverage alcohol companies must be proactive in several overlapping beverage segments to flourish, JBBWorldwide entered the premium wine business in 1998 with the purchase of Geyser Peak Winery in Sonoma County, California. Wines are distributed through many of the same systems as spirits in the United States, so the expansion into wine was easily implemented on a distribution basis. In 2003, JBBWorldwide unveiled Beam and Cola, a new brand of premixed ready-to-drink beverage made from Jim Beam Bourbon and cola. The management staff at JBBWorldwide contends that they are essentially in the entertainment industry and that owning a complete portfolio of products that appeals to a broad audience of consumers who like to embellish their lives with spirits, ready-to-drink beverages and wines is absolutely necessary.

In 2002, Fortune Brands, Inc., a New York Stock Exchange member (NYSE symbol: FO), generated more than $5.6 billion in total revenues. JBBWorldwide accounted for 24 percent of sales and 40 percent of Fortune Brands' profitability through $1.3 billion worth of global sales. JBBWorldwide recently experienced 51 consecutive quarters of profitability. The Jim Beam Bourbon brand alone accounted for about $350 million worth of revenues from sales of more than five million cases worldwide. The other key consumer goods holdings of Fortune Brands currently include companies in the office supply (Acco, Swingline), home (Moen faucets, Aristokraft, Schrock, and Omega cabinets), hardware (Master Lock, Waterloo), and sporting goods (Titleist, Footjoy, and Cobra golfing equipment and sportswear) industries.

"We (Fortune Brands) are a consumer business. We want to be in businesses and in brands that are leaders in their categories. Jim Beam fits that beautifully," says Norm Wesley of Fortune Brands. "We believe that the spirits business has wonderful growth potential."

Rich Reese, still disappointed that Jim Beam Bourbon was passed by Jack Daniel's Tennessee Whiskey, says that he is not satisfied with Jim Beam just being the world's number one bourbon whiskey at a little bit more than five million cases. He and his team currently have their sights set not just on Jack Daniel's but on Johnnie Walker Red Blended Scotch Whisky, the world's largest selling premium whiskey at around six and three-quarter million cases. Says Reese of his top brand, his company's jewel, "People like to have their individual 'badge' in what they drink. Jim Beam is one of the most recognized premium product names around the world. It's a symbol of America. We never forget that bourbon got us here."

While Reese graciously concedes that archrival Brown-Forman Beverages Worldwide in Louisville has done an excellent job promoting Jack Daniel's around the world, he makes the case that Jack Daniel's is not a bourbon whiskey. It is identified as a Tennessee sour mash whiskey. Reese urges consumers to try Jim Beam Kentucky Straight Bourbon Whiskey white label and Jack Daniel's Old Time No. 7 Tennessee Whiskey Black Label side-by-side. "There is a big difference. We believe that through our joint ventures such as Maxxium and Future Brands that we are in a good position to overtake some of our competitors."

Keeping Them Straight: Jim Beam Bourbon and Jack Daniel's Tennessee Sour Mash

Both of these multimillion case, internationally revered American heartland whiskeys are straight whiskeys (straight whiskeys are defined as 100 percent grain distillates that, one, contain no added or artificial flavorings and coloring; two, that are distilled at no higher than 160-proof, or 80 percent alcohol; and, three, that are matured in new charred oak barrels for at least 24 months), but of the two only Jim Beam is considered a straight *bourbon* whiskey. Though Jack Daniel's legally fits the definition of straight bourbon whiskey, because it is produced in Tennessee, a state that officially chooses not to identify its straight whiskeys as "bourbons," it is called a Tennessee straight whiskey.

There is, however, one major difference in production that sets these two acclaimed straight whiskeys apart. Tennessee distillers staunchly defend their decision to differentiate their whiskeys from those of neighboring Kentucky and elsewhere because they employ a filtering sequence called the *Lincoln County Process*, a production step developed in the 1820s by Tennessee distiller Alfred Eaton, that is not used by the bourbon whiskey distillers in any other state. In the Lincoln County Process, the whiskey is filtered through tall vats containing sugar maple charcoal. The charcoal imparts a sooty, ash-like taste to Tennessee whiskeys that is not present in Kentucky bourbon whiskeys.

The only realistic method of discovering the noticeable difference between the two styles is to taste Jim Beam and Jack Daniel's next to each other.

An Illinois Company That Never Loses Sight of Kentucky

For all the boardroom strategizing, focus group testing, and top level planning by bright, dedicated people that occurs daily at the JBB-Worldwide headquarters in Deerfield, Illinois, and at the Fortune Brands nerve center in nearby Lincolnshire, Illinois, the heart of the company still beats steadily as it has for over two centuries 300 miles to the south in the verdant rolling countryside of north-central Kentucky. "The Beam family is a cornerstone of the bourbon industry," says Norm Wesley. "They have been linked to the brand for two hundred years. Our marketing is pointed toward the authenticity and the heritage of the brand. Clearly that's tied to the family. It is very desirable from our standpoint and, I think, from their standpoint, too, to maintain that relationship. Even though we own the brand, the family continues to be the brand's largest champion and worldwide ambassador. If you think about the fact that we're a public company and they're a family . . . for the relationship to have lasted and flourished this long makes it a unique relationship."

The influence of the Beam family character apparently trickles into the everyday dealings of JBBWorldwide in Deerfield where the atmosphere is cordial, informal, and conversational. Says Ron Kapolnek of the Jim Beam approach to business, "There is no ivory tower here. The management team knows people's names. No team is superior to the next. The Beams always bring us back to Earth. The core values of the Beam family stay important. The Beams inflame ambition in us because they're so passionate about what they do."

This company credo holds true by all appearances for the sales staff in the field where the emphasis is placed on face-to-face dealings rather than by e-mail and facsimile communication. "The focus is on personal relationships. The people aspect of this business is key to us. It's important to never lose sight of our customers," says Kapolnek.

One school of thought postulates that the Beams have lasted so long in the bourbon whiskey business because their focus has since fourth generation master distiller Jim Beam been squarely on the distilling side of the industry. Rather than getting bogged down in the financial, sales, and marketing areas where fluctuations due to fads, fates, and world events can cause grave injury, the Beams have been allowed to hone their remarkable artistry by being employees, not employers.

The present-day master distiller Jerry Dalton, the man who succeeded Booker Noe as custodian of Jacob Beam's bourbon whiskey legacy, keeps a close watch on the heartbeat of Jim Beam. Like all master distillers over the ages Dalton is usually the first to show up at the distillery at first light and, most nights, is the person switching off the lights. Dalton was born in southern Kentucky. He earned a PhD in physical chemistry. He has taught mathematics in college and has authored a book on Chinese philosophy called *Backward Down the Path*. He got to know Booker Noe mainly because he lived right behind Booker and Annis years before he was hired at Jim Beam. Dalton recalls "drinking a little snort and talking distilling" and doubtless putting away a few hundred ham biscuits with Booker long before he was hired by Jim Beam.

As far as replacing the larger-than-life Booker goes, Dalton is keenly aware of comparisons and expectations. "It's not difficult to replace Booker. It's impossible. He is a mix of family heritage and extraordinary distilling knowledge that is unique and unmatchable. I couldn't ever replace Booker. But I don't think of myself as replacing Booker as much as I think of myself stepping in and inheriting a lot of good stuff left behind by him. All I can hope to do is bring my own set of skills . . . and hopefully not screw it up."

Though Dalton says that his primary job is to "protect the process that has made Jim Beam the number one bourbon in the world," he has wide latitude to experiment, innovate, and make improvements. While he feels the weight of bearing the Beam distilling mantle, Dalton isn't paralyzed by the reality of it. Muses Dalton of the responsibility that has been handed to him, "During the summertime shutdown sometimes I walk around the distillery or the rackhouses by myself. It's quiet. Nobody's there. Then it will hit me: I'm the first nonfamily member in two hundred years after Booker and Fred to make Jim Beam. It's surreal. It's an amazing responsibility that I'm honored and privileged to bear."

Fred Noe and his father Booker still reside in Bardstown. Booker, now in his seventies, lives in the house of his grandfather Jim Beam. Fred is tall, husky, intelligent, and affable like his famous father. As the Knob Creek brand ambassador, Fred's travels take him literally around the world. Like his father, Fred speaks off the top of his head about the whiskeys he grew up with. He talks about the first time he smelled the pungent, sweet smells of the distillery, of watching his father make the yeast culture in the kitchen, of riding on the distillery's slop trucks and of feeling the cool, moist air of the rackhouses even in the summer. No script for Fred when he is standing in front of the standing room only audiences that he routinely encounters from Sydney to Tokyo to New York. He just says whatever strikes him to relate about the six generations of Beams who distilled whiskey before him and of the family bourbons that are world-famous today. The people come to taste the whiskeys, to be sure, but they really show up more to see and hear a true Kentucky whiskeyman. They come to see the great-grandson of the legendary Jim Beam.

When he's home in Bardstown, Fred helps his father choose the whiskies that will eventually be labeled as Booker's Bourbon. They typically perform that function right there in Booker and Annis' kitchen, the same hallowed place, the holy sanctuary where Jim Beam created the family yeast culture seventy years ago and where today all of Booker's killer ham biscuits are made by Annis and Toogie. Booker takes care to cook the hams himself in the distillery mash cooker. Done so for decades so the ham smells a bit of bourbon. "Gives it a bit o' farh," claims Booker, smacking his lips.

For all the cool efficiencies, modern architecture, and swift electronic communications of the JBBWorldwide and Fortune Brands Illinois corporate headquarters, the spirit of Jim Beam Kentucky Straight Bourbon Whiskey, the world's number one selling straight bourbon whiskey, resides—and always will—in rural Kentucky, the sweet heartland of the United States, shining brightest in Booker's kitchen in Bardstown.

Appendix

Tasting Notes on Jim Beam Bourbons

TASTING DISTILLED SPIRITS PROFESSIONALLY has been one of the most rewarding and demanding experiences of my working life. Propelled by my newsletter *F. Paul Pacult's Spirit Journal*, my first book *Kindred Spirits: The Spirit Journal Guide to the World's Distilled Spirits and Fortified Wines* (Hyperion, 1997) and regular spirits, beer, and wine writing duties for *Sky*, the Delta Air Lines in-flight magazine, the *New York Times*, *Wine Enthusiast Magazine*, and many others, I have, using a strict tasting procedure devised by myself, evaluated over 3,500 distilled spirits and many thousands more beers and wines. Many of the spirits have been whiskeys.

Breaking spirits down through the prism of four senses, sight, smell, taste, and feel; describing them in detail in understandable terminology; then rating them is tedious the majority of days and inspiring only on occasion. The regimen's strength lies in its repetition, the steady adherence to the same format, the best possible equipment, and a conducive environment in which to judge every product in the same, unbiased manner. Price is not a factor in my evaluation system; products earn rating stars based on sensory merit only.

My scoring system is one-to-five stars, five representing the highest achievement. I only recommend the products that receive three or more stars. One star is a disappointing product and is not recommended. Two stars indicate average, acceptable quality but not quite good enough to warrant a recommendation. Three stars mean better than average quality, or, more specifically, a product that displays enough pleasing and distinctive characteristics that advance the product beyond the commonplace and make it, therefore, recommendable. A four star rating means highly recommended and points to a product of superb quality whose virtues are far past what the established standards of the category demand. My least frequently bestowed rating is five stars, or classic, which indicates a product of extraordinary, benchmark quality whose characteristics can be used as a standard of excellence for the entire category. Any product rated five stars receives my highest recommendation designation.

Jim Beam bourbons have over the years provided me with at least seven memorable evaluation moments out of a possible nine. That is a very high ratio, considering the demands I place on every evaluated product. Of the seven very positive moments, six have been genuinely glorious experiences, meriting ratings of four or five rating stars. These are the latest notes and ratings on each of the current Jim Beam bourbons.

Baker's 7 Year Old Kentucky Straight Bourbon Whiskey/Small Batch, 53.5 Percent Alcohol ★★★★

Probably the most overlooked member of the Small Batch Bourbon Collection. Baker's is wonderfully intense and is that rare, flavorful bourbon that reminds me strikingly of a fine XO cognac. The appearance is marked by a deep amber, almost tawny hue. The bouquet offers distant notes of vanilla extract, dark caramel, red cherry, and even a touch of cola nut. In the mouth, Baker's is remarkably refined and sophisticated, emitting layered flavors of yellow fruit, especially pears, and roasted pine nuts. The aftertaste is sweet, warming in the throat, and banana-like. A supremely confident and delicious bourbon.

Basil Hayden's 8 Year Old Kentucky Straight Bourbon Whiskey/Small Batch, 40 Percent Alcohol ★★

The lightest and least impressive bourbon in the Small Batch Bourbon Collection, but then in fairness look at the three imposing bourbons with which it is teamed. The harvest gold color is very pretty and pure. The aroma is lively, grain mash "beer" sweet, and ethereal but honeyed and minty (peppermint, not spearmint). The elementary taste begins in a flowery, almost yeasty manner then turns lazy and dull by the midpalate point, showing only minor flavors of sour apple candy and cotton candy. Basil Hayden's finishes spicily at first then corny sweet and warming in the throat. A decent small batch beginner for the curious who don't want to start out breathing fire.

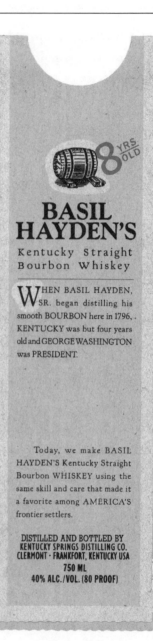

Beam's Choice Kentucky Straight Bourbon Whiskey, 40 Percent Alcohol ★★★

Attractive topaz, honey color. BC smells early on of wet earth, mushrooms, and spice, then after a few more minutes of air contact the minty spiciness takes control, obliterating all other aromatic elements. The palate entry is mildly oaky and a touch sooty, but the complex flavor profile changes markedly at the midpalate stage adding zesty, dry tastes of oak resin, almond, and dry breakfast cereal. The aftertaste is medium-long, dry to off-dry, a bit musty in a pleasantly earthy manner and keenly spicy. An overlooked winner and an excellent value.

Booker's Bourbon Kentucky Straight Bourbon Whiskey/Small Batch, 61 Percent to 63.50 Percent Alcohol ★★★★

The flagship of the Small Batch Bourbon Collection and an authentic one-of-a-kind American whiskey that is stunningly good with every bottling. One particular bottling, the 10th Anniversary edition was a ★★★★★ whiskey. All other incarnations have been borderline four star/five star whiskeys. Bright orange, copper in color, almost like iced tea. The concentrated, intense bouquet is dominated at first by alcohol but then that blows off leaving behind heady scents of sweet oak, vanilla bean, marzipan, and candied almond. The flavor thrust at the palate entry is bracing as intense flavors of wood smoke, tobacco leaf, wood resin, and even wine blanket the taste buds. One of the best finishes in all of whiskey, the extended, seemingly infinite aftertaste of Booker's alone is worth the price as it provides lovely tastes of nuts, spice, sweet oak, and grain mash. I strongly urge everyone, no matter your level of expertise, to add some mineral water to this august spirit after first carefully sampling it neat.

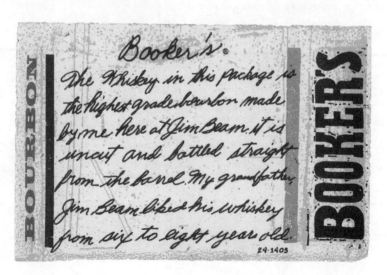

Distillers' Masterpiece 18 Year Old Cognac Cask Finished Kentucky Straight Bourbon Whiskey, 49.5 Percent Alcohol ★★★★★

Luminous amber, rust, new copper penny color. The cutting-edge aroma is faintly spiced at first, then with time in the glass it opens up displaying mature, rich scents of oak, vanilla wafer, and cocoa butter. In the mouth, DM Cognac Cask initially tastes zesty and intensely oaky, then by midpalate the deeply structured flavors turn sweet and fruity. The aftertaste is dominated by the warmth of the heady spirit. The start of a new era, in my opinion, for straight bourbon whiskey by adding the exotic, winy, fruity flavor enhancement of the Cognac cask. Bravo.

Distillers' Masterpiece 20 Year Old Port Cask Finished Kentucky Straight Bourbon Whiskey, 43 Percent Alcohol ★★★★★

A much older than normal bourbon that was placed in barrels that once held port at the end of the maturity cycle. Pretty bronze hue. The first aromas are intensely nutty and floral, with a trace of wine-like sweetness; exposure to air expands the bouquet adding mild, rounded scents of mints, oak char, and ruby port. As tantalizing as the aroma is, this bourbon's true brilliance lies in the taste phase. At palate entry the taste is off-dry and nutty, even nougat-like, then at midpalate the flavor turns succulent, but ultimately dry and resiny as flavors of minerals, apple butter, charred oak, and tobacco leaf keep the taste buds fully occupied. The finish is long, ripe, grapy, and grainy sweet. An American whiskey classic.

Jim Beam 4 Year Old Kentucky Straight Bourbon Whiskey, 40 Percent Alcohol ★★★

Shows an orange, russet hue. In the nasal cavity, JB is pleasantly spirity, kicky, even perfumy, with delicate fragrances of peaches, cocoa, vanilla, and baked apple. In the mouth, it's irresistibly sweet and round, offering opening flavors of light caramel and cigarette smoke, followed by more astringent and mature tastes of oak resin, barrel char, and buttered toast. JB finishes very long, crisp, and zesty. An honest, grainy sweet and zesty bourbon that's more like a favorite old Ford pick-up truck than a Mercedes. That's exactly the intention. The value-for-money ratio is extraordinarily high. No wonder it's number one in the world. *The* house bourbon.

Jim Beam Black 8 Year Old Kentucky Straight Bourbon Whiskey, 43 Percent Alcohol ★★★★

This is a new version of JB Black. The previous incarnation was aged for 7 years and had a proof of 90. The color is like honey, an amber/autumnal gold hue and the purity is perfect. The bouquet is moderately sweet at first with notes of toffee, light caramel, and yellow fruit then after seven more minutes of aeration time the aroma turns dry, slightly baked, and hints of tobacco leaf and oak resin. The palate entry is firm, semisweet, and mildly grainy; by the midpalate point there's a slight oiliness to the texture that I like while the taste becomes narrowly focused on the grain and wood. JB Black finishes elegantly, emitting sophisticated, long, and subtle flavors of toasted grain and oak.

Jim Beam Straight Rye Whiskey, 40 Percent Alcohol ★★

Bronze, pale copper color. The bouquet immediately after the pour is soft to the point of being delicate, even ethereal, then with some exposure to air the aroma fills out, emitting gently fruity, grainy scents that are semisweet and seductive. The palate entry taste is dry, shy, and delightfully spicy while the midpalate flavor point shows greater profile expansion in the forms of subtle spice (nutmeg, perhaps), apple fritter, and fresh flowers. JB Rye concludes with an unexpected flurry of black pepper and oil flavors. Good but uneven.

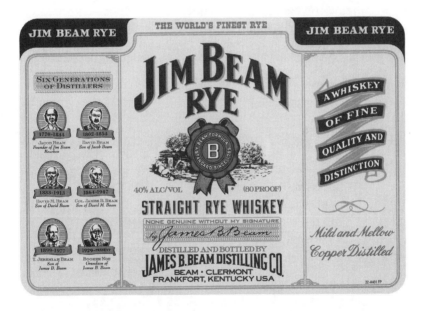

Knob Creek 9 Year Old Kentucky Straight Bourbon Whiskey/Small Batch, 50 Percent Alcohol ★★★★

So, I wonder: how could anyone not love this superbly crafted bourbon, the best-seller of the Small Batch Bourbon Collection? The medium amber, honey-like hue is terribly attractive for starters. Then in the nose KC offers succulent, semisweet, and voluptuous aromas of brandied peaches, roasted chestnuts, toasted breakfast cereal, and honey—it's one of the most bountiful, generous bouquets in the super-premium bourbon realm. In the mouth it's muscle-bound and robust yet elegant and refined, offering a small, smoldering campfire of warmth on the tongue (don't forget that KC is 100-proof) then in the recesses of the throat, but all the while you're found wanting more of the tastes of almonds, kiwi, lime, and black raisins. It closes out warm and fruity, with just a whisper of smoke.

Appendix

The Jim Beam Bourbon Timeline

The Foundations

1620:	Pilgrims land from England in Plymouth, Massachusetts.
1640:	First commercial still is established in Dutch Colony of New Netherland.
1750–1770:	The Long Hunters, including Daniel Boone, explore the territory of western Virginia known as Kentucke.
1755–1760:	**Johannes Jacob Boehm (Beam) born in Pennsylvania.**
1774:	First corn crop harvested in Kentucke.
1775–1781:	Revolutionary War years.
1786:	**Jacob Beam marries Mary Myers in Frederick County, Maryland on September 20.**

1787–1788: Jacob and Mary Myers Beam emigrate from Maryland through the Cumberland Gap to Lincoln County, Kentucky.

1792:   Kentucky becomes a state on June 1.

1791–1794: Whiskey Rebellion in western Pennsylvania quashed by federal troops.

1795:   Jacob Beam sells first barrel of "Old Jake Beam" whiskey.

1802:   David Beam, the tenth child of Jacob and Mary Beam, is born in Washington County, Kentucky.

1810:   2,200 distilleries reported to be operating in Kentucky, producing more than two million gallons of grain whiskey per year.

1820:   David Beam takes over as distiller at "Old Tub" family distillery, making Old Jake Beam.

1824:   David Beam marries Elizabeth Settle on July 19.

Circa 1830: Mary Myers Beam, matriarch of Beam family, dies.

1830–1839: Jacob Beam dies.

1830–1832: David Beam enlarges capacity of Old Tub Distillery to satisfy demand for Old Jake Beam.

1833:   David M. Beam, third child of David and Elizabeth Beam, born in Washington County, Kentucky.

1850:   Louisville & Nashville Railroad formed to connect the cities of Louisville, Kentucky, and Nashville, Tennessee by rail.

1852:   David Beam dies.

1853:   David M. Beam assumes control of Old Tub Distillery. Old Jake Beam now known more commonly as "Old Tub."

1856–1857: David M. Beam relocates Old Tub Distillery to Nelson County, Kentucky to be near L&N Springfield extension line. Names new family company "D.M. Beam & Company."

1861:   David M. Beam marries Margaret Ellen Phillips.

1861–1865:   Civil War years. Kentucky a border state.

The Dynasty

1864:   James Beauregard "Jim" Beam is born.

1868:   William Parker "Park" Beam, brother of Jim, is born.

1880:   Jim Beam begins apprenticeship at family distillery in Nelson County, Kentucky.

1880:   Population of United States passes the 50 million mark. Expansion westward positively impacts bourbon whiskey industry.

1880–1890:   Old Tub becomes national brand of bourbon whiskey with the help of railroad transportation and telegraph lines.

1888:   David M. Beam passes day-to-day operation of Old Tub to Jim Beam and semi-retires.

1892:   David M. Beam retires. Jim Beam assumes full command of family business.

1893:   Panic of 1893 spurs knee-jerk stock market sell-off.

1894:   Jim Beam brings Albert Hart, his brother-in-law, into family business and renames it Beam & Hart Distillery. Distillery operates at 150-bushels per day capacity, has four warehouses with enough room for 10,000 barrels.

1895–1896:   Main markets for Old Tub are western states, Midwest, and Deep South.

1897:   Jim Beam marries Mary Catherine Montgomery.

1898:   Jim Beam reorganizes family business again, bring-
               ing in two Chicago investors, Thomas Dennehy and
               Jeremiah Kenny, to help purchase Clear Springs
               Distillery Company of Bardstown.

1900:   T. Jeremiah Beam is born to Jim and Mary Beam.

1890–1910:   Temperance Movement, preaching abstinence from
               beverage alcohol, gains public and political support.

1913:   David M. Beam, grandson of Jacob Beam, dies at
               the age of 80. Jim Beam purchases F.G. Walker dis-
               tillery in Nelson County for $13,000 for additional
               storage space. Old Tub brand continues to grow.

1916:   Jim Beam elected president of Kentucky Distillers
               Association.

1917:   Eighteenth Amendment that would enact national
               Prohibition on the making, selling, and drinking of
               beverage alcohol is sent to the states for ratification.

1918:   Eighteenth Amendment, also known as the Volstead
               Act, ratified by required 36 states.

1920:   Prohibition goes into effect on January 17. Bourbon
               whiskey distilleries shut down for indefinite period.

1920–1933:   Jim Beam purchases Old Murphy Barber Distillery;
               unsuccessfully runs three nondistilling businesses;
               goes broke; sells Clear Springs to raise cash.

1932:   Franklin Delano Roosevelt defeats Herbert Hoover
               in presidential election, promises to end Prohibition.

1933:   Prohibition repealed by passing of Twenty-First
               Amendment.

1934:   Jim Beam elicits and obtains financial backing
               of Phillip Blum, Oliver Jacobson, and Harry
               Homel of Chicago to create James B. Beam Distill-
               ing Company; incorporates on August 14. Beam

family holds no interest in business. Breaks ground in autumn at Old Murphy Barber Distillery in Clermont, Bullitt County.

1935: After only 120 days, James B. Beam Distilling Company opens for business on March 25. "Old Tub" is brand. Jim Beam is master distiller.

1935: The group of investors that would become Heaven Hill Distillery forms. Joseph L. Beam is among the initial investors.

1935–1941: The Kentucky bourbon whiskey industry is rejuvenated.

1941–1945: World War II years. Most Kentucky whiskey distilleries convert their operations to assist in war effort.

1941: Harry Blum, son of Phillip Blum, buys one-third interests of Oliver Jacobson and Harry Homel for approximately $1 million and takes over as sole proprietor of James B. Beam Distilling Company.

1942: Having lost brand name rights, Jim Beam phases out Old Tub brand in favor of Colonel James B. Beam, then Jim Beam Bourbon brand.

1943: At age 79, Jim Beam relinquishes day-to-day running of James B. Beam Distilling Company to son T. Jeremiah and all distilling responsibilities to nephews Carl and Earl Beam, sons of Park.

1944: Jim Beam officially retires.

1947: Earl Beam leaves Jim Beam to become master distiller at Heaven Hill. Jim Beam dies on Christmas morning.

1949: Park Beam, Jim's younger brother, dies.

1950: F. Booker Noe II, grandson of Jim Beam, is hired by T. Jeremiah Beam.

1953:	James B. Beam Distilling Company acquires 450-acre parcel in Boston. Builds Plant #2.
1957:	Old Crow is the number one brand of bourbon whiskey in the United States. Jim Beam is a distant number four.
1959:	Harry Blum steps down as president. Everett Kovler, Blum's son-in-law, takes the post.
1960:	Booker Noe is named master distiller at Boston Plant #2.
1964:	U.S. Congress passes a resolution naming bourbon whiskey as the nation's "native spirit" and as ". . . a distinctive product of the United States." By law, bourbon can be made only within the United States.
1965:	One-millionth barrel of Beam bourbon since Prohibition is filled on June 2.
1966:	Old Crow is still the number one bourbon whiskey; Jim Beam is closing the gap and is number two, passing Early Times and Ancient Age.
1967:	Harry Blum sells James B. Beam Distilling Company to New Jersey-based American Brands, Inc.
1970:	Jim Beam becomes the top selling bourbon whiskey in America, passing Old Crow.
1971:	Harry Blum dies.
1977:	T. Jeremiah Beam dies.
1984:	Carl Beam dies.
1985:	Jim Beam is the world's top-selling American straight whiskey and bourbon whiskey. Jack Daniel's Black Label, not a bourbon but a Tennessee sour mash whiskey, is second.
1987:	Jim Beam Brands triples in size by purchasing National Distillers, in the process absorbing brands

that include Old Crow Bourbon, Old Grand-Dad Bourbon, Gilbey's Gin, Old Taylor Bourbon, Gilbey's Vodka, and more.

1988: Booker's Bourbon debuts.

1991: Jim Beam Brands buys seven brands from the House of Seagram including Wolfschmidt Vodka, Leroux cordials, and Ronrico rums.

1992: The Small Batch Bourbon Collection (Knob Creek, Booker's, Basil Hayden's, Baker's) debuts.

1997: American Brands, Inc. becomes Fortune Brands, Inc.

1997: Jack Daniel's Black Label, a Tennessee sour mash whiskey, becomes the world's leading American straight whiskey. Jim Beam Bourbon drops to second but remains the best selling bourbon whiskey.

1998: Jim Beam Brands Worldwide, Inc. is formed with Jim Beam Brands Company as a subsidiary. Jim Beam Brands Worldwide, Inc. enters the wine trade with the acquisition of Geyser Peak Winery, Sonoma County, California.

1999: Maxxium Worldwide B.V., an international distribution and sales joint venture, is formed by Jim Beam Brands Worldwide, Inc., Rémy-Cointreau, France, and Highland Distillers, Ltd, Great Britain.

2001: Jim Beam is named "International Distiller of the Year" at International Wine & Spirit Competition in London. Jim Beam Brands Company teams with The Absolut Spirits Company to form Future Brands LLC, a U.S. focused distribution and sales joint venture. Vin & Sprit AB becomes an equal one-fourth partner in Maxxium Worldwide B.V., owning 10 percent of Jim Beam Brands Company. Jim Beam is named "Distiller of the Year" by

Wine Enthusiast Magazine. Jim Beam Brands Worldwide, Inc. sells JBB Greater Europe to Kyndal International.

2002:   The nine-millionth barrel of Jim Beam since the end of Prohibition is filled at Clermont on July 23. This total roughly equates to 280 million cases. Booker Noe wins Lifetime Achievement Award from *Malt Advocate Magazine.*

2003:   Jim Beam Brands Worldwide introduces Beam and Cola, a ready-to-drink beverage.

Bibliography

Disclosed Sources: Books

Alcohol Distiller's Handbook. Cornville, AZ: Desert Publications, 1980.

Axelrod, Alan. *The Complete Idiot's Guide to the Civil War*. New York: Alpha Books, 1998.

Broom, Dave. *Handbook of Whisky: A Complete Guide to the World's Best Malts, Blends and Brands*. London: Octopus Publishing Group Limited, 2000.

Carson, Gerald. *The Social History of Bourbon: An Unhurried Account of Our Star-Spangled American Drink*. Lexington, KY: The University Press of Kentucky, 1963.

Cecil, Sam K. *The Evolution of the Bourbon Whiskey Industry in Kentucky*. Paducah, KY: Turner Publishing Company, 1999.

Clark, Thomas D. *A History of Kentucky*. Ashland, KY: The Jesse Stuart Foundation, 1988.

Crowgey, Henry G. *Kentucky Bourbon: The Early Years of Whiskey-making*. Lexington, KY: The University Press of Kentucky, 1971.

Gabányi, Stefan. *Whisk(e)y*. New York: Abbeville Press, 1997.

Gaurnaccia, Steven, and Bob Sloan. *Hi-Fis & Hi-Balls: The Golden Age of the American Bachelor*. San Francisco: Chronicle Books, 1997.

Getz, Oscar. *Whiskey: An American Pictorial History*. New York: David McCay Company, 1978.

Grimes, William. *Straight Up or on the Rocks: A Cultural History of American Drink*. New York: Simon & Schuster, 1993. Reissued: New York: North Point Press, 2001.

Harrison, Lowell H., and James C. Klotter. *A New History of Kentucky*. Lexington, KY: The University Press of Kentucky, 1997.

Herman, Arthur. *How the Scots Invented the Modern World*. New York: Three Rivers Press, 2001.

Murray, Jim. *The Complete Guide to Whiskey: Selecting, Comparing, and Drinking the World's Great Whiskeys*. Chicago: Triumph Books, 1997.

Pacult, F. Paul. *Kindred Spirits: The Spirit Journal Guide to the World's Distilled Spirits and Fortified Wines*. New York: Hyperion, 1997.

Regan, Gary, and Mardee Haidin Regan. *The Bourbon Companion: A Connoisseur's Guide*. Philadelphia: Running Press, 1998.

Regan, Gary, and Mardee Haidin Regan. *The Book of Bourbon and Other Fine American Whiskeys*. Shelburne, VT: Chapters Publishing, Ltd., 1995.

Smith, Gavin D. *A to Z of Whisky*. Glasgow, Scotland: Neil Wilson Publishing, Ltd., 1997.

Weinstein, Allen, and David Rubel. *The Story of America: Freedom and Crisis from Settlement to Superpower*. New York: Dorling Kindersley Publishing, 2002.

The New York Times Almanac 2002. New York: Penguin Group, 2002.

The World Almanac and Book of Facts 2002. New York: World Almanac Education Group, 2002.

Disclosed Sources: Magazine and Newspaper Articles

Cowdery, Charles K. "Who Invented Bourbon?" *The Malt Advocate*, Vol. 11, No. 4, 2002.

Cowdery, Charles K. "The Beams: America's First Family of Bourbon." *The Malt Advocate*, Vol. 10, No. 2, 2001.

Hansell, John. "Whiskey Man: Booker Noe." *The Malt Advocate*, Vol. 8, No. 3, 1999.

Miller, Marcin. "Kentucky, Where the Good Times Roll." *Whisky Magazine*, No. 6, 1999.

Ramsay, Stuart MacLean. "Booker Noe: Uncut, Unfiltered and Straight from the Barrel." *Whisky Magazine*, No. 13, 2001.

Ramsay, Stuart MacLean. "Sharpest Tack in the Box." *Whisky Magazine*, No. 24, 2003.

Regan, Gary, and Mardee Haidin Regan. "Bourbon Uncovered: The American Whiskey Story: Part I." *Whisky Magazine*, No. 6, 1999.

Regan, Gary, and Mardee Haidin Regan. "Bourbon Uncovered: The American Whiskey Story: Part II." *Whisky Magazine*, No. 7, 2000.

"The Courier-Journal Sunday Magazine," March 21. *Bourbon Whiskey: Pure Water, Quality Grain, A Master Distiller.* Louisville, KY: The Filson Historical Society, 1966.

Information Sources: Family Records and Genealogical Compilations

Jo Ann Beam. *Descendents of Jacob Beam.*

Jo Ann Beam. *Master Distiller Joe L. Beam and 7 Sons.*

Information Sources: Archival Materials from Historical Societies, Museums, and Libraries

Audio tapes 18G15, 18G3(a), 18G3(b), 18G13. Tape recorded interviews with Jack Muir, Jack Stiles, and Thomas Moore McGinnis. *Prohibition in Nelson County*. Frankfort, KY: Kentucky Oral History Commission, Kentucky Historical Society.

Basham, Thomas E., Col. *Distilleries of Old Kentucky*. Special Collections and Archives. Lexington, KY: University of Kentucky, Margaret I. King Library.

Elliott, Sam Carpenter. *The Nelson County Record: An Illustrated Historical & Industrial Supplement 1896*. Nazareth, KY: Nazareth Archival Center, 1896.

Jim Beam Collection. Bardstown, KY: The Oscar Getz Museum of Whiskey History.

Genealogy records, Pennsylvania, Maryland, Virginia; nineteenth century newspaper collection. Louisville, KY: The Filson Library, The Filson Historical Society.

Photograph Credits and Sources

Courtesy of Jim Beam Brands Company, Jim Beam Brands Worldwide, Inc. Deerfield, IL.

Index